# IN THE KITCHEN WITH

## AMERICA'S

# FAVORITE
# BRAND NAME

### ★★★ RECIPES ★★★

All recipes and photographs that contain specific brand names are copyrighted by those companies and/or associations, unless otherwise specified. Photographs, except those on pages 33, 35, 47, 69, 75, 77, 85, 93, 97, 103, 165, 203, 257, 269, 271, 273, 279, 297, 301, 303, 329, 341, 351, 357, 359, copyright © Publications International, Ltd.

Some of the products listed in this publication may be in limited distribution.

Front cover photography by Peter Dean Ross Photography.

**Pictured on the front cover** *(clockwise from top left):* Stuffed Pork Tenderloin *(page 94)*, Triple Layer Cheesecake *(page 322)*, Shrimp on the Barbie *(page 151)*, Classic Arroz Con Pollo *(page 157)*, Three-Berry Tart *(page 309)*, Turkey Shanghai *(page 130)* and Chicken Enchiladas *(page 156)*.

**Pictured on the back cover** *(top to bottom):* Tarragon Chicken Salad Sandwiches *(page 212)*, Cinnamon Buns *(page 242)* and Cheddar and Leek Strata *(page 238)*.

ISBN: 0-7853-2399-6

Library of Congress Catalog Card Number: 95-72457

Manufactured in U.S.A.

8 7 6 5 4 3 2 1

**Microwave Cooking:** Microwave ovens vary in wattage. The microwave cooking times given in this publication are approximate. Use the cooking times as guidelines and check for doneness before adding more time. Consult manufacturer's instructions for suitable microwave-safe cooking dishes.

# IN THE KITCHEN WITH
## AMERICA'S
# FAVORITE
# BRAND NAME
### ★★RECIPES★★

PUBLICATIONS INTERNATIONAL, LTD.

# CONTENTS

# CONTENTS

# SNAPPY STARTERS

*Add pizzazz to premeal munching with this delightful sampling of appetizers. These creamy spreads, tasty dips and mouthwatering finger foods are just the things to get an impromptu gathering or elegant open house into full swing.*

## Fresh Garden Dip

1½ **cups fat free or reduced fat mayonnaise**
1½ **cups finely shredded DOLE® Carrots**
 1 **cup finely chopped DOLE® Broccoli Florets**
 ⅓ **cup finely chopped DOLE® Green Onions**
 2 **teaspoons dill weed**
 ¼ **teaspoon garlic powder**

• **Stir** together mayonnaise, carrots, broccoli, green onions, dill and garlic powder in medium bowl until blended.

• **Spoon** into serving bowl. Cover and chill 1 hour or overnight. Serve with DOLE® Broccoli Florets, Cauliflower Florets and Peeled Mini Carrots. Garnish with fresh dill sprigs, if desired. Refrigerate any leftover dip in airtight container up to 1 week.

*Makes 14 servings*

**Prep Time:** 15 minutes
**Chill Time:** 1 hour

*Top to bottom: Fresh Garden Dip, Fiesta Quesadillas with Fruit Salsa (page 16)*

## Roasted Red Pepper Dip

1 envelope LIPTON® Recipe Secrets®
   Onion Soup Mix
1 package (8 ounces) cream cheese,
   softened
1 jar (7 ounces) roasted red peppers
   packed in oil, undrained
½ teaspoon dried basil leaves, crushed
   (optional)
¼ teaspoon dried oregano leaves,
   crushed (optional)
   Suggested Dippers*

*Suggested Dippers:* Use mozzarella sticks,
bread sticks, sliced pepperoni, cooked
tortellini, pitted ripe olives or cherry tomatoes.

In food processor, process all ingredients
except Suggested Dippers until smooth.
Cover; chill 2 hours. Serve with Suggested
Dippers.                      *Makes 2 cups*

## Mediterranean Feta Dip

1 envelope LIPTON® Recipe Secrets®
   Vegetable Soup Mix
1 container (16 ounces) sour cream
½ cup diced seeded cucumber
4 ounces feta or blue cheese,
   crumbled
2 tablespoons chopped red onion
½ teaspoon dried oregano leaves,
   crushed (optional)
   Suggested Dippers*

*Suggested Dippers:* Serve with assorted
fresh vegetables and pita bread triangles.

In medium bowl, thoroughly blend all
ingredients except Suggested Dippers.
Cover; chill. Serve with Suggested
Dippers.              *Makes about 2½ cups*

## Classic Salsa

4 medium tomatoes
1 small onion, finely chopped
¼ cup chopped fresh cilantro
2 to 3 jalapeño peppers or serrano
   chilies, seeded and minced
2 tablespoons lime juice
1 small clove garlic, minced
   Salt and ground black pepper to
   taste

Cut tomatoes in half; remove seeds.
Coarsely chop tomatoes. Combine
tomatoes, onion, cilantro, jalapeños, lime
juice and garlic in medium bowl. Add salt
and pepper. Cover; refrigerate 1 hour or
up to 3 days for flavors to blend.

*Makes about 2½ cups*

## Vegetable-Topped Hummus

1 can (about 15 ounces) garbanzo
   beans, rinsed and drained
2 tablespoons tahini
2 tablespoons lemon juice
1 clove garlic
¾ teaspoon salt
1 tomato, seeded, diced
2 green onions, finely chopped
2 tablespoons chopped fresh parsley
   Pita bread wedges

In food processor or blender combine
beans, tahini, lemon juice, garlic and salt;
process until smooth. Combine tomato,
onions and parsley in small bowl. Spoon
bean mixture into medium serving bowl;
top with tomato mixture. Serve with pita
bread.                    *Makes 8 servings*

## Hidden Valley — Boursin Cheese —

2 packages (8 ounces each) cream
    cheese, softened
½ cup butter or margarine, softened
1 package (1 ounce) HIDDEN VALLEY
    RANCH® Milk Recipe Original
    Ranch® Salad Dressing Mix
1 tablespoon Dijon mustard
1 teaspoon minced garlic
    Round French bread

In large bowl, beat all ingredients except
bread with electric mixer until blended.
Spoon into 3-cup serving bowl. Cover
tightly and refrigerate overnight. Let stand
at room temperature 30 minutes before
serving. To serve, slice off top of French
bread. Remove inside, leaving ¼-inch-thick
shell. Spoon cheese mixture into bread
shell. Garnish with parsley and serve with
additional French bread and vegetables, as
desired. *Makes 2 cups*

## Hot Artichoke — and Tuna Spread —

1 can (6 ounces) STARKIST® Solid
    White or Chunk Light Tuna,
    drained
1 jar (12 ounces) marinated artichoke
    hearts, drained
1 to 2 cloves garlic
1 cup shredded mozzarella cheese
½ cup grated Parmesan cheese
¼ cup chopped canned green chilies
1 tablespoon minced green onion
2 to 3 tablespoons mayonnaise
    Hot pepper sauce to taste
    French bread or assorted crackers

In food processor bowl with metal blade,
place all ingredients except bread.
Process until well blended but not
puréed. Transfer mixture to ovenproof
serving dish. Bake, uncovered, in 350°F
oven about 30 minutes or until mixture is
golden. Serve hot with French bread.

*Makes 12 servings*

## Cheesy — Guacamole —

¼ pound VELVEETA® Pasteurized
    Process Cheese Spread, cubed
½ cup sour cream
2 avocados, peeled, coarsely chopped
1 tomato, coarsely chopped
½ small onion, coarsely chopped
1 fresh jalapeño pepper, seeded,
    coarsely chopped
1 tablespoon lemon juice
    Few drops hot pepper sauce

**PLACE** all ingredients in food processor
container with steel blade attached;
process until blended. Serve with tortilla
chips. *Makes 3 cups*

## Guacamole

2 large avocados, peeled, mashed
¼ cup finely chopped seeded tomato
2 tablespoons grated onion
2 tablespoons lime juice
½ teaspoon salt
¼ teaspoon hot pepper sauce
    Ground black pepper to taste
    Additional chopped tomato

Combine avocados, tomato, onion, lime
juice, salt and pepper sauce in medium
bowl; mix well. Add pepper. Serve
immediately or cover and refrigerate up
to 2 hours. Garnish with additional
chopped tomato. *Makes 2 cups*

## Venetian Canapés

12 slices firm white bread
5 tablespoons butter or margarine,
   divided
2 tablespoons all-purpose flour
½ cup milk
3 ounces fresh mushrooms (about
   9 medium), finely chopped
6 tablespoons grated Parmesan
   cheese, divided
2 teaspoons anchovy paste
¼ teaspoon salt
⅛ teaspoon ground black pepper
   Green and ripe olive slices, red and
   green bell pepper strips and
   rolled anchovy fillets, for garnish

Preheat oven to 350°F. Cut rounds out of bread slices with 2-inch round cutter. Melt 3 tablespoons butter in small saucepan. Brush both sides of bread rounds lightly with butter. Bake bread rounds on ungreased baking sheets 5 to 6 minutes per side or until golden. Remove to wire rack. Cool completely. *Increase oven temperature to 425°F.*

Melt remaining 2 tablespoons butter in same small saucepan. Stir in flour; cook and stir over medium heat until bubbly. Whisk in milk; cook and stir 1 minute or until sauce thickens and bubbles. (Sauce will be very thick.) Place mushrooms in large bowl; stir in sauce, 3 tablespoons cheese, anchovy paste, salt and black pepper until well blended.

Spread heaping teaspoonful mushroom mixture onto each toast round; place on ungreased baking sheets. Sprinkle remaining 3 tablespoons cheese over bread rounds, dividing evenly. Garnish, if desired. Bake 5 to 7 minutes or until tops are light brown. Serve warm.

*Makes 8 to 10 servings*

## Molletes

IMPERIAL® Margarine
8 to 10 French rolls, cut lengthwise
   into halves or quarters
LAWRY'S® Garlic Powder with
   Parsley
1 can (16 ounces) refried beans
   Salsa
2 cups (8 ounces) shredded Cheddar
   or Monterey Jack cheese

Spread margarine on cut sides of rolls; lightly sprinkle with Garlic Powder with Parsley. Toast under broiler until just golden. Spread each with equally divided portions of refried beans and salsa. Top with cheese. Broil until heated through and cheese is melted.

*Makes 16 to 20 appetizers*

**Presentation:** Serve with guacamole.

*Venetian Canapés*

# Herbed Croutons with Savory Bruschetta

½ cup regular or reduced fat mayonnaise
¼ cup FRENCH'S® Dijon Mustard
1 tablespoon finely chopped green onion
1 clove garlic, minced
¾ teaspoon dried oregano leaves
1 long thin loaf (18 inches) French bread, cut crosswise into ½-inch-thick slices
Savory Bruschetta (recipe follows)

Combine mayonnaise, mustard, onion, garlic and oregano in small bowl; mix well. Spread herbed mixture onto one side of each slice of bread.

Place bread, spread-sides up, on grid. Grill over medium-low coals 1 minute or until lightly toasted. Prepare Savory Bruschetta; spoon onto croutons. Serve warm.

*Makes 6 servings*

## Savory Bruschetta

1 pound ripe plum tomatoes, cored, seeded and chopped
1 cup finely chopped fennel bulb or celery
¼ cup chopped fresh basil leaves
3 tablespoons FRENCH'S® Dijon Mustard
3 tablespoons olive oil
3 tablespoons balsamic vinegar
2 cloves garlic, minced
½ teaspoon salt

Combine all ingredients in medium bowl; toss until well blended. *Makes 3 cups*

# Bruschetta al Pomodoro with Two Cheeses

1 loaf (1 pound) country Italian bread, cut diagonally into 12 (1-inch) slices
2 teaspoons minced garlic
⅓ cup extra virgin olive oil
¼ teaspoon crushed red pepper flakes
4 large ripe plum tomatoes, thinly sliced crosswise
1 medium-size red onion, slivered
⅓ cup slivered fresh basil leaves *or* 1 tablespoon dried basil
Red wine vinegar
½ cup (2 ounces) shredded ALPINE LACE® Fat Free Pasteurized Process Skim Milk Cheese Product—For Mozzarella Lovers
¼ cup (1 ounce) shredded ALPINE LACE® Fat Free Pasteurized Process Skim Milk Cheese Product—For Parmesan Lovers

**1.** Preheat the broiler. Place the bread slices in a single layer on a baking sheet and toast both sides until golden brown. Immediately rub one side of each bread slice with the garlic.

**2.** In a small saucepan, heat the oil and red pepper flakes over medium heat until warm. Brush each slice with the oil.

**3.** Top each bruschetta with 2 or 3 tomato slices, then add a few slivers of onion and basil. Sprinkle each with a little vinegar. Sprinkle the bruschetta with the mozzarella and the Parmesan. Broil 6 inches from the heat for 4 minutes or until cheese is bubbly.

*Makes 12 servings*

*Herbed Croutons with Savory Bruschetta*

## Potato Skins with Cheddar Melt

4 medium-size Idaho baking potatoes (about 2 pounds)
4 slices lean turkey bacon
2 tablespoons vegetable oil
2 cups (8 ounces) shredded ALPINE LACE® Reduced Fat Cheddar Cheese
¼ cup fat free sour cream
2 tablespoons finely chopped chives or green onions
1 tablespoon minced jalapeño pepper

**1.** Place a piece of foil on the bottom rack of the oven and preheat the oven to 425°F. Scrub the potatoes well and pierce the skins a few times with a sharp knife. Place the potatoes directly on the middle oven rack and bake for 1 hour or until tender.

**2.** Meanwhile, in a small skillet, cook the bacon over medium heat until crisp. Drain on paper towels, then crumble the bacon.

**3.** Using a sharp knife, cut the potatoes in half lengthwise. With a small spoon, scoop out the pulp, leaving ¼-inch-thick shells. (Save the potato pulp for another use.) Cut the skins into appetizer-size triangles.

**4.** Place the skins on a baking sheet, brush the insides with the oil and bake for 15 minutes or until crisp.

**5.** Remove the skins from the oven, sprinkle with the cheese and return to the oven for 5 minutes or until the cheese melts. Top the skins with the sour cream, then sprinkle with the chives, pepper and bacon. *Makes about 24 servings*

## Polenta Triangles

3 cups cold water
1 cup yellow cornmeal
1 envelope LIPTON® Recipe Secrets® Golden Onion or Onion Soup Mix
1 can (4 ounces) mild chopped green chilies, drained
½ cup thawed frozen or drained canned whole kernel corn
⅓ cup finely chopped roasted red pepper
½ cup shredded sharp Cheddar cheese (about 2 ounces)

In 3-quart saucepan, bring water to a boil over high heat. With wire whisk, stir in cornmeal, then golden onion soup mix. Reduce heat to low and simmer uncovered, stirring constantly, 25 minutes or until thickened. Stir in chilies, corn and roasted red pepper. Spread into lightly greased 9-inch square baking pan; sprinkle with cheese. Let stand 20 minutes or until firm; cut into triangles. Serve at room temperature or heat in oven at 350°F for 5 minutes or until warm. *Makes about 24 triangles*

*Potato Skins with Cheddar Melt*

# Fiesta Quesadillas with Fruit Salsa

1 can (11 ounces) DOLE® Mandarin Oranges, drained and finely chopped
1 tablespoon chopped fresh cilantro or parsley
1 tablespoon lime juice
4 (8-inch) whole wheat or flour tortillas
¾ cup (3 ounces) shredded low fat Monterey Jack, mozzarella or Cheddar cheese
⅔ cup finely chopped DOLE® Pitted Dates or Pitted Prunes
⅓ cup crumbled feta cheese
2 tablespoons chopped DOLE® Green Onion

•**Combine** mandarin oranges, cilantro and lime juice in small bowl for salsa; set aside.

•**Place** 2 tortillas on large baking sheet. Sprinkle half of shredded cheese, dates, feta cheese and green onion over each tortilla to within ½ inch of edge; top with remaining tortillas.

•**Bake** at 375°F 5 to 8 minutes or until hot. Cut each quesadilla into 6 wedges.

•**Drain** salsa just before serving, if desired; serve over warm quesadillas. Garnish with fresh cilantro sprigs, if desired. *Makes 6 servings*

**Prep Time:** 15 minutes
**Bake Time:** 8 minutes

# Chicken Sesame with Oriental Crème

⅓ cup reduced sodium soy sauce
2 teaspoons minced garlic
1 teaspoon dark sesame oil
½ teaspoon ground ginger
1 pound boneless, skinless chicken breasts, cut into 4×½-inch strips
6 ounces (1 carton) ALPINE LACE® Fat Free Cream Cheese with Garlic & Herbs
2 tablespoons finely chopped green onion
2 tablespoons sesame seeds, toasted
1 tablespoon extra virgin olive oil

**1.** In a small bowl, whisk the soy sauce, garlic, sesame oil and ginger. Reserve 2 tablespoons and pour the remaining marinade into a self-sealing plastic bag. Add the chicken pieces and seal the bag. Turn the bag to coat all the chicken, then refrigerate for at least 2 hours, turning bag occasionally.

**2.** To make the Oriental Crème: In another small bowl, place the cream cheese. Whisk in the reserved 2 tablespoons of marinade and stir in the green onion. Cover and refrigerate.

**3.** Remove the chicken from the marinade and discard any remaining marinade. Spread the sesame seeds on a plate and roll the chicken strips in them until lightly coated. In a large nonstick skillet, heat the olive oil over medium-high heat. Add the chicken and stir-fry for 6 minutes or until the juices run clear when the chicken is pierced with a fork. Serve with the Oriental Crème.

*Makes 24 servings*

*Chicken Sesame with Oriental Crème*

# Tri-Colored Tuna Stuffed Mushrooms

**30 medium mushrooms, cleaned and stems removed**
**2 tablespoons melted butter**
**1 cup finely chopped onion**
**1 tablespoon vegetable oil**
**1 can (6 ounces) STARKIST® Solid White or Chunk Light Tuna, drained and flaked**
**½ cup shredded smoked Gouda cheese, divided**
**1 red bell pepper, seeded and puréed***
**1 package (10 ounces) frozen spinach soufflé**
**¼ cup mayonnaise, divided**
**¼ cup grated Parmesan cheese, divided**
**½ teaspoon curry powder**

*\*Place coarsely chopped red pepper in blender. Blend until puréed.*

Lightly coat mushroom caps with melted butter; divide into 3 groups of 10. Sauté onion in hot oil until tender. *In each of 3 small bowls,* place ⅓ tuna and ⅓ sautéed onion. In first small bowl, add ¼ cup Gouda cheese and red bell pepper purée. In second small bowl, add ¼ cup spinach soufflé,** 2 tablespoons mayonnaise, 2 tablespoons Parmesan cheese and curry powder. In third small bowl, add remaining ¼ cup Gouda cheese, remaining 2 tablespoons mayonnaise and remaining 2 tablespoons Parmesan cheese. Fill 10 mushrooms with filling from each bowl. Arrange on baking sheet; bake in 350°F oven 10 to 12 minutes. Serve hot.          *Makes 30 servings*

*\*\*Keep remainder frozen until ready to use.*

# Sweet 'n Sour Oriental Meatball Hors d'Oeuvres

**MEATBALLS**
**½ cup KELLOGG'S CORN FLAKES® Cereal**
**¼ cup finely chopped onion**
**¼ teaspoon salt**
**¼ teaspoon garlic powder**
**⅛ teaspoon ground white pepper**
**1 tablespoon Worcestershire sauce**
**1 egg white**
**½ pound lean ground turkey Vegetable cooking spray**

**SAUCE**
**1 cup pineapple juice**
**½ cup cider vinegar**
**½ cup firmly packed brown sugar**
**2 teaspoons soy sauce**
**2 tablespoons cornstarch**
**2 tablespoons water**
**⅛ teaspoon ground ginger**

**1.** To make Meatballs, preheat oven to 375°F. In medium bowl mix together Kellogg's Corn Flakes® Cereal, onion, salt, garlic powder, pepper, Worcestershire sauce and egg white.

**2.** Add ground turkey to cereal mixture, mixing only until evenly combined (mixture will be soft). Divide mixture evenly into balls using rounded measuring tablespoon. Roll into balls and place in shallow baking pan coated with cooking spray.

**3.** Bake about 12 minutes or until meatballs are no longer pink.

**4.** To make Sauce, combine pineapple juice, vinegar, sugar and soy sauce in medium saucepan. Bring to a boil. Dissolve cornstarch in water; stir into pineapple juice mixture. Stir in ginger and simmer about 2 minutes. Add meatballs and simmer until meatballs are hot.

*Makes 21 meatballs, 1¾ cups sauce*

## Beefy Stuffed Mushrooms

 1 pound lean ground beef
 2 teaspoons prepared horseradish
 1 teaspoon chopped fresh chives
 1 clove garlic, minced
 ¼ teaspoon ground white pepper
 18 large mushrooms
 ⅔ cup dry white wine

Preheat oven to 350°F. Combine ground beef, horseradish, chives, garlic and pepper in medium bowl until well blended. Remove stems from mushrooms; reserve stems for another use. Stuff mushroom caps with beef mixture. Place stuffed mushrooms in shallow baking dish; pour wine over mushrooms. Bake 20 minutes or until meat is no longer pink.

*Makes 1½ dozen*

## Baked Mozzarella Sticks

 **Butter-flavored nonstick cooking spray**
 **12 ounces (2 blocks) ALPINE LACE® Fat Free Pasteurized Process Skim Milk Cheese Product—For Mozzarella Lovers**
 **½ cup egg substitute *or* 2 large eggs**
 **1 cup Italian seasoned dry bread crumbs**
 **¼ cup minced fresh parsley**

**1.** Preheat the oven to 400°F. Spray 2 large baking sheets with the cooking spray.

**2.** Cut each block of cheese in half crosswise, then each half lengthwise into 3 equal sticks (about 3×¾ inches), making a total of 12 sticks.

**3.** In a medium-size bowl, whisk the egg substitute (or the whole eggs) until frothy. On a plate, toss the bread crumbs with the parsley.

**4.** Dip each cheese stick first into the egg substitute, then roll in the bread crumbs, pressing them slightly as you go. Arrange the cheese in a single layer on the baking sheets.

**5.** Spray the sticks lightly with the cooking spray. Bake for 10 minutes or until golden brown and crispy.

*Makes 12 cheese sticks*

## Ranch-Style Crab Caliente

1 package (8 ounces) cream cheese, softened
1 cup mayonnaise
1 package (0.4 ounces) HIDDEN VALLEY RANCH® Buttermilk Recipe Original Ranch® Salad Dressing Mix
2 tablespoons lemon juice
1 large tomato, seeded and chopped
½ cup chopped green onions
6 ounces fresh or canned crabmeat
1 tablespoon diced seeded jalapeño pepper
Parsley and paprika

Preheat oven to 350°F. In medium bowl, blend cream cheese, mayonnaise, salad dressing mix and lemon juice. Stir in tomato, green onions, crabmeat and jalapeño. Spoon mixture into small casserole dish; bake 15 minutes. Remove from oven; garnish with parsley and lightly dust surface with paprika. Serve immediately. *Makes 8 to 10 servings*

## Scallops à la Schaller

1 pound bacon, cut in half crosswise
2 pounds small sea scallops
½ cup olive oil
½ cup dry vermouth
2 tablespoons chopped fresh parsley
1 teaspoon garlic powder
1 teaspoon black pepper
½ teaspoon onion powder
⅛ teaspoon dried oregano leaves

Wrap 1 bacon piece around each scallop; secure with wooden toothpicks, if necessary. Place in 13×9-inch baking dish. Blend oil, vermouth, parsley, garlic powder, pepper, onion powder and oregano in small bowl. Pour over scallops; cover. Marinate in refrigerator at least 4 hours. Remove scallops from marinade; discard marinade. Arrange on rack of broiler pan. Broil, 4 inches from heat, 12 to 15 minutes or until bacon is brown and scallops are opaque, turning once. Remove toothpicks. Arrange on greens-lined platter and garnish with strips of lemon peel, if desired. *Makes 8 servings*

Favorite recipe from **New Jersey Department of Agriculture**

## Crab Cakes Canton

7 ounces thawed frozen cooked crabmeat, drained and flaked
1½ cups fresh bread crumbs
¼ cup thinly sliced green onions
1 clove garlic, minced
1 teaspoon minced fresh ginger
2 egg whites, slightly beaten
1 tablespoon teriyaki sauce
2 teaspoons vegetable oil, divided
Prepared sweet and sour sauce (optional)

Combine crabmeat, bread crumbs, onions, garlic and ginger in medium bowl. Add egg whites and teriyaki sauce; mix well. Shape into patties about ½ inch thick and 2 inches in diameter. Heat 1 teaspoon oil in large nonstick skillet over medium heat until hot. Add 3 cakes to skillet. Cook 2 minutes per side or until golden brown. Repeat with remaining 1 teaspoon oil and crab cakes. Serve with sweet and sour sauce, if desired. *Makes 6 servings*

*Scallops à la Schaller*

## Ranch Buffalo Wings

½ cup butter or margarine, melted
¼ cup hot pepper sauce
3 tablespoons vinegar
24 chicken wing drumettes
1 package (1 ounce) HIDDEN VALLEY RANCH® Milk Recipe Original Ranch® Salad Dressing Mix
½ teaspoon paprika
1 cup prepared HIDDEN VALLEY RANCH® Original Ranch® Salad Dressing
Celery sticks

Preheat oven to 350°F. In small bowl, whisk together butter, pepper sauce and vinegar. Dip drumettes into butter mixture; arrange in single layer in large baking pan. Sprinkle with 1 package salad dressing mix. Bake 30 to 40 minutes or until chicken is browned and juices run clear. Sprinkle with paprika. Serve with 1 cup prepared salad dressing and celery sticks. *Makes 6 to 8 servings*

## Buffalo Wings

24 chicken wings (about 4 pounds)
1 envelope LIPTON® Recipe Secrets® Golden Onion Soup Mix
½ cup margarine or butter, melted
2 tablespoons white vinegar
2 tablespoons water
2 cloves garlic
1½ to 2 teaspoons ground red pepper
1 teaspoon ground cumin (optional)
1 cup WISH-BONE® Chunky Blue Cheese Dressing

Cut tips off chicken wings (save tips for a soup). Cut chicken wings in half at joint.

In food processor or blender, process golden onion soup mix, margarine, vinegar, water, garlic, pepper and cumin until blended; set aside.

Broil chicken 12 minutes or until brown, turning after 6 minutes. Brush with ½ of the soup mixture, then broil 2 minutes or until crisp. Turn, then brush with remaining soup mixture and broil 1 minute. Serve with Wish-Bone Chunky Blue Cheese Dressing and, if desired, celery sticks. *Makes 48 appetizers*

•*Also terrific with LIPTON® Recipe Secrets® Onion Soup Mix.*

*Ranch Buffalo Wings*

## Grilled Fruit Kabobs

⅓ cup dairy sour cream
⅓ cup apricot preserves
¼ cup A.1.® Steak Sauce
1½ cups pineapple chunks (fresh or canned)
1 cup seedless grapes
1 orange, sectioned
1 large banana, cut into 12 chunks
1 tablespoon FLEISCHMANN'S® Margarine, melted

Soak 12 (10-inch) wooden skewers in water for at least 30 minutes. In small bowl, combine sour cream, apricot preserves and 1 tablespoon steak sauce; set aside.

Thread fruit pieces alternately onto skewers. In small bowl, combine remaining 3 tablespoons steak sauce with melted margarine; brush kabobs with margarine mixture. Grill fruit over medium heat for 5 minutes or until warm and very lightly browned, turning and basting with remaining margarine mixture. Serve warm with reserved sour cream sauce for dipping.

*Makes 12 servings*

## Baked Garlic Bundles

½ of 16-ounce package frozen phyllo dough, thawed to room temperature
¾ cup butter, melted
3 large heads fresh garlic,* separated into cloves and peeled
½ cup finely chopped walnuts
1 cup Italian-style bread crumbs

*The whole garlic bulb is called a head.*

Preheat oven to 350°F. Remove phyllo from package; unroll and place on large sheet of waxed paper. Using scissors, cut phyllo crosswise into 2-inch-wide strips. Cover with large sheet of waxed paper and damp kitchen towel. (Phyllo dries out quickly if not covered.)

Lay 1 phyllo strip on flat surface; brush immediately with melted butter. Place 1 clove of garlic at 1 end of strip. Sprinkle about 1 teaspoon walnuts over length of strip. Roll up garlic clove and walnuts in strip, tucking in side edges as you roll. Brush bundle with melted butter; roll in bread crumbs to coat. Repeat with remaining phyllo strips, garlic cloves, walnuts, butter and bread crumbs until all but smallest garlic cloves are used. Place bundles on rack in shallow roasting pan. Bake 20 minutes or until crispy.

*Makes 24 to 27 appetizers*

Favorite recipe from **Christopher Ranch Garlic**

*Grilled Fruit Kabobs*

## Southwestern — Chilies Rellenos —

2 tablespoons olive oil
½ teaspoon ground white pepper
½ teaspoon salt
½ teaspoon ground red pepper
¼ teaspoon ground cloves
2 cans (4 ounces each) whole green
    chilies, drained, halved, seeded
1½ cups (6 ounces) shredded Wisconsin
    Cheddar cheese
1½ cups (6 ounces) shredded Monterey
    Jack cheese
1 package (16 ounces) egg roll
    wrappers
1 egg yolk
1 teaspoon water
    Vegetable oil

Combine olive oil, white pepper, salt, red pepper and cloves in small bowl. Add chilies; toss to coat. Let stand at room temperature 1 hour. Combine cheeses in another small bowl. Place 1 chili half in center of each egg roll wrapper; top with ¼ cup cheese mixture. Beat egg yolk and water in small cup; brush edges of wrapper with mixture. Fold wrapper in half; press together, working out any air bubbles. Press ends together. Fold ends under; pinch to seal. Repeat with remaining ingredients. Heat ½ inch vegetable oil in large, heavy saucepan over medium-high heat until oil reaches 375°F; maintain temperature. Fry chilies rellenos, a few at a time, in hot oil 2 to 3 minutes or until golden brown, turning once. Remove with slotted spoon; drain on paper towels. *Makes 6 servings*

Favorite recipe from **Wisconsin Milk Marketing Board**

## Thai Lamb & — Couscous Rolls —

16 large napa or Chinese cabbage
    leaves, stems trimmed
2 tablespoons minced fresh ginger
1 teaspoon crushed red pepper
⅔ cup uncooked quick-cooking
    couscous
½ pound ground lean lamb
½ cup chopped green onions
3 cloves garlic, minced
¼ cup plus 2 tablespoons chopped
    fresh cilantro or mint, divided
2 tablespoons reduced-sodium soy
    sauce
1 tablespoon lime juice
1 teaspoon Oriental sesame oil
1 cup plain nonfat yogurt

Place 4 cups water in medium saucepan; bring to a boil over high heat. Drop cabbage leaves into water; cook 30 seconds. Drain. Rinse leaves under cold water until cool; pat dry with paper towels. Place 1 cup water, ginger and red pepper in medium saucepan; bring to a boil over high heat. Stir in couscous; cover. Remove saucepan from heat; let stand 5 minutes.

Spray large saucepan with nonstick cooking spray; add lamb, onions and garlic. Cook and stir over medium-high heat 5 minutes or until lamb is no longer pink. Combine couscous, lamb, ¼ cup cilantro, soy sauce, lime juice and oil in medium bowl. Spoon evenly over centers of cabbage leaves. Fold ends of cabbage leaves over filling; roll up. Combine yogurt and remaining 2 tablespoons cilantro in small bowl; spoon evenly over rolls. Serve warm. *Makes 16 appetizers*

*Thai Lamb & Coucous Rolls*

# – Grilled Antipasto –

⅔ cup A.1.® Steak Sauce
¼ cup lemon juice
2 tablespoons olive oil
1 teaspoon dried basil leaves
2 cloves garlic, minced
16 medium scallops (about ⅔ pound)
16 medium shrimp, shelled and
    deveined (about ¾ pound)
12 mushrooms
2 ounces thinly sliced cooked roast
    beef or ham
16 (2×½-inch) eggplant strips
1 (6½-ounce) jar marinated artichoke
    hearts, drained
1 red bell pepper, thickly sliced
    Lettuce leaves for garnish

Soak 12 (10-inch) wooden skewers in water for at least 30 minutes. In medium bowl, combine steak sauce, lemon juice, olive oil, basil and garlic; set aside.

Thread 4 scallops onto each of 4 skewers. Thread 4 shrimp onto each of 4 skewers. Thread 6 mushrooms onto each of 2 skewers. Cut roast beef or ham into 3×1-inch strips; wrap 1 strip around each eggplant strip and secure with wooden toothpick. Wrap remaining beef or ham around artichoke hearts; thread onto remaining 2 skewers. Place skewers, eggplant bundles and pepper slices on baking sheet; brush with steak sauce mixture.

Grill over medium heat for 7 to 10 minutes or until seafood is opaque and vegetables are tender, turning and basting several times. Remove each item from grill as it is done; place on large lettuce-lined serving platter. *Makes 8 servings*

# Fruit Antipasto Platter

1 DOLE® Fresh Pineapple
2 medium, firm DOLE® Bananas,
    sliced diagonally
2 DOLE® Oranges, peeled and sliced
½ cup thinly sliced DOLE® Red Onion
½ pound low fat sharp Cheddar
    cheese, cut into 1-inch cubes
2 jars (6 ounces each) marinated
    artichoke hearts, drained and
    halved
    DOLE® Green or Red Leaf Lettuce
½ cup fat free or light Italian salad
    dressing

• **Twist** crown from pineapple. Quarter pineapple lengthwise; remove core. Cut whole fruit from skin; slice fruit into thin wedges.

• **Arrange** pineapple, bananas, oranges, onion, cheese and artichoke hearts on lettuce-lined platter; serve with dressing. Garnish with orange peel and fresh herbs, if desired. *Makes 10 servings*

**Prep Time:** 25 minutes

*Grilled Antipasto*

## — Fruit Empanadas —

1 can (8 ounces) DEL MONTE®
   Pineapple Tidbits In Its Own Juice
1 can (17½ ounces) refried beans
1 ripe medium banana, mashed
¾ cup firmly packed brown sugar
⅓ cup DEL MONTE® Seedless Raisins
⅓ cup chopped nuts
½ teaspoon ground cinnamon
4 pastry sticks or pastry for 2 double-
   crust pies
1 egg
1 tablespoon milk or cream

Drain pineapple, reserving juice for other use. Combine pineapple, beans, banana, brown sugar, raisins, nuts and cinnamon in saucepan. Cook over low heat 10 minutes; cool. Prepare pastry as package directs; roll out to ⅛-inch thickness. Cut into 4-inch circles. Combine egg and milk in small bowl. For each empanada, place 2 tablespoons filling in center of each circle. Brush egg-milk mixture on edges. Fold in half; crimp edges with fork to seal. Place empanadas on ungreased baking sheet; brush each with egg-milk mixture. Bake at 400°F, 15 to 20 minutes or until golden. Serve warm or cold.

*Makes about 3 dozen*

## Cajun Ham Mini — Sandwiches —

12 ounces light beer
1 small onion, chopped
1 clove garlic, quartered
1 bay leaf
1 cinnamon stick
4 whole cloves
½ teaspoon crushed red pepper
¼ teaspoon dried thyme leaves
16 slices (12 ounces) cooked smoked
   lean ham
   Peach Mustard Spread (recipe
   follows)
16 cocktail-size buns, split in half
4 slices (3 ounces) Swiss cheese,
   quartered

**MICROWAVE DIRECTIONS:** Combine beer, onion, garlic, bay leaf, cinnamon stick, cloves, pepper and thyme in 4-cup microwave-safe glass measure. Cover with plastic wrap, venting corner; microwave at HIGH 5 minutes. Cool; strain into bowl. (May be made up to 24 hours ahead.) Add ham slices; cover. Marinate 30 minutes in refrigerator. Drain marinade; discard. Meanwhile, prepare Peach Mustard Spread; spread scant teaspoonful onto cut side of each bun. Place cheese square on bottom; top with folded ham slice and top of bun. Place 4 sandwiches on microwave-safe plate at a time; cover with paper towels. Microwave at HIGH 45 seconds. *Makes 16 sandwiches*

***Peach Mustard Spread:*** Combine ⅓ cup peach fruit spread and 2 teaspoons horseradish or Dijon mustard.

*Makes ⅓ cup*

Favorite recipe from **National Cattlemen's Beef Association**

## Meat-Filled Oriental Pancakes

**6 Oriental Pancakes (recipe follows)**
**1 tablespoon cornstarch**
**3 tablespoons KIKKOMAN® Soy Sauce**
**1 tablespoon dry sherry**
**¾ pound ground beef**
**½ pound ground pork**
**⅔ cup chopped green onions and tops**
**1 teaspoon minced fresh gingerroot**
**1 clove garlic, pressed**

Prepare Oriental Pancakes. Combine cornstarch, soy sauce and sherry in large bowl. Add beef, pork, green onions, ginger and garlic; mix until thoroughly combined. Spread ½ cup meat mixture evenly over each pancake, leaving about a ½-inch border on 1 side. Starting with opposite side, roll up pancake jelly-roll fashion. Place rolls, seam-side down, in single layer on heatproof plate; place plate on steamer rack. Set rack in large pot or wok of boiling water. Cover and steam 15 minutes. (For best results, steam all rolls at the same time.) Just before serving, cut rolls diagonally into quarters. Arrange on serving platter and serve hot.

*Makes 2 dozen appetizers*

**Oriental Pancakes:** Beat *4 eggs* in large bowl with wire whisk. Combine *½ cup water, 3 tablespoons cornstarch, 2 teaspoons KIKKOMAN® Soy Sauce* and *½ teaspoon sugar;* add to eggs and beat well. Heat an 8-inch omelet or crepe pan over medium heat. Brush bottom of pan with *½ teaspoon vegetable oil;* reduce heat to low. Beat egg mixture; pour ¼ cup into skillet, lifting and tipping pan from side to side to form a thin round pancake. Cook 1 to 1½ minutes, or until firm. Carefully lift with spatula and transfer to sheet of waxed paper. Continue procedure, adding *½ teaspoon oil* to pan for each pancake. *Makes 6 pancakes*

## Black Bean Tortilla Pinwheels

**1 (8-ounce) package cream cheese, softened**
**1 cup dairy sour cream**
**1 cup (4 ounces) shredded Wisconsin Monterey Jack cheese**
**¼ cup chopped red onion**
**¼ cup chopped drained pimiento-stuffed green olives**
**½ teaspoon seasoned salt**
**⅛ teaspoon garlic powder**
**1 (15-ounce) can black beans, drained**
**5 (10-inch) flour tortillas**
**Salsa**

Blend cream cheese and sour cream in medium bowl. Stir in Monterey Jack cheese, onion, olives, salt and garlic powder. Cover; refrigerate 2 hours. Process beans in food processor until smooth. Spread thin layer beans and thin layer cheese mixture over tortillas. Roll tortillas up tightly. Wrap in plastic wrap; refrigerate until chilled. Cut tortillas crosswise into ¾-inch-thick slices. Serve with salsa. *Makes 12 to 16 servings*

Favorite recipe from **Wisconsin Milk Marketing Board**

# DOWN-HOME SOUPS & STEWS

*Savor the superheroes of comfort food—delicious soups, creamy chowders, chunky chilies and hearty stews—simmered to soothe the soul. Team them up with simple sides for informal meals or serve them on their own as elegant starters.*

## Chicken Vegetable Soup

1 bag SUCCESS® Rice
5 cups chicken broth
1½ cups chopped uncooked chicken
1 cup sliced celery
1 cup sliced carrots
½ cup chopped onion
¼ cup chopped fresh parsley
½ teaspoon pepper
½ teaspoon dried thyme leaves, crushed
1 bay leaf
1 tablespoon lime juice

Prepare rice according to package directions.

Combine broth, chicken, celery, carrots, onion, parsley, pepper, thyme and bay leaf in large saucepan or Dutch oven. Bring to a boil over medium-high heat, stirring once or twice. Reduce heat to low; simmer 10 to 15 minutes or until chicken is no longer pink in center. Remove bay leaf; discard. Stir in rice and lime juice. Garnish, if desired. *Makes 4 servings*

*Chicken Vegetable Soup*

# Creamy Shell
## Soup

4 cups water
3 to 4 chicken pieces
1 cup diced onions
¼ cup chopped celery
¼ cup minced parsley *or* 1 tablespoon
    dried parsley flakes
1 bay leaf
1 teaspoon salt
¼ teaspoon white pepper
2 medium potatoes, diced
4 to 5 green onions, chopped
3 chicken bouillon cubes
½ teaspoon seasoned salt
½ teaspoon poultry seasoning
4 cups milk
2 cups medium shell macaroni,
    cooked and drained
¼ cup butter or margarine
¼ cup all-purpose flour
    Ground nutmeg
    Chopped fresh parsley

Simmer water, chicken, diced onions, celery, minced parsley, bay leaf, salt and pepper in Dutch oven until chicken is tender. Remove bay leaf; discard. Remove chicken; cool. Skin, debone and cut into small cubes; set aside.

Add potatoes, green onions, bouillon cubes, seasoned salt and poultry seasoning to broth. Simmer 15 minutes. Add milk, macaroni and chicken; return to simmer.

Melt butter in skillet over medium heat. Add flour, stirring constantly, until mixture begins to brown. Add to soup; blend well.

Let soup simmer on very low heat 20 minutes to blend flavors. Season to taste. Garnish with nutmeg and chopped parsley.                    *Makes 8 servings*

Favorite recipe from **North Dakota Wheat Commission**

# Louisiana Shrimp
# and Chicken
## Gumbo

3 tablespoons vegetable oil
¼ cup all-purpose flour
2 medium onions, chopped
1 cup chopped celery
1 large green bell pepper, chopped
2 cloves garlic, minced
3 cups chicken broth
1 can (16 ounces) whole tomatoes in
    juice, undrained
1 package (10 ounces) frozen sliced
    okra
1 bay leaf
1 teaspoon TABASCO® pepper sauce
¾ pound shredded cooked chicken
½ pound medium shrimp, peeled,
    deveined
    Hot cooked rice

Heat oil in large saucepan or Dutch oven. Add flour; cook over low heat until mixture turns dark brown and develops nutty aroma; stir frequently. Add onions, celery, bell pepper and garlic; cook 5 minutes or until vegetables are tender. Gradually add broth. Stir in tomatoes with juice, okra, bay leaf and TABASCO sauce; bring to a boil. Add chicken and shrimp; cook 3 to 5 minutes or until shrimp turn pink. Remove bay leaf. Serve with rice.

*Makes 6 servings*

*Creamy Shell Soup*

## Turkey-Olive
## — Ragoût en Crust —

½ pound boneless white or dark
   turkey meat, cut into 1-inch cubes
1 clove garlic, minced
1 teaspoon vegetable oil
¼ cup (about 10) small frozen pearl
   onions
½ cup reduced-sodium chicken
   bouillon or turkey broth
½ teaspoon dried parsley flakes
⅛ teaspoon dried thyme, crumbled
1 small bay leaf
1 medium red potato, skin on, cut
   into ½-inch cubes
10 frozen snow peas
8 whole small pitted ripe olives
1 can (4 ounces) refrigerated crescent
   rolls
½ teaspoon dried dill weed, crumbled

**1.** Preheat oven to 375°F.

**2.** In medium skillet over medium heat, cook and stir turkey and garlic in oil 3 to 4 minutes or until no longer pink; remove and set aside. Add onions to skillet; cook and stir until lightly browned. Add bouillon, parsley, thyme, bay leaf and potato. Bring mixture to a boil. Reduce heat; cover. Simmer 10 minutes or until potato is tender. Remove and discard bay leaf.

**3.** Combine turkey mixture with potato mixture. Stir in snow peas and olives. Divide mixture between 2 (1¾-cup) individual ovenproof casseroles.

**4.** Divide crescent rolls into 2 rectangles; press perforations together to seal. If necessary, roll out each rectangle to make dough large enough to cover top of each casserole. Sprinkle dough with dill weed,

pressing lightly into dough. Cut small decorative shape from each dough piece; discard cutouts or place on baking sheet and bake in oven with casseroles. Place dough over turkey-vegetable mixture in casseroles. Trim dough to fit; press dough to edge of each casserole to seal. Bake 7 to 8 minutes or until pastry is golden brown. *Makes 2 servings*

***Note:*** *For more golden crust, brush top of dough with beaten egg yolk before baking.*

**Lattice Crust Variation:** With pastry wheel or knife, cut each rectangle lengthwise into 6 strips. Arrange strips, lattice-fashion, over turkey-vegetable mixture; trim dough to fit. Press ends of dough to edge of each casserole to seal.

Favorite recipe from **National Turkey Federation**

## Spicy Quick and
## —— Easy Chili ——

1 pound ground beef
1 large clove garlic, minced
1 can (15¼ ounces) DEL MONTE®
   Whole Kernel Golden Sweet Corn,
   drained
1 can (16 ounces) kidney beans,
   drained
1 can (14½ ounces) DEL MONTE® Chili
   Style Chunky Tomatoes
1 can (4 ounces) diced green chilies
   Green onions (optional)

In large saucepan, brown meat with garlic; drain. Add remaining ingredients. Simmer, uncovered, 10 minutes, stirring occasionally. Garnish with green onions, if desired. *Makes 4 servings*

*Turkey-Olive Ragoût en Crust*

# Chili Burrito Cups

1 (2½-pound) boneless beef chuck pot roast
1 medium onion, sliced
½ teaspoon salt
¼ teaspoon black pepper
1 large onion, chopped
1 tablespoon vegetable oil
1 can (about 16 ounces) pinto, kidney or pink beans, drained
1 can (14½ to 16 ounces) whole peeled tomatoes, with juice
1 can (6 ounces) tomato paste
1 can (4 ounces) chopped green chilies
1 tablespoon chili powder
8 Microwave Tortilla Cups (recipe follows)
Sour cream and guacamole (optional)

Cut boneless beef chuck pot roast into three to four pieces. Place beef, sliced onion, salt and pepper in Dutch oven. Add water to measure ½ inch up side of pan; cover tightly. Cook at low heat on range top or in 300°F oven 2 to 2½ hours or until beef is tender. Cool slightly. Skim off fat. Pour off juices, reserving 1 cup. Shred beef along the grain using two forks; reserve. In same Dutch oven, cook and stir chopped onion in oil until tender. Add reserved shredded beef, reserved 1 cup juices, beans, tomatoes, tomato paste, chilies and chili powder. Bring to a boil; reduce heat and simmer 1 hour or until thickened, stirring occasionally.

Meanwhile, prepare Microwave Tortilla Cups. Spoon an equal amount of beef mixture into each tortilla cup. Serve with sour cream and guacamole, if desired.

*Makes 8 servings*

**Microwave Tortilla Cups:** Gently press four 7- to 8-inch flour tortillas into four 10-ounce custard cups. Microwave at HIGH (100% power) 2 minutes. Rotate and rearrange custard cups; continue cooking at HIGH (100% power) 1 to 2 minutes. Carefully lift tortillas out and cool on wire rack for 5 minutes. Repeat procedure to make eight tortilla cups.

Favorite recipe from **Beef Industry Council**

# Cider Stew

2 pounds stew beef, cut into 1-inch cubes
2 tablespoons FLEISCHMANN'S® Margarine
¼ cup all-purpose flour
2 cups water
1 cup apple cider
½ cup A.1.® Steak Sauce
2 teaspoons dried thyme leaves
½ teaspoon ground black pepper
1 bay leaf
3 medium potatoes, peeled and cut into 1-inch cubes
3 medium carrots, sliced
1 medium onion, chopped
1 (10-ounce) package frozen cut green beans

In large heavy pot, over medium-high heat, brown half the beef at a time in margarine. Return beef to pot. Stir in flour. Gradually stir in water, cider and steak sauce. Over high heat, bring to a boil; stir in thyme, pepper and bay leaf. Reduce heat to low; cover and simmer for 2 hours.

Add potatoes, carrots, onion and beans. Cover and cook for 30 minutes more or until vegetables are tender. Discard bay leaf before serving.

*Makes 6 to 8 servings*

## Arizona Pork Chili

1½ pounds boneless pork, cut into ¼-inch cubes
1 tablespoon vegetable oil
1 onion, coarsely chopped
2 cloves garlic, minced
1 can (15 ounces) black, pinto or kidney beans, drained
1 can (14½ ounces) DEL MONTE® Chili Style Chunky Tomatoes
1 can (4 ounces) diced green chilies
1 teaspoon ground cumin
Tortillas and sour cream (optional)

In large skillet, brown meat in oil over medium-high heat. Add onion and garlic; cook until onion is tender. Season with salt and pepper, if desired. Add remaining ingredients except tortillas and sour cream. Simmer 10 minutes, stirring occasionally. Serve with tortillas and sour cream, if desired.  *Makes 6 servings*

**Prep Time:** 10 minutes
**Cook Time:** 25 minutes

## Ginger Wonton Soup

4 ounces lean ground pork
½ cup reduced-fat ricotta cheese
½ tablespoon minced fresh cilantro
½ teaspoon ground black pepper
⅛ teaspoon Chinese 5-spice powder
20 fresh or frozen, thawed wonton skins
1 teaspoon vegetable oil
⅓ cup chopped red bell pepper
1 teaspoon grated fresh ginger
2 cans (14½ ounces each) fat-free reduced-sodium chicken broth
2 teaspoons reduced-sodium soy sauce
4 ounces fresh pea pods
1 can (8¾ ounces) baby corn, rinsed and drained
2 green onions, thinly sliced

Cook pork in small nonstick skillet over medium-high heat until no longer pink. Cool slightly; stir in ricotta cheese, cilantro, black pepper and 5-spice powder. Place 1 teaspoon filling in center of each wonton skin. Fold top corner of wonton over filling. Lightly brush remaining corners with water. Fold left and right corners over filling. Tightly roll filled end toward remaining corner in jelly-roll fashion. Moisten edges with water to seal. Cover and set aside.

Heat oil in large saucepan. Add bell pepper and ginger; cook 1 minute. Add chicken broth and soy sauce; bring to a boil. Add pea pods, baby corn and wontons. Reduce heat to medium-low; simmer 4 to 5 minutes or until wontons are tender. Sprinkle with onions.

*Makes 4 servings*

# Zesty Noodle Soup

1 pound BOB EVANS FARMS® Zesty
   Hot Roll Sausage
2½ cups water
1 (16-ounce) can whole tomatoes,
   undrained
½ pound fresh mushrooms, sliced
1 large onion, chopped
1 small green bell pepper, chopped
2½ cups tomato juice
¼ cup chopped fresh parsley
1 teaspoon celery seeds
1 teaspoon lemon juice
1 teaspoon Worcestershire sauce
½ teaspoon salt
½ teaspoon dried thyme
1 cup uncooked egg noodles

Crumble sausage into 3-quart saucepan.
Cook over medium-high heat until
browned, stirring occasionally. Drain off
any drippings. Add water, tomatoes with
juice, mushrooms, onion and pepper;
cook until vegetables are tender, stirring
well to break up tomatoes. Stir in all
remaining ingredients except noodles.
Bring to a boil over high heat. Reduce
heat to low; simmer, covered, 30 minutes.
Add noodles; simmer just until noodles
are tender, yet firm. Serve hot. Refrigerate
leftovers.                    *Makes 6 servings*

**Serving Suggestion:** Serve with crusty
French bread.

# Ravioli Soup

¾ pound hot Italian sausage, crumbled
   and cooked
1 can (14½ ounces) DEL MONTE®
   Italian Recipe Stewed Tomatoes
1 can (14 ounces) beef broth
1 package (9 ounces) fresh or frozen
   cheese ravioli or tortellini, cooked
   and drained
1 can (14½ ounces) DEL MONTE®
   Italian Green Beans, drained
2 green onions, sliced
   Grated Parmesan cheese (optional)

**1.** In 5-quart pot, combine sausage,
tomatoes, broth and 1¾ cups water; bring
to a boil over high heat.

**2.** Reduce heat to low; stir in ravioli,
green beans and onions. Gently cook until
ravioli are heated through. Season with
pepper and sprinkle with grated
Parmesan cheese, if desired.

*Makes 4 servings*

*Ravioli Soup*

# Country Bean Soup

1¼ cups dried navy beans or lima beans, rinsed and drained
4 ounces salt pork or fully cooked ham, chopped
¼ cup chopped onion
½ teaspoon dried oregano leaves
¼ teaspoon salt
¼ teaspoon ground ginger
¼ teaspoon dried sage
¼ teaspoon ground black pepper
2 cups skim milk
2 tablespoons butter

Place navy beans in large saucepan; add enough water to cover beans. Bring to a boil. Reduce heat; simmer 2 minutes. Remove from heat; cover and let stand for 1 hour. (Or, cover beans with water and soak overnight.)

Drain beans and return to saucepan. Stir in 2½ cups water, salt pork, onion, oregano, salt, ginger, sage and pepper. Bring to a boil; reduce heat. Cover and simmer 2 to 2½ hours or until beans are tender. (If necessary, add more water during cooking.) Add milk and butter, stirring until mixture is heated through and butter is melted. Season with additional salt and pepper, if desired.

*Makes 6 servings*

Favorite recipe from **Wisconsin Milk Marketing Board**

# Ham and Cauliflower Chowder

1 bag (16 ounces) BIRDS EYE® frozen Cauliflower
2 cans (10¾ ounces each) cream of mushroom or cream of celery soup
2½ cups milk or water
½ pound ham, cubed
⅓ cup shredded colby cheese (optional)

• Cook cauliflower according to package directions.

• Combine cauliflower, soup, milk and ham in saucepan; mix well.

• Cook over medium heat 4 to 6 minutes, stirring occasionally. Top individual servings with cheese.

*Makes 4 to 6 servings*

**Prep Time:** 2 minutes
**Cook Time:** 10 to 12 minutes

*Country Bean Soup*

# Chicken, Andouille Smoked Sausage and Tasso Jambalaya

3 tablespoons unsalted butter or margarine
½ pound tasso or other smoked ham, diced
½ pound andouille smoked sausage or other smoked pork sausage such as Polish sausage (kielbasa), cut into ¼-inch slices
¾ pound boneless chicken, cut into bite-size pieces
2 bay leaves
2 tablespoons Chef Paul Prudhomme's POULTRY MAGIC®
1 cup chopped onion, divided
1 cup chopped celery, divided
1 cup chopped green bell pepper, divided
1 tablespoon minced garlic
½ cup canned tomato sauce
1 cup peeled, chopped tomatoes
2½ cups chicken stock or water
1½ cups uncooked rice (preferably converted)

Melt butter in 4-quart saucepan over high heat. Add tasso and andouille sausage; cook until meat starts to brown, 4 to 5 minutes, stirring frequently and scraping pan bottom well. Add chicken; continue cooking until chicken is brown, 4 to 5 minutes, stirring frequently and scraping pan bottom as needed. Stir in bay leaves, Poultry Magic® and ½ cup *each* of onion, celery and bell pepper; add garlic. Cook until vegetables are tender, about 6 to 8 minutes, stirring and scraping pan bottom frequently. Stir in tomato sauce; cook about 1 minute, stirring often. Stir in tomatoes, remaining onion, celery and bell pepper. Stir in stock and rice; mix well. Bring mixture to a boil, stirring occasionally. Reduce heat and simmer, covered, over very low heat until rice is tender but still chewy, about 30 minutes. (If you prefer to finish this dish by baking it once stock and rice are added, transfer mixture to an ungreased 13×9-inch baking pan and bake, uncovered, at 350°F until rice is tender but still chewy, about 1 hour.) Stir well; remove bay leaves. Let sit, uncovered, 5 minutes before serving. To serve, arrange 2 heaping ½-cup mounds of rice on each serving plate.

*Makes 6 main-dish servings*

# Seafood Bisque

2 leeks, cut in half lengthwise
2 tablespoons margarine
3 cups milk
2 cups chopped peeled potatoes
1 (8-ounce) package imitation crab flakes, rinsed
½ teaspoon dried thyme leaves, crushed
⅛ to ¼ teaspoon hot pepper sauce
½ pound VELVEETA® Pasteurized Process Cheese Spread, cubed
2 tablespoons dry sherry (optional)

**THINLY** slice white portion and 1 inch of light green portion of leeks; sauté in margarine.

**ADD** all remaining ingredients except process cheese spread and sherry.

**BRING** to boil. Reduce heat to low; cover. Simmer 15 minutes or until potatoes are tender.

**ADD** process cheese spread and sherry; stir until process cheese spread is melted. Garnish with fresh chives and lemon peel. *Makes 6 servings*

**Prep Time:** 40 minutes

## — Seafood Gumbo —

1 bag SUCCESS® Rice
1 tablespoon reduced-calorie
    margarine
¼ cup chopped onion
¼ cup chopped green bell pepper
2 cloves garlic, minced
1 can (28 ounces) whole tomatoes, cut
    up, undrained
2 cups chicken broth
½ teaspoon ground red pepper
½ teaspoon dried thyme leaves,
    crushed
½ teaspoon dried basil leaves, crushed
¾ pound whitefish, cut into 1-inch
    pieces
1 package (10 ounces) frozen cut
    okra, thawed and drained
½ pound medium shrimp, peeled and
    deveined

Prepare rice according to package directions. Melt margarine in large saucepan over medium-high heat. Add onion, bell pepper and garlic; cook and stir until crisp-tender. Stir in tomatoes, broth, red pepper, thyme and basil. Bring to a boil. Reduce heat to low; simmer, uncovered, until thoroughly heated, 10 to 15 minutes. Stir in fish, okra and shrimp; simmer until fish flakes easily with fork and shrimp curl and turn pink. Add rice; heat thoroughly, stirring occasionally, 5 to 8 minutes. *Makes 4 servings*

## Albacore Corn — Chowder —

2 tablespoons butter or margarine
½ cup sliced celery
½ cup chopped onion
¾ cup chopped carrots
2 to 3 tablespoons flour
1 teaspoon dried thyme or Italian
    seasoning
1 can (17 ounces) cream-style corn
2 cups milk
1 can (12 ounces) STARKIST® Solid
    White Tuna, drained and flaked
1 cup water
1 teaspoon chicken flavor instant
    bouillon

In medium saucepan, melt butter over medium heat; sauté celery, onion and carrots about 3 minutes. Add flour and thyme; blend well. Cook 3 more minutes. Add corn, milk, tuna, water and bouillon, stirring to blend. Cover and simmer *(do not boil)* 5 minutes to heat through, stirring occasionally. *Makes 4 servings*

**Prep Time:** 20 minutes

# Creamy Gazpacho

1 cup undiluted CARNATION®
    Evaporated Skimmed Milk
1¾ cups (14.5-ounce can) CONTADINA®
    Recipe Ready Diced Tomatoes
2 cups tomato juice
3 tablespoons lemon juice
2 tablespoons olive oil
1 clove garlic, minced
½ teaspoon salt
¼ teaspoon ground black pepper
¼ teaspoon red pepper sauce
2 cups (2 medium) peeled, seeded and
    diced cucumbers
½ cup diced green bell pepper
½ cup diced onion
    Garnishes: Plain low fat or nonfat
    yogurt, diced cucumber, bell
    pepper and onion (optional)

Place evaporated skimmed milk, tomatoes, tomato juice, lemon juice, olive oil, garlic, salt, black pepper and red pepper sauce in blender; cover and blend thoroughly. (Blender container will be very full.)

Pour into serving bowl or tureen and add cucumber, bell pepper and onion; stir thoroughly. Chill. Serve cold; garnish as desired.           *Makes about 7 servings*

# Vichyssoise

¼ cup margarine
4 medium leeks, sliced
1 medium onion, sliced
2 pounds potatoes, pared and thinly
    sliced (about 6 medium)
4 cups chicken broth
2½ cups milk
⅛ teaspoon salt
2 cups half-and-half

Melt margarine in large saucepan over medium-high heat. Add leeks and onion; cook and stir 5 minutes or until tender. Add potatoes and broth; bring to a boil over high heat. Reduce heat to medium-low; simmer 30 minutes.

Place potato mixture in food processor. Process until smooth. Return mixture to saucepan. Add milk and salt. Bring to a boil over high heat; remove saucepan from heat. Cool. Strain mixture through fine sieve. Add half-and-half; chill.

*Makes 8 to 10 servings*

*Creamy Gazpacho*

# Cream of Asparagus Soup

1 pound fresh asparagus, cut into 1-inch pieces
3½ cups fat-free reduced-sodium chicken broth, divided
¼ cup margarine
¼ cup all-purpose flour
½ cup half-and-half
½ teaspoon salt
⅛ teaspoon ground black pepper

Combine asparagus and 1 cup broth in medium saucepan; cook 12 to 15 minutes or until tender. Melt margarine in large saucepan. Add flour. Gradually add remaining 2½ cups broth; cook, stirring occasionally, until slightly thickened. Stir in half-and-half, salt and pepper; cook until thickened. Add asparagus. Heat thoroughly. *Makes 6 to 8 servings*

# Southwestern Soup

1 bag (16 ounces) BIRDS EYE® frozen Corn
½ cup chopped green pepper
2 cans (15 ounces each) chili
1 cup hot water

• Combine all ingredients in saucepan.

• Cook over medium heat 10 to 12 minutes. *Makes 4 to 6 servings*

**Prep Time:** 1 to 2 minutes
**Cook Time:** 10 to 12 minutes

# Potato & Cheddar Soup

2 cups water
2 cups peeled cubed red potatoes
3 tablespoons butter or margarine
1 small onion, finely chopped
3 tablespoons all-purpose flour
Red and black pepper to taste
3 cups milk
½ teaspoon sugar
1 cup (4 ounces) shredded Cheddar cheese
1 cup cubed cooked ham
Chopped fresh parsely (optional)

Bring water to a boil in large saucepan. Add potatoes; cook until tender. Drain, reserving liquid. Measure 1 cup, adding water if necessary. Melt butter in saucepan over medium heat. Add onion; cook and stir until tender but not brown. Add flour; season with red and black pepper. Cook 3 to 4 minutes. Gradually add potatoes, reserved liquid, milk and sugar to onion mixture; stir well. Add cheese and ham. Simmer over low heat 30 minutes, stirring frequently. Garnish with chopped fresh parsley, if desired. *Makes 12 servings*

## Tomato Soup

1 tablespoon vegetable oil
1 cup chopped onion
2 cloves garlic, coarsely chopped
½ cup chopped carrot
¼ cup chopped celery
2 cans (28 ounces each) crushed
    tomatoes in tomato puree
3½ cups chicken broth*
1 tablespoon Worcestershire sauce
½ to 1 teaspoon salt
½ teaspoon dried thyme leaves
¼ to ½ teaspoon ground black pepper
2 to 4 drops hot pepper sauce

*Substitute 2 cans (10½ ounces each)
condensed chicken broth and 1 cup water
for 3½ cups chicken broth.

Heat oil in large Dutch oven over
medium-high heat. Add onion and garlic;
cook and stir 1 to 2 minutes or until
onion is tender. Add carrot and celery;
cook 7 to 9 minutes or until tender,
stirring frequently. Stir in tomatoes, broth,
Worcestershire sauce, salt, thyme, pepper
and hot pepper sauce. Reduce heat to
low. Cover; simmer 20 minutes, stirring
frequently.

For a smoother soup: Remove from heat.
Let cool about 10 minutes. Process soup
in food processor or blender in small
batches until smooth. Return soup to
Dutch oven; simmer 3 to 5 minutes until
heated through.            *Makes 6 servings*

## Double Pea Soup

1 tablespoon vegetable oil
1 large white onion, finely chopped
3 cloves garlic, finely chopped
2 cups dried split peas
1 bay leaf
1 teaspoon ground mustard
1½ cups frozen green peas
1 teaspoon salt
¼ teaspoon ground black pepper
    Nonfat sour cream (optional)

Heat oil in large saucepan or Dutch oven
over medium-high heat until hot. Add
onion; cook 5 minutes or until onion is
tender, stirring occasionally. Add garlic;
cook and stir 2 minutes.

Stir 2 cups water, split peas, bay leaf and
mustard into saucepan. Bring to a boil
over high heat. Cover; reduce heat to
medium-low. Simmer 45 minutes or until
split peas are tender, stirring occasionally.

Stir green peas, salt and pepper into
saucepan; cover. Cook 10 minutes or until
green peas are tender. Remove bay leaf;
discard. Blend using hand-held blender
until smooth or process small batches in
blender or food processor until smooth.

Top each serving with sour cream, if
desired. Garnish as desired.

*Makes 6 servings*

**Note:** *If a smoky flavor is desired, a chipotle
chili can be added during the last 5 minutes
of cooking.*

*Double Pea Soup*

# SALAD SENSATIONS

*Forget the plain bowl of lettuce—here's a collection of flavor-packed salads that really make the meal. Crispy garden, juicy fruit and creamy potato salads are perfect complements for any meal. And char-broiled chicken, tasty seafood and hot-off-the-grill beef salads are fit for a feast.*

## Southwest Caesar Salad

1 package (10 ounces) DOLE®
   Complete Caesar Salad
2 cups cubed cooked
   chicken breast
1 can (14 to 16 ounces) low-
   sodium kidney, black or
   pinto beans, drained
1 can (8 ounces) low-sodium
   whole kernel corn,
   drained
1 medium tomato, cut into
   wedges
1 medium DOLE® Red,
   Yellow or Green Bell
   Pepper, thinly sliced
½ medium onion, thinly
   sliced

•**Combine** romaine, croutons and Parmesan cheese from salad bag with chicken, beans, corn, tomato, bell pepper and onion in large serving bowl.

•**Pour** dressing from packet over salad; toss to evenly coat.
*Makes 4 servings*

**Prep Time:** 10 minutes

***Note:*** *Refrigerate salad blends, complete salads and vegetable combinations in their original bags as soon as you get them home. Since the bags have been designed with a special material to keep vegetables at their freshest, you can store any leftovers in the same bags, tightly closed, in your refrigerator crisper.*

*Southwest Caesar Salad*

# Chicken Caesar Salad

1 tablespoon plus 1½ teaspoons olive oil
4 boneless skinless chicken breast halves (¾ to 1 pound), cut into strips
4 to 5 cups torn romaine lettuce (1 large head)
1 large roma *or* 1 medium tomato, diced
½ cup grated fresh Parmesan cheese
1 bottle (8 ounces) LAWRY'S® Creamy Caesar with Cracked Pepper Dressing or LAWRY'S® Classic Caesar with Imported Anchovies Dressing
Seasoned croutons

In large skillet, heat oil. Add chicken. Sauté 7 to 10 minutes or until no longer pink in center, stirring frequently. In large salad bowl, combine lettuce, tomato, Parmesan cheese and chicken; mix lightly. Refrigerate. Before serving, add enough dressing to coat all ingredients; toss lightly. Sprinkle with croutons.

*Makes 4 servings*

**Hint:** For extra flavor, grill chicken breast halves until no longer pink in center; slice thinly. Serve on salad.

# Warm Mushroom Salad

2 quarts mixed salad greens (such as spinach, arugula, curly endive and romaine)
3 tablespoons FILIPPO BERIO® Olive Oil
1 (10-ounce) package mushrooms, cleaned and quartered or sliced
3 shallots, chopped
1 clove garlic, crushed
2 tablespoons chopped fresh chives
2 tablespoons lemon juice
2 tablespoons balsamic vinegar
1 teaspoon sugar
1½ cups purchased garlic croutons
Shavings of Parmesan cheese
Salt and freshly ground black pepper

Tear salad greens into bite-size pieces. Arrange on 4 serving plates. In medium skillet, heat olive oil over medium heat until hot. Add mushrooms, shallots and garlic; cook and stir 3 to 5 minutes or until mushrooms are tender. Stir in chives, lemon juice, vinegar and sugar; simmer 30 seconds. Spoon mixture over salad greens. Top with croutons and Parmesan cheese. Season to taste with salt and pepper.

*Makes 4 to 6 servings*

*Chicken Caesar Salad*

# Marinated Tomatoes & Mozzarella

1 medium bunch fresh basil leaves, divided
1 pound Italian tomatoes, sliced
½ pound fresh packed buffalo mozzarella cheese, sliced
¼ cup olive oil
3 tablespoons chopped fresh chives
2 tablespoons red wine vinegar
2 teaspoons sugar
½ teaspoon dried oregano
½ teaspoon LAWRY'S® Seasoned Pepper
½ teaspoon LAWRY'S® Garlic Powder with Parsley

Divide basil in half; reserve one half for garnish. Chop remaining basil leaves; set aside. In shallow dish, place tomato slices and cheese. Combine oil, chives, vinegar, sugar, oregano, Seasoned Pepper and Garlic Powder with Parsley in small bowl; pour over tomatoes and cheese. Cover. Refrigerate at least 30 minutes. To serve, arrange tomato and cheese slices on serving plate. Sprinkle with chopped basil leaves. Garnish with reserved whole basil leaves.
*Makes 4 to 6 servings*

**Presentation:** Serve with grilled chicken sandwiches or as a zesty Italian appetizer.

# Pride of the Crowns' Salad

1 teaspoon dry mustard
1 teaspoon LAWRY'S® Seasoned Salt
1 teaspoon LAWRY'S® Seasoned Pepper
1 teaspoon LAWRY'S® Pinch of Herbs
¼ teaspoon LAWRY'S® Garlic Powder with Parsley
½ cup red wine vinegar
¾ cup olive oil
2 heads Bibb lettuce, torn into bite-size pieces
½ to ¾ cup chopped walnuts
¼ pound bacon, diced, cooked and drained
½ cup (2 ounces) coarsely shredded Gruyère cheese
1½ cups seasoned croutons

In container with stopper or lid, combine mustard, seasonings and vinegar; cover and shake well. Add olive oil; cover and shake until blended. Refrigerate several hours to blend flavors. In large salad bowl, combine remaining ingredients. Shake dressing. Add to salad; toss lightly to coat.
*Makes 6 servings*

**Presentation:** Serve on chilled salad plates with a chilled salad fork.

*Marinated Tomatoes & Mozzarella*

# Crunchy Onion Layered Salad with Dilly Dijon Dressing

## LAYERED SALAD

4 cups washed and torn salad greens

8 ounces boiled ham, cut into cubes

4 hard-cooked eggs, chopped

2 ripe tomatoes, chopped

1 bell pepper (green, red or yellow), seeded and chopped

1 bunch radishes, sliced

1 package (9 ounces) frozen peas, thawed and drained

1 can (2.8 ounces) FRENCH'S® French Fried Onions

## DILLY DIJON DRESSING

1 cup regular or reduced fat mayonnaise

1 cup buttermilk or whole milk

¼ cup FRENCH'S® Dijon Mustard

1 package (1 ounce) ranch salad dressing mix

½ teaspoon dried dill weed

Layer salad ingredients in 3-quart straight-sided glass bowl. Combine Dilly Dijon Dressing ingredients in small bowl; mix well. Spoon over salad just before serving. Garnish as desired.

*Makes 4 main-dish or 6 side-dish servings*

**Prep Time:** 30 minutes

**Tip:** For extra-crispy flavor, place French Fried Onions on a microwave-safe plate. Microwave on HIGH 1 to 2 minutes until golden.

# Layered Mexican Salad

1 small head romaine lettuce, washed, cored

1 cup salsa

1 can (15 ounces) black turtle beans, rinsed, drained

1 cup frozen whole kernel corn, thawed, drained

1 large cucumber, peeled

1 can (2¼ ounces) sliced black ripe olives, drained

1 large lemon

¾ cup nonfat mayonnaise

3 tablespoons plain nonfat yogurt

2 to 3 cloves garlic, minced

½ cup (2 ounces) shredded low-fat Cheddar cheese

1 green onion, thinly sliced

Layer romaine leaves and slice crosswise into ½-inch strips. Place half of lettuce in large serving bowl. Layer salsa, beans and corn over lettuce. Halve cucumber lengthwise; scoop out and discard seeds. Slice thinly. Place cucumber on top of corn; sprinkle with olives. Top with remaining lettuce.

Grate lemon peel; blend with mayonnaise, yogurt and garlic. Juice lemon; stir 3 to 4 tablespoons juice into dressing. Spread dressing evenly on top of salad. Sprinkle with cheese and green onion. Cover salad; refrigerate 2 hours or up to 1 day.

*Makes 12 servings*

## French Salad Dressing

½ teaspoon salt
1 clove garlic, crushed
¼ teaspoon dry mustard
¼ teaspoon freshly ground black
   pepper
¼ teaspoon dried salad seasoning
¼ cup white wine vinegar or lemon
   juice, divided
¼ cup FILIPPO BERIO® Olive Oil

In small bowl, combine salt, garlic, mustard, pepper and salad seasoning. Whisk in vinegar and olive oil until thoroughly mixed. Store dressing, in tightly covered container, in refrigerator up to 1 week. Shake well before using.

*Makes about ½ cup*

## Classic Vinaigrette

¼ cup FILIPPO BERIO® Olive Oil
¼ cup white wine vinegar
1 teaspoon Dijon mustard
¼ teaspoon sugar
   Salt and freshly ground black
   pepper

In small screw-topped jar, combine olive oil, vinegar, mustard and sugar. Cover and shake vigorously until well blended. Season to taste with salt and pepper. Store dressing in refrigerator up to 1 week. Shake well before using.

*Makes about ½ cup*

**Garlic Vinaigrette:** Add 1 small, halved garlic clove to oil mixture; let stand 1 hour. Discard garlic. Store and serve as directed above.

**Lemon Vinaigrette:** Use 2 tablespoons lemon juice in place of vinegar; add finely grated peel of 1 small lemon to oil mixture. Store and serve as directed above.

**Herb Vinaigrette:** Whisk 1 to 2 tablespoons finely chopped fresh herbs (basil, oregano or chives) into dressing just before serving. Store and serve as directed above.

**Shallot Vinaigrette:** Add 1 to 2 finely chopped shallots to oil mixture; let stand at least 1 hour before serving. Store and serve as directed above.

## Lime and Lemon Cream Dressing

   Finely grated peel and juice of
      1 lime
   Finely grated peel and juice of
      1 lemon
2 teaspoons sugar
3 tablespoons FILIPPO BERIO® Olive
   Oil
½ cup half-and-half
   Few drops hot pepper sauce
2 shallots, finely chopped
   Salt and freshly ground black
   pepper

In small bowl, combine lime peel and juice, lemon peel and juice and sugar. Whisk in olive oil. Gradually whisk in half-and-half and hot pepper sauce. Stir in shallots. Season to taste with salt and pepper. Store dressing, in tightly covered container, in refrigerator 1 to 2 days.

*Makes about ¾ cup*

## Southwestern Bean and Corn Salad

1 can (about 15 ounces) pinto beans, rinsed and drained
1 cup fresh (about 2 ears) or thawed frozen whole kernel corn
1 red bell pepper, finely chopped
4 green onions, finely chopped
2 tablespoons cider vinegar
2 tablespoons honey
½ teaspoon salt
½ teaspoon ground mustard
½ teaspoon ground cumin
⅛ teaspoon cayenne pepper

Combine beans, corn, bell pepper and onions in large bowl. Blend vinegar and honey in small bowl until smooth. Stir in salt, mustard, cumin and cayenne pepper. Pour over bean mixture; toss until well blended. Cover; refrigerate at least 1 hour before serving. Serve on lettuce leaves, if desired.        *Makes 4 servings*

## French Lentil Salad

1½ cups lentils, rinsed, sorted, drained*
4 green onions, finely chopped
3 tablespoons balsamic vinegar
2 tablespoons chopped fresh parsley
1 tablespoon olive oil
¾ teaspoon salt
½ teaspoon dried thyme leaves
¼ teaspoon ground black pepper
¼ cup chopped walnuts, toasted

*Packages may contain grit and tiny stones. Thoroughly rinse. Then sort through and discard grit or any unusual looking pieces.*

Combine 2 quarts water and lentils in large saucepan; bring to a boil. Cover; reduce heat to medium-low. Simmer 30 minutes or until lentils are tender, stirring occasionally. Drain; discard liquid.

Combine lentils, onions, vinegar, parsley, oil, salt, thyme and pepper in large bowl. Cover; refrigerate at least 1 hour before serving. Serve on lettuce leaves, if desired. Top with walnuts just before serving. Garnish as desired.        *Makes 4 servings*

## Far East Tabbouleh

¾ cup uncooked bulgur
1¾ cups boiling water
2 tablespoons teriyaki sauce
2 tablespoons lemon juice
1 tablespoon olive oil
¾ cup diced seeded cucumber
¾ cup diced seeded tomato
½ cup thinly sliced green onions
½ cup minced fresh cilantro or parsley
1 tablespoon minced fresh ginger
1 clove garlic, crushed

Combine bulgur and boiling water in small bowl. Cover with plastic wrap; let stand 45 minutes or until bulgur is puffed, stirring occasionally. Drain in wire mesh sieve; discard liquid.

Combine bulgur, teriyaki sauce, lemon juice and oil in large bowl. Stir in cucumber, tomato, onions, cilantro, ginger and garlic until well blended. Cover; refrigerate 4 hours, stirring occasionally.
        *Makes 4 servings*

*Southwestern Bean and Corn Salad*

## Hot German Potato Salad

1½ **pounds new or boiling-type potatoes, cut into ¾-inch cubes**
1⅓ **cups water, divided**
½ **teaspoon salt**
½ **pound bacon, cut crosswise into thin strips**
2 **tablespoons cider vinegar**
4 **teaspoons sugar**
1 **tablespoon FRENCH'S® Worcestershire Sauce**
2 **teaspoons cornstarch**
¼ **teaspoon ground black pepper**
1 **can (2.8 ounces) FRENCH'S® French Fried Onions, divided**
1 **cup chopped celery**
1 **cup chopped green bell pepper**
¼ **cup chopped pimento**

**MICROWAVE DIRECTIONS:** Place potatoes, *1 cup* water and salt in 3-quart microwave-safe dish. Cover and microwave on HIGH 15 minutes or until potatoes are tender, stirring once. Drain in colander; set aside.

Place bacon in same dish. Microwave, uncovered, on HIGH 5 minutes or until bacon is crisp, stirring once. Remove bacon with slotted spoon; set aside. Pour off all but ¼ *cup* bacon drippings. Stir in remaining ⅓ *cup* water, vinegar, sugar, Worcestershire, cornstarch and black pepper. Microwave, uncovered, on HIGH 1 to 2 minutes or until dressing has thickened, stirring once.

Return potatoes to dish. Add ½ *can* French Fried Onions, celery, bell pepper, pimento and reserved bacon; toss well to coat evenly. Microwave, uncovered, on HIGH 2 minutes. Stir. Sprinkle with remaining onions. Microwave on HIGH 1 minute or until onions are golden. Serve warm. *Makes 6 servings*

## Apple Slaw with Poppy Seed Dressing

1 **cup coarsely chopped unpeeled Jonathan apple**
1 **teaspoon lemon juice**
2 **tablespoons nonfat sour cream**
1 **tablespoon plus 1½ teaspoons skim milk**
1 **tablespoon frozen apple juice concentrate, thawed**
1 **teaspoon sugar**
¾ **teaspoon poppy seeds**
½ **cup sliced carrot**
⅓ **cup shredded green cabbage**
⅓ **cup shredded red cabbage**
2 **tablespoons finely chopped green bell pepper**

Combine apple and lemon juice in resealable plastic food storage bag. Seal bag; turn to coat. Blend sour cream, milk, apple juice concentrate, sugar and poppy seeds in small bowl. Add apple mixture, carrot, cabbages and pepper; toss until well blended. Cover; refrigerate at least 1 hour before serving. Serve on cabbage leaves, if desired. *Makes 2 servings*

*Apple Slaw with Poppy Seed Dressing*

## Four-Season Fruit Slaw

1 package (16 ounces) DOLE® Classic Cole Slaw
1 cup DOLE® Seedless Red or Green Grapes, halved
¾ cup DOLE® Chopped Dates or Pitted Prunes
⅓ cup sliced DOLE® Green Onions
¾ cup fat free or reduced fat mayonnaise
3 tablespoons apricot or peach fruit spread
½ cup DOLE® Slivered Almonds, toasted

•**Mix** cole slaw, grapes, dates and onions in large serving bowl.

•**Stir** mayonnaise and fruit spread until blended in small bowl. Spoon over cole slaw mixture; toss to evenly coat. Cover.

•**Chill** 30 minutes. Stir in almonds just before serving.               *Makes 6 servings*

**Prep Time:** 15 minutes
**Chill Time:** 30 minutes

## Minted Fruit Rice Salad

⅔ cup DOLE® Pineapple Orange Juice or Mandarin Tangerine Juice
⅓ cup water
1 cup uncooked instant rice
1 can (11 ounces) DOLE® Mandarin Oranges, drained
1 can (8 ounces) DOLE® Crushed Pineapple
½ cup chopped cucumber
⅓ cup chopped DOLE® Red Onion
3 tablespoons chopped fresh mint

•**Combine** juice and water in medium saucepan. Bring to boil. Stir in rice. Remove from heat; cover. Let stand 10 minutes.

•**Stir** together rice, mandarin oranges, undrained pineapple, cucumber, onion and mint in medium serving bowl. Serve at room temperature or chilled. Garnish with fresh mint leaves, if desired.

*Makes 4 servings*

## Fruity Brown Rice Salad with Raspberry Vinaigrette

2 cups cooked brown rice
2 cups small broccoli flowerets, blanched and chilled
2 cups fresh or canned pineapple chunks
1 can (11 ounces) mandarin oranges, drained
½ cup slivered red bell pepper
½ cup chopped red onion
    Raspberry Vinaigrette Dressing (page 65)
1 can (12 ounces) STARKIST® Solid White Tuna, drained and chunked
6 to 8 Bibb lettuce cups

In large bowl, mix together rice, broccoli, pineapple, oranges, red pepper and onion. Add Raspberry Vinaigrette Dressing; toss. Refrigerate several hours before serving. Just before serving, add tuna; toss gently. Serve in lettuce cups.

*Makes 6 to 8 servings*

## Raspberry Vinaigrette Dressing

¼ cup raspberry vinegar or apple
 cider vinegar
2 tablespoons orange or lemon juice
1 tablespoon brown sugar
1 teaspoon seasoned salt
½ teaspoon crushed red pepper
1 medium clove garlic, finely minced
 or pressed
½ cup olive oil

In small bowl, whisk together vinegar, orange juice, brown sugar, seasoned salt, crushed red pepper and garlic. Slowly add oil, whisking continuously until well blended.

## Sparkling Berry Salad

2 cups cranberry juice
2 packages (4-serving size each) *or*
 1 package (8-serving size) JELL-O®
 Brand Sugar Free Gelatin, any red
 flavor
1½ cups cold club soda
¼ cup crème de cassis liqueur
1 teaspoon lemon juice
1 cup raspberries
1 cup blueberries
½ cup sliced strawberries
½ cup whole strawberries, cut into
 fans

**BRING** cranberry juice to a boil in medium saucepan. Completely dissolve gelatin in boiling cranberry juice. Stir in club soda, liqueur and lemon juice. Chill until slightly thickened.

**RESERVE** a few raspberries and blueberries for garnish, if desired. Stir remaining raspberries, blueberries and the sliced strawberries into gelatin mixture. Spoon into 6-cup mold that has been lightly sprayed with nonstick cooking spray. Chill until firm, about 4 hours. Unmold. Surround with reserved berries and the strawberry fans.

*Makes 8 servings*

**Variation:** Omit crème de cassis liqueur. Increase cranberry juice to 2¼ cups.

## Sunset Yogurt Salad

2 packages (4-serving size each) *or*
 1 package (8-serving size) JELL-O®
 Brand Orange or Lemon Flavor
 Sugar Free Gelatin
2 cups boiling water
1 container (8 ounces) plain low fat
 yogurt
¼ cup cold water
1 can (8 ounces) crushed pineapple in
 unsweetened juice, undrained
1 cup shredded carrots

**COMPLETELY** dissolve gelatin in boiling water. Measure 1 cup gelatin into medium mixing bowl; chill until slightly thickened. Stir in yogurt. Pour into medium serving bowl. Chill until set but not firm.

**ADD** cold water to the remaining gelatin. Stir in pineapple and carrots. Chill until slightly thickened. Spoon over gelatin-yogurt mixture in bowl. Chill until firm, about 4 hours. Garnish if desired.

*Makes 10 servings*

# Bow Tie Pasta Salad

16 ounces uncooked bow ties, rotini, ziti or other shaped pasta
1 bag (16 ounces) BIRDS EYE® frozen Farm Fresh Mixtures Broccoli, Cauliflower and Carrots*
1 cup Italian, creamy Italian or favorite salad dressing
1 bunch green onions, thinly sliced
1 cup pitted ripe olives, halved (optional)

*Or, substitute any other BIRDS EYE® frozen Farm Fresh Mixtures variety.*

Cook pasta according to package directions; drain. Cook vegetables according to package directions; drain. Combine pasta and vegetables with remaining ingredients in large bowl. Cover and chill until ready to serve.

*Makes about 8 servings*

# Pepperoni Pasta Salad

1 bag (16 ounces) BIRDS EYE® frozen Farm Fresh Mixtures Broccoli, Red Peppers, Onions and Mushrooms
2 cups cooked macaroni
1 package (3 ounces) thinly sliced pepperoni
1/4 to 1/2 cup peppercorn or ranch salad dressing

Cook vegetables according to package directions. Combine vegetables and macaroni in large bowl. Chill. Toss with pepperoni and dressing. Add salt and pepper to taste.

*Makes 4 to 6 servings*

# Grilled Vegetable and Ravioli Salad

1 package (9 ounces) CONTADINA® Refrigerated Fat Free Garden Vegetable Ravioli, cooked and drained
1 pound assorted fresh vegetables, such as zucchini, onion, eggplant or red, yellow or green bell peppers, grilled and diced
1 cup lightly packed, torn assorted salad greens
1 2/3 cups (12-ounce container) CONTADINA® Refrigerated Light Garden Vegetable Sauce
2 tablespoons olive oil
2 tablespoons red wine vinegar

In medium bowl, combine ravioli, vegetables and salad greens. In small bowl, combine garden vegetable sauce, oil and vinegar; mix well. Add to pasta; toss well. Serve immediately.

*Makes 4 servings*

*Bow Tie Pasta Salad*

# Thai-Style Tuna and Fruit Salad with Sweet-Sour-Spicy Dressing

8 lettuce leaves (use different varieties for color)
2 tablespoons chopped fresh cilantro
2 tablespoons chopped fresh mint leaves
1 can (6 ounces) STARKIST® Solid White Tuna, drained and chunked
⅓ cup sliced cucumber
⅓ cup drained mandarin oranges
⅓ cup red seedless grape halves
¼ cup thinly sliced red onion
Sweet-Sour-Spicy Dressing (recipe follows)
⅓ cup chopped cashews or peanuts

On platter, arrange half of lettuce. Break up remaining lettuce into bite-size pieces and place on lettuce on platter. Sprinkle cilantro and mint over lettuce. Arrange tuna, cucumber, oranges, grapes and onion on top. Refrigerate, covered, while preparing Sweet-Sour-Spicy Dressing. Pour dressing over salad; sprinkle with cashews.                   *Makes 4 servings*

## Sweet-Sour-Spicy Dressing

1 lime
3 cloves garlic
2 serrano chilies, halved, seeded and cut in pieces
¼ cup lime juice
1½ tablespoons nam pla (fish sauce) or soy sauce
1 tablespoon sugar

Peel ½ of lime with vegetable peeler. Place peel in blender or small food processor; add garlic, chilies, lime juice, nam pla and sugar. Process until mixture is blended and lime peel, garlic and chilies are finely chopped.

**Prep Time:** 20 minutes

# Tuna Pasta Primavera Salad

2 cups cooked and chilled small shell pasta
1½ cups halved cherry tomatoes
½ cup thinly sliced carrots
½ cup sliced celery
½ cup chopped seeded peeled cucumber
½ cup thinly sliced radishes
½ cup thawed frozen peas
¼ cup slivered red bell pepper
2 tablespoons minced green onion, including tops
1 can (12 ounces) STARKIST® Solid White or Chunk Light Tuna, drained and chunked
1 cup salad dressing of choice
Bibb or red leaf lettuce
Fresh herbs, for garnish

In large bowl, combine all ingredients except lettuce and herbs. Chill several hours. If using oil and vinegar dressing, stir salad mixture occasionally to evenly marinate ingredients. Place lettuce leaves on each plate; spoon salad over lettuce. Garnish with fresh herbs, if desired.

*Makes 6 servings*

**Prep Time:** 25 minutes

*Thai-Style Tuna and Fruit Salad with Sweet-Sour-Spicy Dressing*

# Thai Chicken Broccoli Salad

4 ounces uncooked linguine
Nonstick cooking spray
½ pound boneless skinless chicken
breasts, cut into 2×½-inch pieces
2 cups broccoli flowerets
⅔ cup chopped red bell pepper
6 green onions, sliced diagonally into
1-inch pieces
¼ cup reduced-fat creamy peanut
butter
2 tablespoons reduced-sodium soy
sauce
2 teaspoons Oriental sesame oil
½ teaspoon crushed red pepper
⅛ teaspoon garlic powder
¼ cup unsalted peanuts, chopped

Cook pasta according to package directions, omitting salt. Drain. Spray large nonstick skillet with cooking spray; heat over medium-high heat until hot. Add chicken; stir-fry 5 minutes or until chicken is no longer pink. Remove chicken from skillet. Add broccoli and 2 tablespoons cold water to skillet. Cook, covered, 2 minutes. Uncover; cook and stir 2 minutes or until broccoli is crisp-tender. Remove broccoli from skillet. Combine pasta, chicken, broccoli, bell pepper and onions in large bowl.

Blend peanut butter, 2 tablespoons hot water, soy sauce, oil, red pepper and garlic powder in small bowl. Pour over pasta mixture; toss until well blended. Top with peanuts before serving. Serve immediately. *Makes 4 servings*

# Szechuan Pork Salad

½ pound boneless lean pork
4 tablespoons KIKKOMAN® Teriyaki
Sauce, divided
⅛ to ¼ teaspoon crushed red pepper
1 cup water
2 tablespoons cornstarch
1 tablespoon distilled white vinegar
2 tablespoons vegetable oil, divided
1 onion, chunked and separated
12 radishes, thinly sliced
2 medium zucchini, cut into julienne
strips
Salt
4 cups shredded lettuce

Cut pork across grain into thin slices, then into narrow strips. Combine pork, 1 tablespoon teriyaki sauce and red pepper in small bowl; set aside. Combine water, cornstarch, remaining 3 tablespoons teriyaki sauce and vinegar; set aside. Heat 1 tablespoon oil in hot wok or large skillet over high heat. Add pork; stir-fry 2 minutes; remove. Heat remaining 1 tablespoon oil in same pan. Add onion; stir-fry 2 minutes. Add radishes and zucchini; lightly sprinkle with salt. Stir-fry 1 minute longer. Stir in pork and teriyaki sauce mixture. Cook and stir until mixture boils and thickens. Spoon over bed of lettuce on serving platter; serve immediately. *Makes 2 to 3 servings*

# Grilled Steak and — Asparagus Salad —

½ cup bottled light olive oil vinaigrette
⅓ cup A.1.® Steak Sauce
1 (1-pound) beef top round steak
1 (10-ounce) package frozen
  asparagus spears, cooked and
  cooled
½ cup thinly sliced red bell pepper
8 large lettuce leaves
1 tablespoon toasted sesame seed

In small bowl, blend vinaigrette and steak sauce. Place steak in glass dish; coat with ¼ cup vinaigrette mixture. Cover; chill 1 hour, turning once.

In small saucepan, over medium heat, heat remaining vinaigrette mixture to a boil. Reduce heat and simmer 1 minute; keep warm.

Remove steak from marinade. Grill over medium heat for 12 minutes or until done, turning occasionally. Thinly slice steak. Arrange steak, asparagus and red pepper on lettuce leaves. Pour warm vinaigrette mixture over salad; sprinkle with sesame seed. Serve immediately.

*Makes 4 servings*

# — Thai Beef Salad —

**DRESSING**

1 cup prepared olive oil vinaigrette
  salad dressing
⅓ cup FRANK'S® Original RedHot®
  Cayenne Pepper Sauce
3 tablespoons chopped peeled fresh
  ginger
3 tablespoons sugar
3 cloves garlic, chopped
2 teaspoons FRENCH'S®
  Worcestershire Sauce
1 cup packed fresh mint or basil
  leaves, coarsely chopped

**SALAD**

1 flank steak (about 1½ pounds)
6 cups washed and torn mixed salad
  greens
1 cup sliced peeled cucumber
⅓ cup chopped peanuts

Place Dressing ingredients in blender or food processor. Cover; process until smooth. Reserve 1 cup Dressing. Place steak in large resealable plastic food storage bag. Pour remaining Dressing over steak. Seal bag and marinate in refrigerator 30 minutes.

Place steak on grid, reserving marinade. Grill over hot coals about 15 minutes for medium-rare, basting frequently with marinade. Let steak stand 5 minutes. To serve, slice steak diagonally and arrange on top of salad greens and cucumber. Sprinkle with nuts and drizzle with reserved 1 cup Dressing. Serve warm. Garnish as desired.          *Makes 6 servings*

# STICK-TO-YOUR-RIBS MEATS

*Sink your teeth into the best of the butcher's bounty—beef, pork, lamb and veal—prepared to tender and juicy perfection.*

## Sizzling Steak Fajitas

½ cup A.1.® Steak Sauce

½ cup prepared picante sauce

1 pound flank or bottom round steak, thinly sliced

1 medium onion, thinly sliced

1 medium green bell pepper, cut into strips

1 tablespoon FLEISCHMANN'S® Margarine

8 (8-inch) flour tortillas, warmed

Sour cream, chopped tomatoes, avocado slices, shredded cheese and prepared guacamole (optional)

In small bowl, blend steak sauce and picante sauce. Place steak in shallow nonmetal dish; pour marinade over steak. Cover; chill for at least 2 hours, stirring occasionally.

In large skillet, over medium-high heat, cook onion and green pepper in margarine for 3 minutes or until vegetables are tender. Remove with slotted spoon; reserve. Add steak with marinade to same skillet; cook and stir for 8 minutes or until cooked to desired doneness. Add reserved vegetables; cook until heated through. Serve steak mixture in tortillas with desired fajita toppings.

*Makes 4 servings*

*Sizzling Steak Fajita*

# Mexican Flank Steak with Mock Tamales

1½ pounds beef flank steak
⅓ cup fresh lemon juice
⅓ cup extra virgin olive oil
6 tablespoons minced jalapeño peppers
1 tablespoon chopped fresh cilantro
1 teaspoon salt
1 teaspoon freshly ground black pepper
Linda's Sassy Salsa (recipe follows)
Mock Tamales (recipe follows)
Lemon slices, jalapeño peppers and cilantro sprigs, for garnish

Place beef flank steak in shallow dish. Combine lemon juice, oil, jalapeño peppers, cilantro, salt and black pepper in medium bowl; add steak, turning to coat. Cover; refrigerate 6 to 8 hours or overnight. Prepare Linda's Sassy Salsa and Mock Tamales. Remove steak from marinade; reserve marinade. Place steak on grid over medium-hot coals. Place Mock Tamales around outer edge of grid. Grill steak 12 to 15 minutes or to desired doneness (rare or medium), turning once and basting occasionally with marinade. Turn tamales halfway through cooking time. Place steak and tamales on serving platter. Spoon ¼ cup salsa over tamales. Garnish platter with lemon slices, whole jalapeño peppers and cilantro sprigs. Carve steak across grain into thin slices and serve with remaining salsa.

*Makes 6 servings*

# Linda's Sassy Salsa

2 tomatillos, hulls and tough skins removed
3 large cloves garlic, peeled
2 plum tomatoes, minced
3 plum tomatoes, coarsely chopped
3 jalapeño peppers, thinly sliced
¼ cup coarsely chopped fresh cilantro
1 tablespoon fresh lemon juice
1 teaspoon freshly ground black pepper

Process tomatillos and garlic in food processor or blender until finely chopped. Combine tomatillo mixture, tomatoes, jalapeño peppers, cilantro, lemon juice and black pepper in medium bowl. Refrigerate, covered, 1 hour or overnight to blend flavors.

*Makes 2 cups*

# Mock Tamales

1 cup (4 ounces) shredded sharp Cheddar cheese
1 cup (4 ounces) shredded Muenster cheese
2 tablespoons minced green onion and tops
6 (7-inch) flour tortillas

Combine cheeses and onions in medium bowl. Place equal portion of cheese mixture in center of each tortilla. Fold bottom side of each tortilla over filling. Fold two sides over filling; fold top side over filling, envelope fashion. Wrap each tamale in 12×8-inch piece of foil, twisting each end. *Makes 6 servings*

Favorite recipe from **National Beef Cook-Off**®

*Mexican Flank Steak with Mock Tamale*

## Pepper Stuffed Flank Steak with French's Signature Steak Sauce

1 flank steak (about 1½ pounds)
    Salt and black pepper
2 cups thinly sliced bell peppers
1 small onion, thinly sliced
    French's Signature Steak Sauce
    (recipe follows)

Lay steak on baking sheet lined with plastic wrap. Cover; freeze about 2 hours or until nearly firm. Place steak on cutting board. Cut steak in half lengthwise. Thaw in refrigerator. Sprinkle inside of each piece with salt and black pepper. Arrange bell peppers and onion on steak, leaving ½-inch edge. Tightly roll up jelly-roll style; tie with kitchen string. Place steak on oiled grid. Grill over medium-high coals 25 minutes for medium doneness, turning often. Baste with some of French's Signature Steak Sauce during last 10 minutes of cooking. Remove string. Let steak stand 5 minutes. Slice steak diagonally. Serve with remaining sauce.

*Makes 6 servings*

### French's Signature Steak Sauce

½ cup ketchup
¼ cup FRENCH'S® Worcestershire
    Sauce
1 to 2 tablespoons FRANK'S® Original
    RedHot® Cayenne Pepper Sauce or
    to taste
2 cloves garlic, minced

Combine ingredients for French's Signature Steak Sauce in small bowl; stir until smooth.

*Makes ¼ cup*

## Beef Kabobs with Zucchini and — Cherry Tomatoes —

¼ cup FILIPPO BERIO® Olive Oil
2 tablespoons chopped fresh parsley
2 tablespoons red wine vinegar
1 clove garlic, minced
½ teaspoon salt
⅛ teaspoon ground black pepper
1 pound lean beef top sirloin or top
    round steak, well trimmed, cut
    into 1-inch cubes
1 small zucchini, cut into ½-inch-thick
    slices
12 cherry tomatoes
6 metal skewers

In medium bowl, whisk together first six ingredients. Add beef, zucchini and tomatoes; toss to coat. Cover; marinate 2 hours or overnight in refrigerator. Drain, reserving marinade. Alternately thread beef and vegetables onto skewers, ending with beef. Brush barbecue grid with olive oil. Grill kabobs, on covered grill, over hot coals 6 to 8 minutes for medium-rare or until desired doneness, turning and brushing with reserved marinade halfway through grilling time. Or, broil kabobs, 4 inches from heat, 6 to 8 minutes for medium-rare or until desired doneness, turning and brushing with reserved marinade halfway through broiling time.

*Makes 6 servings*

*Pepper Stuffed Flank Steak with
French's Signature Steak Sauce*

## Peppercorn Beef Kabobs

**1 pound boneless beef sirloin steak, cut 1 inch thick**
**1½ teaspoons black peppercorns, crushed**
**½ teaspoon salt**
**½ teaspoon paprika**
**1 clove garlic, minced**
**1 medium onion, cut into 12 wedges**

Preheat broiler. Cut beef steak into 1-inch pieces. Combine peppercorns, salt, paprika and garlic in shallow dish. Add beef; turn to coat. Thread an equal number of beef pieces and 3 onion wedges onto each of 4 (12-inch) metal skewers. (If using bamboo skewers, soak in water 20 minutes before using to prevent them from burning.) Spray rack of broiler pan with nonstick cooking spray. Place kabobs on rack. Broil 4 inches from heat, 9 to 12 minutes or until desired doneness, turning occasionally. Garnish with tomatoes, if desired.

*Makes 4 servings*

Favorite recipe from **National Cattlemen's Beef Association**

## Stuffed Sirloin Roast

**1 boneless sirloin steak, 2 inches thick (about 3 pounds), well trimmed**
**½ teaspoon salt**
**½ teaspoon freshly ground black pepper**
**2 tablespoons unsalted butter substitute**
**8 ounces mushrooms, chopped**
**2 teaspoons minced garlic**
**1 cup (4 ounces) shredded ALPINE LACE® Reduced Fat Baby Swiss Cheese**
**1 tablespoon snipped fresh rosemary leaves *or* 1 teaspoon dried rosemary**
**2 teaspoons snipped fresh thyme leaves *or* ½ teaspoon dried thyme**
**Sprigs of fresh rosemary**

**1.** Preheat the oven to 350°F. Fit a large roasting pan with a rack. Cut the steak horizontally with a sharp pointed knife almost, but not completely, through. Open the steak like a book. Sprinkle with the salt and pepper.

**2.** In a medium-size skillet, melt the butter over medium-high heat. Add the mushrooms and garlic and sauté for 5 minutes or until all the liquid has evaporated. Spread the mushroom mixture evenly onto the steak. In a small bowl, toss the cheese with the rosemary and thyme and sprinkle on top of the mushroom mixture.

**3.** Starting with one of the wide ends, roll up the steak, jelly-roll style. Tie with a piece of cotton string at 2-inch intervals. Place the roast, seam-side down, on the rack. Bake, uncovered, for 45 minutes for rare (55 minutes for medium-rare) or until it's the way you like it. Garnish with the rosemary sprigs and serve immediately!

*Makes 12 servings*

## Marinated Beef Tenderloin

¾ **cup dry vermouth**
¼ **cup olive oil**
¼ **cup chopped shallots**
1 **teaspoon LAWRY'S® Garlic Powder with Parsley**
1 **teaspoon dried rosemary**
¾ **teaspoon LAWRY'S® Seasoned Salt**
¾ **teaspoon dried thyme, crushed**
¾ **teaspoon LAWRY'S® Seasoned Pepper**
1½ **pounds beef tenderloin**

In small bowl, combine all ingredients except meat. Pierce meat several times with fork. In large resealable plastic bag or glass baking dish, place meat and marinade. Seal bag or cover dish. Marinate in refrigerator at least 1 hour or overnight, turning occasionally. Bake at 400°F, uncovered, 50 minutes to 1 hour or until internal meat temperature reaches 180°F. Let stand 5 minutes before slicing.

*Makes 4 to 6 servings*

**Presentation:** Serve with garlic potatoes and your favorite vegetables.

## Hunan Chili Beef

1 **pound beef flank steak**
1 **tablespoon cornstarch**
3 **tablespoons low-sodium soy sauce**
3 **tablespoons vegetable oil, divided**
1 **tablespoon rice wine or dry sherry**
2 **teaspoons brown sugar**
1 **jalapeño pepper, halved, seeded***
3 **green onions with tops**
¼ **small red bell pepper**
1 **cup drained canned baby corn**
1 **small piece fresh ginger (1 inch long), peeled and minced**
2 **cloves garlic, minced**
1 **teaspoon hot chili oil**
**Hot cooked rice**

*\*Jalapeño peppers can sting and irritate the skin; wear rubber gloves when handling peppers and do not touch eyes.*

Cut beef across grain into 2×¼-inch slices. Blend cornstarch, soy sauce, 1 tablespoon vegetable oil, wine and brown sugar in medium bowl until smooth. Add beef and toss to coat; set aside. Cut jalapeño lengthwise into strips. Cut onions into 1-inch pieces. Remove seeds from red pepper. Rinse, dry and cut into ¼-inch strips. Set aside.

Heat wok over high heat until hot. Drizzle 1 tablespoon vegetable oil into wok and heat 30 seconds. Add half the beef mixture; stir-fry until well browned. Remove to large bowl. Repeat with remaining 1 tablespoon vegetable oil and beef mixture. Reduce heat to medium. Add corn, onions, ginger and garlic to wok; stir-fry 1 minute. Add jalapeño and red pepper; stir-fry 1 minute. Return beef and any accumulated juices to wok; add chili oil. Toss to combine; cook until heated through. Serve with rice.

*Makes 4 servings*

## Moo Shu Beef

½ **pound deli roast beef, cut ⅛ inch thick**
1 **tablespoon dry sherry**
2 **teaspoons cornstarch, divided**
1 **teaspoon minced fresh ginger**
3 **teaspoons low-sodium soy sauce, divided**
1 **clove garlic, minced**
½ **teaspoon sugar**
¼ **cup beef broth**
3 **tablespoons peanut oil or vegetable oil, divided**
1 **egg, slightly beaten**
1 **cup shredded carrots**
3 **green onions with tops, cut into ½-inch pieces**
1 **can (8 ounces) sliced bamboo shoots, drained and cut into thin strips**
   **Hoisin\* or plum sauce**
8 **flour tortillas (7 to 8 inches), warmed**

*\*Hoisin sauce is a thick, dark brown sauce made from soybeans, flour, sugar, spices, garlic, chili and salt. It has a sweet, spicy flavor.*

Cut beef into thin strips. Blend sherry, 1 teaspoon cornstarch, ginger, 1 teaspoon soy sauce, garlic and sugar in large bowl until smooth. Add beef; toss to coat. Marinate 10 minutes. Blend broth, ½ cup water, remaining 2 teaspoons soy sauce and remaining 1 teaspoon cornstarch in cup until smooth; set aside.

Heat wok over high heat until hot. Drizzle 1 tablespoon oil into wok; heat 30 seconds. Pour egg into wok; tilt to coat bottom. Scramble egg, breaking into small pieces as it cooks. Remove from wok. Add remaining 2 tablespoons oil to wok; heat 30 seconds. Add carrots; stir-fry 1 minute. Add beef mixture, onions and bamboo shoots; stir-fry 1 minute. Stir broth mixture until smooth; add to wok. Cook and stir 1 minute or until sauce boils and thickens. Cook 1 minute more. Stir in egg.

Spread equal amount of hoisin on each tortilla. Spoon beef mixture over sauce. Fold bottom of tortilla up over filling, then fold sides over filling. Transfer to serving plate.     *Makes 4 servings*

## Teriyaki Beef

¾ **pound sirloin tip steak, cut into thin strips**
½ **cup teriyaki sauce**
¼ **cup water**
1 **tablespoon cornstarch**
1 **teaspoon sugar**
1 **bag (16 ounces) BIRDS EYE® frozen Farm Fresh Mixtures Broccoli, Carrots and Water Chestnuts**

• Spray large skillet with nonstick cooking spray; cook beef strips over medium-high heat 7 to 8 minutes, stirring occasionally.

• Combine teriyaki sauce, water, cornstarch and sugar; mix well.

• Add teriyaki sauce mixture and vegetables to beef. Bring to boil; quickly reduce heat to medium.

• Cook 7 to 10 minutes or until broccoli is heated through, stirring occasionally.

*Makes 4 to 6 servings*

**Prep Time:** 5 to 10 minutes
**Cook Time:** 20 minutes

*Moo Shu Beef*

# Herb-Crusted Roast Beef and Potatoes

1 (4½-pound) eye of round or sirloin tip beef roast
¾ cup plus 2 tablespoons FILIPPO BERIO® Olive Oil, divided
Salt and freshly ground black pepper
2 tablespoons paprika
2 pounds small red skin potatoes, cut in half
1 cup dry bread crumbs
1 teaspoon dried thyme leaves
1 teaspoon dried rosemary leaves
½ teaspoon salt
¼ teaspoon freshly ground black pepper

Preheat oven to 325°F. Brush roast with 2 tablespoons olive oil. Season to taste with salt and pepper. Place in large roasting pan; insert meat thermometer into center of thickest part of roast. Roast 45 minutes.

Meanwhile, in large bowl, combine ½ cup olive oil and paprika. Add potatoes; toss until lightly coated. In small bowl, combine remaining ¼ cup olive oil, bread crumbs, thyme, rosemary, ½ teaspoon salt and ¼ teaspoon pepper.

Carefully remove roast from oven. Place potatoes around roast. Press bread crumb mixture on top of roast to form crust. Sprinkle any remaining bread crumb mixture over potatoes. Roast 40 to 45 minutes or until thermometer registers 145°F for medium-rare or until desired doneness is reached. Transfer roast to carving board; tent with foil. Let stand 5 to 10 minutes before carving. Serve with potatoes.  *Makes 8 servings*

# Family Swiss Steak and Potatoes

½ cup all-purpose flour
1½ teaspoons salt
½ teaspoon pepper
2½ pounds round steak, about 1½ inches thick
2 tablespoons CRISCO® Oil
2 cups sliced onions
1 can (14½ ounces) whole tomatoes, cut up, liquid reserved
½ cup water
½ teaspoon dried thyme leaves
1 bay leaf
8 medium potatoes, peeled

**1. Combine** flour, salt and pepper in shallow dish. **Add** meat. **Coat** both sides with flour mixture. **Pound** flour into meat.

**2. Heat** Crisco Oil in large deep skillet or Dutch oven on medium heat. **Add** meat. **Brown** on both sides, adding onions during last 2 to 3 minutes.

**3. Add** tomatoes with liquid, water, thyme and bay leaf. **Bring** to a boil. **Reduce** heat to low. **Cover. Simmer** 1 hour 15 minutes. **Turn** meat over. **Add** potatoes. **Simmer** until meat and potatoes are tender.

**4. Arrange** meat and potatoes on platter. **Remove** bay leaf from sauce. **Pour** sauce over meat and potatoes.

*Makes 8 servings*

*Herb-Crusted Roast Beef and Potatoes*

# Stuffed Salisbury Steak with Mushroom & Onion Topping

2 pounds ground beef
¼ cup FRENCH'S® Worcestershire
    Sauce
2 cans (2.8 ounces each) FRENCH'S®
    French Fried Onions, divided
1 teaspoon garlic salt
½ teaspoon ground black pepper
4 ounces Cheddar cheese, cut into
    6 sticks (about 2 × ½ × ½ inches)
    Mushroom Topping (recipe follows)

Combine beef, Worcestershire, *1 can*
French Fried Onions, garlic salt and
pepper in medium bowl. Divide meat
evenly into 6 portions. Place 1 stick
cheese in center of each portion, shaping
meat into ovals around cheese. Place
steaks on grid. Grill over medium-high
coals 15 minutes or until meat
thermometer inserted into beef reaches
160°F, turning once. Serve with
Mushroom Topping and sprinkle with
remaining *1 can* French Fried Onions.

*Makes 6 servings*

## Mushroom Topping

2 tablespoons butter or margarine
1 package (12 ounces) mushrooms,
    wiped clean and quartered
2 tablespoons FRENCH'S®
    Worcestershire Sauce

Melt butter in large skillet over medium-
high heat. Add mushrooms; cook
until browned, stirring often. Add
Worcestershire. Reduce heat to low.
Cook 5 minutes, stirring occasionally.

*Makes 6 servings*

# Margarita Pork Kabobs

1 pound pork tenderloin, cut into
    1-inch cubes
1 cup margarita mix *or* 1 cup lime
    juice, 4 teaspoons sugar and
    ½ teaspoon salt
1 teaspoon ground coriander
1 clove garlic, minced
2 tablespoons butter, softened
1 tablespoon minced fresh parsley
2 teaspoons lime juice
⅛ teaspoon sugar
2 ears corn, cut into 8 pieces
1 large green or red bell pepper, cut
    into 1-inch chunks

Combine margarita mix, coriander and
garlic. Place pork cubes in heavy resealable
plastic bag; pour marinade over to cover.
Seal bag; marinate in refrigerator for at
least 30 minutes. Blend together butter,
parsley, lime juice and sugar; set aside.
Thread pork cubes onto skewers,
alternating with pieces of corn and
chunks of bell pepper. (If using bamboo
skewers, soak in water 20 to 30 minutes
before using.) Grill over hot coals, basting
with butter mixture, for 10 to 15 minutes,
turning frequently.    *Makes 4 servings*

Favorite recipe from **National Pork Producers Council**

*Margarita Pork Kabob*

# Cajun Chops with Creole Rice

1 tablespoon paprika
1 teaspoon seasoned salt
1 teaspoon rubbed sage
½ teaspoon garlic powder
½ teaspoon cayenne pepper
½ teaspoon black pepper
8 (4-ounce) lean boneless center-cut pork loin chops, ½ inch thick
2 teaspoons CRISCO® Oil
  Creole Beans and Rice (recipe follows)

**1. Combine** paprika, seasoned salt, sage, garlic powder, cayenne pepper and black pepper in shallow dish. **Add** meat. **Coat** on both sides with seasoning mixture.

**2. Heat** Crisco Oil in large nonstick skillet on high heat. **Add** meat. **Reduce** heat to medium. **Cook** on both sides 6 to 8 minutes or until dark brown. **Serve** with Creole Beans and Rice.

*Makes 8 servings*

# Creole Beans and Rice

2 cans (14½ ounces each) peeled no salt added tomatoes, undrained
1 cup uncooked rice
2 tablespoons CRISCO® Oil
½ cup chopped onion
4 cloves garlic, minced
1 cup chopped celery
1 cup chopped carrots
1 cup chopped green bell pepper
1 tablespoon ground cumin
1 tablespoon chili powder
1 teaspoon dried basil leaves
½ teaspoon cayenne pepper
2 cans (15½ ounces each) kidney beans, drained
1 can (6 ounces) no salt added tomato paste
3 tablespoons vinegar
1 tablespoon Worcestershire sauce
1 teaspoon sugar

**1. Drain** tomatoes, reserving liquid. **Add** enough water to reserved liquid to measure 2 cups. **Pour** into medium saucepan. **Add** rice. **Bring** to a boil. **Reduce** heat to low. **Simmer** 20 minutes or until rice is tender.

**2. Heat** Crisco Oil in large saucepan over medium heat. **Add** onion and garlic. **Cook** and stir until tender. **Add** celery and carrots. **Cook** and stir until crisp-tender. **Add** green pepper, cumin, chili powder, basil and cayenne. **Cook** and stir until green pepper is tender.

**3. Add** tomatoes. **Break** up with spoon. **Stir** in rice, beans, tomato paste, vinegar, Worcestershire sauce and sugar. **Reduce** heat to low. **Heat** thoroughly, stirring occasionally.

*Makes 8 servings*

# Jalapeño Pork & Peaches

1 can (16 ounces) peach halves in syrup
1½ teaspoons white wine vinegar
1¼ teaspoons minced jalapeño pepper
4 thin lean pork chops
¼ cup seasoned dry bread crumbs
1½ teaspoons LAWRY'S® Seasoned Salt
1¼ teaspoons LAWRY'S® Garlic Powder with Parsley
1 tablespoon vegetable oil
1 teaspoon cornstarch
½ teaspoon sugar

Drain peaches; reserve ½ cup syrup. Quarter peaches; set aside. In small bowl, combine reserved ½ cup syrup, vinegar and jalapeño pepper. Place pork chops and syrup mixture in resealable plastic bag. Marinate pork chops in refrigerator 30 minutes. In shallow dish, combine bread crumbs, Seasoned Salt and Garlic Powder with Parsley. Remove pork chops from bag, reserving marinade. Dredge pork chops in crumb mixture. In large skillet, heat oil and brown pork chops 4 to 5 minutes on each side or until golden. In small saucepan, combine reserved marinade, cornstarch and sugar. Bring to a boil; reduce heat and simmer 1 minute. Stir in peaches; heat through. Serve sauce over pork chops.

*Makes 4 servings*

# Spareribs with Tex-Mex Barbecue Sauce

6 pounds pork spareribs, cut into 2-rib portions
½ cup HELLMANN'S® or BEST FOODS® Real or Light Mayonnaise or Low Fat Mayonnaise Dressing
½ cup ketchup
¼ cup Worcestershire sauce
3 tablespoons chili powder
1 clove garlic, minced or pressed
⅛ teaspoon hot pepper sauce

In large shallow roasting pan, arrange ribs in single layer on rack. Roast in 325°F oven 1½ hours or until tender. Meanwhile, prepare Tex-Mex Barbecue Sauce: In small bowl with wire whisk, combine mayonnaise, ketchup, Worcestershire sauce, chili powder, garlic and pepper sauce until smooth. Brush sauce on ribs, turning frequently, during last 20 minutes of roasting time.

*Makes 6 servings*

**Homestyle Barbecue Sauce:** Follow recipe for Tex-Mex Barbecue Sauce, omitting chili powder and garlic and adding ¼ cup prepared mustard and ¼ cup KARO® Dark Corn Syrup *or* ¼ cup firmly packed brown sugar.

**Sweet and Sour Barbecue Sauce:** Follow recipe for Tex-Mex Barbecue Sauce, omitting Worcestershire sauce, chili powder, garlic and hot pepper sauce and adding ¾ cup apricot preserves, ¼ cup soy sauce and 1 teaspoon ground ginger.

# Jamaican Pork Chops with Tropical Fruit Salsa

⅔ cup prepared Italian salad dressing
⅓ cup FRANK'S® Original RedHot® Cayenne Pepper Sauce
⅓ cup lime juice
2 tablespoons brown sugar
2 teaspoons dried thyme leaves
1 teaspoon ground allspice
½ teaspoon ground nutmeg
½ teaspoon ground cinnamon
6 loin pork chops, cut 1 inch thick (about 2½ pounds)
Tropical Fruit Salsa (recipe follows)

Place salad dressing, RedHot sauce, lime juice, sugar and seasonings in blender or food processor. Cover and process until smooth. Reserve *½ cup* dressing mixture for Tropical Fruit Salsa. Place pork chops in large resealable plastic food storage bag. Pour remaining dressing mixture over chops. Seal bag and marinate in refrigerator 1 hour.

Place chops on grid, reserving marinade. Grill over medium coals 30 minutes or until pork is juicy and barely pink in center, turning and basting frequently with dressing mixture. (Do not baste during last 5 minutes of cooking.) Serve chops with Tropical Fruit Salsa. Garnish as desired. *Makes 6 servings*

## Tropical Fruit Salsa

1 cup finely chopped fresh pineapple
1 ripe mango, peeled, seeded and finely chopped
2 tablespoons finely chopped red onion
1 tablespoon minced fresh cilantro leaves

Combine pineapple, mango, onion, cilantro and reserved *½ cup* dressing mixture in small bowl. Refrigerate until chilled. *Makes about 2½ cups*

**Prep Time:** 20 minutes
**Marinate Time:** 1 hour
**Cook Time:** 30 minutes

*Jamaican Pork Chop with Tropical Fruit Salsa*

## Dijon Baby Back — Barbecued Ribs —

2 to 3 teaspoons LAWRY'S® Seasoned Salt
4 pounds pork baby back ribs
1 bottle (12 ounces) LAWRY'S® Dijon & Honey Barbecue Sauce

Sprinkle Seasoned Salt onto both sides of ribs. In resealable bag or shallow glass baking dish, place ribs; seal bag or cover dish. Refrigerate at least 2 hours. Heat grill. Grill ribs, 4 to 5 inches from heat source, 45 to 60 minutes or until ribs are tender, turning and basting with Dijon & Honey Barbecue Sauce after 30 minutes.

*Makes 4 to 6 servings*

## Thai Ribs

¼ cup creamy peanut butter
¼ cup Kikkoman® Soy Sauce
3 tablespoons vinegar
2 tablespoons sugar
1½ teaspoons TABASCO® pepper sauce
1 large clove garlic, pressed
3 to 4 pounds pork spareribs, cut into 2-rib pieces

Measure peanut butter into small bowl; gradually blend in soy sauce and vinegar until mixture is smooth and creamy. Stir in sugar, TABASCO sauce and garlic. Place ribs, meaty-side down, in shallow, foil-lined baking pan. Brush ribs thoroughly with peanut butter mixture. Cover pan tightly with foil; bake in 350°F oven 1

hour. Discard foil; drain off drippings. Brush ribs with sauce; bake, uncovered, 15 minutes. Turn ribs over and brush with remaining sauce. Bake 15 minutes longer, or until ribs are golden brown and tender.

*Makes 4 to 6 servings*

## Spareribs with Zesty Honey — Sauce —

1 cup chili sauce
½ to ¾ cup honey
¼ cup minced onion
2 tablespoons dry red wine (optional)
1 tablespoon Worcestershire sauce
1 teaspoon Dijon mustard
3 pounds pork spareribs
Salt and pepper

Combine chili sauce, honey, onion, wine, if desired, Worcestershire sauce and mustard in small saucepan. Cook and stir over medium heat until mixture comes to a boil. Reduce heat to low and simmer, uncovered, 5 minutes.

Sprinkle spareribs with salt and pepper. Place on rack in roasting pan; cover with foil. Roast at 375°F 35 to 45 minutes. Uncover and brush generously with sauce. Roast 45 minutes, brushing with sauce every 15 minutes, until spareribs are fully cooked and tender. Cut spareribs into serving portions and serve with remaining sauce. *Makes 4 servings*

Favorite recipe from **National Honey Board**

*Dijon Baby Back Barbecued Ribs*

# Honey Nut Stir-Fry

1 pound pork steak or loin or boneless chicken breast
¾ cup orange juice
⅓ cup honey
3 tablespoons soy sauce
1 tablespoon cornstarch
¼ teaspoon ground ginger
2 tablespoons vegetable oil, divided
2 large carrots, sliced diagonally
2 stalks celery, sliced diagonally
½ cup cashews or peanuts
Hot cooked rice

Cut pork into thin strips; set aside. Combine orange juice, honey, soy sauce, cornstarch and ginger in small bowl; mix well. Heat 1 tablespoon oil in large skillet over medium-high heat. Add carrots and celery; stir-fry about 3 minutes. Remove vegetables; set aside. Add remaining 1 tablespoon oil to skillet. Add meat; stir-fry about 3 minutes. Return vegetables to skillet. Stir sauce mixture; add to skillet with nuts. Cook and stir over medium-high heat until sauce comes to a boil and thickens. Serve over rice.

*Makes 4 to 6 servings*

Favorite recipe from **National Honey Board**

# Mandarin Pork Stir-Fry

1½ cups DOLE® Mandarin Tangerine Juice or Pineapple Orange Juice, divided
Vegetable cooking spray
12 ounces lean pork tenderloin or boneless skinless chicken breast halves, cut into thin strips
1 tablespoon finely chopped fresh ginger *or* ½ teaspoon ground ginger
2 cups DOLE® Shredded Carrots
½ cup chopped DOLE® Pitted Prunes
4 DOLE® Green Onions, diagonally cut into 1-inch pieces
2 tablespoons low-sodium soy sauce
1 teaspoon cornstarch
Hot cooked rice (optional)

•**Heat** 2 tablespoons juice over medium-high heat in large, nonstick skillet sprayed with vegetable cooking spray until juice bubbles.

•**Add** pork and ginger. Cook and stir 3 minutes or until pork is no longer pink; remove pork from skillet.

•**Heat** 3 tablespoons juice in skillet. Add carrots, prunes and green onions; cook and stir 3 minutes.

•**Stir** soy sauce and cornstarch into remaining juice; add to carrot mixture in skillet. Return pork to skillet; cover. Cook 2 minutes or until heated through and sauce is slightly thickened. Serve over rice and garnish with green onions and orange peel, if desired. *Makes 4 servings*

*Honey Nut Stir-Fry*

## Stuffed Pork Tenderloin

2 teaspoons minced garlic
2 teaspoons snipped fresh rosemary
   *or* ½ teaspoon dried rosemary
2 teaspoons snipped fresh thyme
   leaves *or* ½ teaspoon dried thyme
1 teaspoon salt
½ teaspoon freshly ground black
   pepper
1 boneless end-cut rolled pork loin
   with tenderloin attached
   (4 pounds), tied
1 tablespoon unsalted butter
   substitute
2 large tart apples, peeled, cored and
   thinly sliced (2 cups)
1 cup thin strips yellow onion
10 thin slices (½ ounce each) ALPINE
   LACE® Reduced Fat Swiss Cheese
1 cup apple cider or apple juice

**1.** Preheat the oven to 325°F. Fit a 13×9×3-inch baking pan with a rack. In a small bowl, combine the garlic, rosemary, thyme, salt and pepper. Untie and unroll the pork loin, laying it flat. Rub half of the spice mixture onto the pork.

**2.** In a medium skillet, melt the butter over medium-high heat. Add the apples and onion and sauté for 5 minutes or until tender. Spread this mixture evenly on the pork; cover with cheese slices. Starting from one of the widest ends, re-roll the pork, jelly-roll style. Tie the roast with cotton string at 1-inch intervals and rub the outside with the remaining spice mixture. Place the roast on the rack in the pan and pour the apple cider over it. Roast, uncovered, basting frequently with drippings for 2 hours or until an instant-read thermometer inserted in the thickest part registers 155°F. Let stand for 15 minutes before slicing.          *Makes 16 servings*

## Pork Tenderloin Mole

2 whole pork tenderloins (1¼ to
   1½ pounds)
2 tablespoons oil
½ cup chopped onion
1 clove garlic, minced
1 cup Mexican-style chili beans,
   undrained
¼ cup raisins
¼ cup bottled chili sauce
2 tablespoons water
1 tablespoon peanut butter
1 teaspoon unsweetened cocoa
   Dash *each* salt, cinnamon and
   cloves

Place tenderloins in shallow baking pan. Roast at 350°F for 30 to 40 minutes or until pork is barely pink in center. Heat oil in medium saucepan; cook onion and garlic over low heat for 5 minutes. Combine remaining ingredients in blender; process until almost smooth. Stir sauce mixture into saucepan. Heat thoroughly, stirring frequently. Serve sauce over pork tenderloin slices.

*Makes 6 servings*

Favorite recipe from **National Pork Producers Council**

## Mushroom Sausage Spinach Strudel

½ pound **BOB EVANS FARMS® Original Recipe Roll Sausage**
3 tablespoons olive oil
1 small onion, chopped
¼ pound fresh mushrooms, sliced
¼ cup chopped red bell pepper
1 clove garlic, minced
½ pound fresh spinach, washed, torn into small pieces and drained
¼ cup (1 ounce) shredded Swiss cheese
Salt and black pepper to taste
4 sheets phyllo dough, thawed according to package directions
¼ cup butter or margarine, melted
3 tablespoons dry bread crumbs
Fresh thyme sprig and red pepper strips (optional)

Crumble sausage into medium skillet. Cook over medium-high heat until browned, stirring occasionally. Drain off any drippings. Remove sausage to paper towels; set aside. Heat oil in same skillet until hot. Add onion, mushrooms, chopped red pepper and garlic; cook and stir until vegetables are tender. Stir in sausage, spinach, cheese, salt and black pepper; cook until vegetables are tender. Set aside until cool.

Preheat oven to 375°F. Place 1 phyllo sheet on work surface. Brush entire sheet with some melted butter and sprinkle with ¼ of bread crumbs. (To keep remaining sheets from drying out, cover with damp kitchen towel.) Repeat layers three times. Spread sausage mixture over top; roll up, starting at one short side, until roll forms. Place on ungreased baking sheet. Brush with remaining butter; bake 15 minutes or until golden. Let stand 5 minutes. Cut into 1-inch slices. Garnish with thyme and pepper strips, if desired. Serve hot. Refrigerate leftovers. *Makes 4 to 6 servings*

## Sausage Stroganoff in Puffed Pastry Shells

2 (10-ounce) packages **BOB EVANS FARMS® Skinless Link Sausage**
1 medium onion, sliced
1 (10½-ounce) can condensed cream of mushroom soup
1 cup sour cream
1 (4-ounce) can sliced mushrooms, drained
2 tablespoons ketchup
2 teaspoons Worcestershire sauce
8 frozen puffed pastry shells, thawed according to package directions

Preheat oven to 250°F. Cut sausage into bite-size pieces. Cook in large skillet over medium heat until browned, stirring occasionally. Remove sausage; set aside. Add onion to drippings; cook and stir until just tender. Stir in sausage, soup, sour cream, mushrooms, ketchup and Worcestershire sauce. Cook over low heat until heated through. Warm shells in oven. Spoon sausage mixture into shells. Serve hot. Refrigerate leftovers and reheat slowly in top of large double boiler over hot, not boiling, water. *Makes 8 servings*

## Hickory Smoked Ham with Maple-Mustard Sauce

**Hickory chunks or chips for smoking**
**1 fully cooked boneless ham (about 5 pounds)**
**¾ cup maple syrup**
**¾ cup spicy brown mustard or Dijon mustard**

Soak about 4 wood chunks or several handfuls of wood chips in water; drain. If using a canned ham, scrape off any gelatin. If using another type of fully cooked ham, such as a bone-in shank, trim most of the fat, leaving a ⅛-inch layer. (The thinner the fat layer, the better the glaze will adhere to the ham.)

Arrange low KINGSFORD® Briquets on each side of a rectangular metal or foil drip pan. Pour in hot tap water to fill pan half full. Add soaked wood (all the chunks; part of the chips) to the fire.

Oil hot grid to help prevent sticking. Place ham on grid directly above drip pan. Grill ham, on a covered grill, 20 to 30 minutes per pound, until a meat thermometer inserted in the thickest part registers 140°F. If your grill has a thermometer, maintain a cooking temperature of about 200°F. For best flavor, cook slowly over low coals, adding a few briquets to both sides of the fire every hour, or as necessary to maintain a constant temperature. Add more soaked hickory chips every 20 to 30 minutes.

Meanwhile, prepare Maple-Mustard Sauce by mixing maple syrup and mustard in small bowl; set aside most of the syrup mixture to serve as a sauce. Brush ham with remaining mixture several times during the last 45 minutes of cooking. Let ham stand 10 minutes before slicing. Slice ham and serve with Maple-Mustard Sauce.

*Makes 12 to 15 servings*

## Mandarin Medallions

**1 pork tenderloin, about 1 pound**
**1 tablespoon vegetable oil**
**½ cup orange juice**
**¼ cup orange marmalade**
**2 tablespoons lemon juice**
**1 tablespoon cornstarch**
**1 teaspoon prepared horseradish**
**½ teaspoon ground cinnamon**
**1 (10-ounce) can mandarin orange segments, drained**

Slice tenderloin crosswise into eight pieces. Flatten pieces slightly. Heat oil in large heavy skillet over medium-high heat. Brown pork pieces quickly, about 1 minute per side. Blend remaining ingredients except mandarin oranges; add to skillet. Cook and stir until sauce thickens. Reduce heat; simmer 3 to 4 minutes or until pork is barely pink in center. Remove to serving platter; garnish with mandarin oranges.

*Makes 4 servings*

Favorite recipe from **National Pork Producers Council**

*Mandarin Medallions*

# Apple-icious Lamb Kabobs

1 cup apple juice or cider
2 tablespoons Worcestershire sauce
½ teaspoon lemon pepper
2 cloves garlic, peeled and sliced
1½ pounds fresh American lamb, cut into 1¼-inch cubes
Apple Barbecue Sauce (recipe follows)
1 large apple, cut into 12 wedges
Assorted vegetables, cut into wedges

Combine apple juice, Worcestershire sauce, lemon pepper and garlic in large resealable plastic food storage bag; add lamb. Seal bag; turn to coat. Marinate in refrigerator 2 to 24 hours, turning occasionally.

To prevent sticking, spray grill with nonstick cooking spray. Prepare coals for grilling. Prepare Apple Barbecue Sauce; set aside.

Remove meat from marinade. Alternately thread meat, apple and vegetables onto skewers. (If using bamboo skewers, soak in water 20 minutes before using to prevent them from burning.) Place kabobs on grill, 4 inches from medium coals. Grill 10 to 12 minutes or until desired doneness, turning occasionally and brushing with Apple Barbecue Sauce.

*Makes 6 servings*

## Apple Barbecue Sauce

½ cup finely chopped onion
½ cup apple juice or cider
1 cup chili sauce
½ cup unsweetened applesauce
2 tablespoons brown sugar
1 tablespoon Worcestershire sauce
1 teaspoon dry mustard
5 drops hot pepper sauce

Combine onion and apple juice in 1-quart saucepan; simmer 2 minutes. Stir in chili sauce, applesauce, sugar, Worcestershire sauce, mustard and pepper sauce. Simmer 10 minutes. *Makes about 2 cups*

Favorite recipe from **American Lamb Council**

*Apple-icious Lamb Kabob*

# Lamb Rib Roast Dijon

1 (6-rib) lamb rib roast (about 1½ to
1¾ pounds)
1 tablespoon Dijon mustard
⅓ cup soft bread crumbs
½ teaspoon dried basil leaves
Dash garlic powder
Lemon slices (optional)
Italian parsley (optional)

Trim fat from lamb rib roast; spread mustard on roast. Combine bread crumbs, basil and garlic powder; press mixture into mustard. Place roast, fat-side up, on rack in shallow roasting pan. Insert meat thermometer into thickest part of roast, not touching bone or fat. *Do not add water. Do not cover.* Roast in 375°F oven to desired degree of doneness. Allow 30 to 35 minutes per pound for rare; 35 to 40 minutes for medium. Remove roast when meat thermometer registers 135°F for rare; 155°F for medium. Cover roast with aluminum foil tent and allow to stand 15 to 20 minutes before carving. Roast will continue to rise approximately 5°F in temperature to reach 140°F for rare; 160°F for medium. Garnish with lemon slices and Italian parsley, if desired.

*Makes 2 servings*

Favorite recipe from **National Cattlemen's Beef Association**

# Saltimbocca

4 boneless thin veal slices cut from
the leg or thinly sliced veal cutlets
(about 1¼ pounds)
1 tablespoon FILIPPO BERIO® Olive
Oil
1 clove garlic, thinly sliced
4 slices prosciutto, cut in half
8 fresh sage leaves*
½ cup beef broth
5 tablespoons Marsala wine or
medium sherry
¼ cup half-and-half
Freshly ground black pepper

*\*Omit sage if fresh is unavailable. Do not substitute dried sage leaves.*

Pound veal between 2 pieces waxed paper with flat side of meat mallet or rolling pin until very thin. Cut each piece in half to make 8 small pieces. In large skillet, heat olive oil with garlic over medium heat until hot. Add veal; cook until brown, turning occasionally. Top each piece with slice of prosciutto and sage leaf. Add beef broth and Marsala. Cover; reduce heat to low and simmer 5 minutes or until veal is cooked through and tender. Transfer veal to warm serving platter; keep warm. Add half-and-half to mixture in skillet; simmer 5 to 8 minutes, stirring occasionally, until liquid is reduced and thickened, scraping bottom of skillet to loosen browned bits. Remove garlic. Spoon sauce over veal. Season to taste with pepper.

*Makes 4 servings*

*Saltimbocca*

# PERFECT POULTRY

Enjoy your favorite poultry—chicken, turkey or duck—tucked into stir-fries, smothered in salsas and sauces or stuffed with flavorful fixings. Whether you make them with easy, after-work preparations or jazz them up with festive touches, you won't want to blow the whistle on this fowl play!

## Chicken Cordon Bleu

4 large boneless skinless chicken breast halves (about 1¼ pounds)
4 slices lean baked ham, divided
4 ounces Swiss cheese, cut into 4 sticks, divided
2 tablespoons butter or margarine
1 cup sliced fresh mushrooms
¼ teaspoon dried thyme leaves
⅛ teaspoon ground nutmeg
⅛ teaspoon pepper
2 tablespoons dry white wine
1 jar (12 ounces) HEINZ® HomeStyle Chicken Gravy
Slivered almonds (optional)

Place chicken between 2 pieces of waxed paper or plastic wrap. Pound with flat side of meat mallet or rolling pin to ¼-inch thickness. Place 1 ham slice and 1 cheese stick on each breast. Roll up chicken lengthwise, jelly-roll fashion, tucking ends in; secure with wooden toothpicks. In large skillet, brown chicken on all sides in butter; remove. In same skillet, cook and stir mushrooms, thyme, nutmeg and pepper until mushrooms are tender. Stir in wine, then add gravy. Return chicken to skillet. Cook over low heat, covered, 10 minutes or until chicken is no longer pink in center, turning once. Remove toothpicks before serving. Garnish with almonds, if desired.

*Makes 4 servings*

*Chicken Cordon Bleu*

# Chicken Wellington

6 large boneless skinless chicken
   breast halves
¾ teaspoon salt, divided
¼ teaspoon ground black pepper,
   divided
¼ cup butter or margarine, divided
12 ounces mushrooms (button or
   crimini), finely chopped
½ cup finely chopped shallots or
   onion
2 tablespoons port wine or cognac
1 tablespoon fresh thyme *or*
   1 teaspoon dried thyme leaves
1 package (17¼ ounces) frozen puff
   pastry, thawed
1 egg, separated
1 tablespoon country or Dijon
   mustard
1 teaspoon milk

Sprinkle chicken with ¼ teaspoon
salt and ⅛ teaspoon pepper. Melt 2
tablespoons butter in large skillet over
medium heat. Add 3 breasts; cook 10
minutes or until golden brown, turning
once. Transfer to plate; cook remaining
3 chicken breast halves. Set aside to cool
slightly.

Melt remaining 2 tablespoons butter in
same skillet over medium heat. Add
mushrooms and shallots. Cook and stir
about 5 minutes or until tender. Add
wine, thyme, remaining ½ teaspoon salt,

remaining ⅛ teaspoon pepper and any
juices that have accumulated around
chicken; simmer 10 to 12 minutes or until
liquid evaporates, stirring frequently. Cool.

Roll out each pastry sheet into 15×12-
inch rectangle. Cut each rectangle into
three 12×5-inch rectangles. Beat egg
white in small bowl; brush over pastry
rectangles.

Place 1 breast on each rectangle. Spread
½ teaspoon mustard and ¼ cup cooled
mushroom mixture over each breast. Fold
opposite half of pastry over chicken. Fold
edges of bottom dough over top, pressing
edges together to seal. Place on ungreased
baking sheet.

Beat egg yolk with milk. Brush over
surface of pastry. Cover loosely with
plastic wrap. Refrigerate until cold 1 to
4 hours before baking.

Preheat oven to 400°F. Remove plastic
wrap. Bake Chicken Wellington 25 to 30
minutes or until deep golden brown and
temperature of chicken reaches 160°F.
Garnish, if desired. *Makes 6 servings*

*Chicken Wellington*

## Stuffed Chicken Breasts à la Française

6 boneless skinless chicken breast
    halves with pockets (6 ounces
    each)
6 ounces (1 carton) ALPINE LACE® Fat
    Free Cream Cheese with Garlic &
    Herbs
½ cup finely chopped green onions
    (tops only)
2 teaspoons snipped fresh rosemary
    *or* ¾ teaspoon dried rosemary
½ cup all-purpose flour
1 teaspoon ground black pepper
⅓ cup low sodium chicken broth
⅓ cup dry white wine or low sodium
    chicken broth
8 sprigs fresh rosemary, about
    3 inches long (optional)

**1.** Preheat the oven to 350°F. Spray a 13×9×2-inch baking dish with nonstick cooking spray. Rinse the chicken and pat dry with paper towels. In a medium-size bowl, mix the cream cheese with the green onions and rosemary until well blended. Stuff the pockets of the chicken breasts with this mixture.

**2.** On a piece of wax paper, blend the flour and pepper. Roll chicken breasts in seasoned flour, then arrange in baking dish. Pour broth and wine over chicken.

**3.** Cover the dish tightly with foil and bake for 30 minutes. Uncover and bake 10 minutes more or until the juices run clear when the thickest piece of chicken is pierced with a fork. Transfer the chicken to a serving platter and garnish each with a sprig of rosemary, if you wish.

*Makes 6 servings*

## Crab-Stuffed — Chicken Breasts —

1 package (8 ounces) cream cheese,
    softened
6 ounces frozen crabmeat or imitation
    crabmeat, thawed and drained
1 envelope LIPTON® Recipe Secrets®
    Savory Herb with Garlic Soup Mix
6 boneless skinless chicken breast
    halves (about 1½ pounds)
¼ cup all-purpose flour
2 eggs, beaten
¾ cup plain dry bread crumbs
2 tablespoons olive or vegetable oil
1 tablespoon margarine or butter

Preheat oven to 350°F. In bowl, combine cream cheese, crabmeat and savory herb with garlic soup mix; set aside.

With knife blade parallel to cutting board, slice horizontally through each chicken breast, stopping 1 inch from opposite edge; open breasts. Evenly spread each breast with cream cheese mixture. Close each chicken breast, securing open edge with wooden toothpicks.

Dip chicken in flour, then eggs, then bread crumbs, coating well. In 12-inch skillet, heat oil and margarine over medium-high heat and cook chicken 10 minutes or until golden, turning once. Transfer chicken to 13×9-inch baking dish and bake uncovered 15 minutes or until chicken is done. Remove toothpicks before serving. *Makes about 6 servings*

**Menu Suggestion:** Serve with a mixed green salad and warm garlic bread.

*Crab-Stuffed Chicken Breast*

## Sausage Stuffed Chicken Breast Olé

6 boneless skinless chicken breast halves

1 pound BOB EVANS FARMS® Original Recipe or Zesty Hot Roll Sausage

1 (8-ounce) block Monterey Jack cheese, divided

4 tablespoons butter or margarine, divided

1 large green bell pepper, sliced into rings

1 large onion, sliced into rings

2 cloves garlic, minced

2 (16-ounce) cans stewed tomatoes, undrained

1 (12-ounce) can large black olives, drained, sliced and divided

¼ cup chopped fresh cilantro

3 tablespoons chopped jalapeño peppers (optional)

Fresh cilantro sprigs (optional)

Pound chicken into uniform thin rectangles with meat mallet or rolling pin. Divide uncooked sausage into 6 equal pieces. Cut 6 (½-inch-thick) sticks from cheese block. Shred remaining cheese; set aside. Wrap each sausage piece around each cheese stick to enclose cheese completely. Place 1 sausage bundle on each chicken piece at one narrow end; roll up and secure with toothpicks.

Melt 2 tablespoons butter in large Dutch oven or skillet over medium heat until hot. Add chicken bundles; cook, covered, about 5 to 7 minutes on each side or until browned, turning occasionally. Remove chicken; set aside.

Melt remaining 2 tablespoons butter in same Dutch oven. Add bell pepper, onion and garlic; cook and stir until onion is lightly browned. Stir in tomatoes with juice, half the olives, chopped cilantro and jalapeños, if desired. Cook and stir over medium-low heat about 10 minutes. Add reserved chicken bundles. Cook, covered, 30 to 40 minutes. Spoon tomato sauce mixture on top of chicken. Sprinkle with remaining cheese and olives, if desired. Garnish with fresh cilantro, if desired.

*Makes 6 servings*

## Ixtapa Stuffed Peppers

4 large red or green bell peppers

1 pound boneless skinless chicken breasts, cut into ¼-inch pieces

½ cup chopped green bell pepper

½ cup frozen corn or canned corn, drained

½ cup salsa

1 to 1½ teaspoons chili powder

½ to 1 teaspoon ground cumin

4 cups Corn CHEX® brand cereal

Preheat oven to 350°F. Grease 11×7-inch baking dish. Cut peppers in half lengthwise. Remove stems and seeds. Combine chicken, chopped green pepper, corn, salsa, chili powder and cumin; mix well. Add cereal; mix well. Fill each pepper half with about 1 cup chicken mixture. Place in prepared baking dish. Bake, covered, 20 minutes; remove cover and bake an additional 20 to 25 minutes or until chicken is no longer pink. Top with additional salsa, if desired. Serve immediately.

*Makes 4 servings*

*Sausage Stuffed Chicken Breast Olé*

## Chiles Rellenos – Chicken Roll-Ups –

6 boneless skinless chicken breast
  halves (about 1½ pounds)
1½ cups (6 ounces) shredded Monterey
  Jack cheese
3 tablespoons diced green chilies
3 tablespoons sliced pimientos
30 RITZ® Crackers, coarsely crushed
  (about 1½ cups crumbs)
½ teaspoon chili powder
¼ teaspoon ground cumin
2 tablespoons all-purpose flour
1 egg, beaten
3 tablespoons FLEISCHMANN'S®
  Margarine, melted
1 (16-ounce) jar prepared mild,
  medium or hot thick and chunky
  salsa

Pound each chicken breast with flat side
of meat mallet to ¼-inch thickness. On
waxed paper, mix cheese, chilies and
pimientos. Divide and spoon cheese
mixture over each chicken breast. Roll up
chicken from short edge; secure with
wooden toothpicks. Mix cracker crumbs,
chili powder and cumin. Coat chicken
rolls with flour; dip in egg, then roll in
crumb mixture. Place chicken rolls in
12×8×2-inch baking pan. Drizzle
margarine over chicken. Bake at 350°F for
35 to 40 minutes or until chicken is
tender and juices run clear; remove
wooden toothpicks before serving. Serve
topped with salsa.          *Makes 6 servings*

## Tex-Mex Chicken Fajitas

6 boneless skinless chicken breast
  halves (about 1½ pounds), cut
  into strips
½ cup LAWRY'S® Mesquite Marinade
  with Lime Juice*
3 tablespoons plus 1½ teaspoons
  vegetable oil, divided
1 small onion, sliced and separated
  into rings
1 medium-sized green bell pepper, cut
  into strips
¾ teaspoon LAWRY'S® Garlic Powder
  with Parsley
½ teaspoon hot pepper sauce
1 medium tomato, cut into wedges
2 tablespoons chopped fresh cilantro
  Flour tortillas, warmed
1 medium lime, cut into wedges

*\*1 package (1.27 ounces) LAWRY'S® Spices &
Seasonings for Fajitas, ¼ cup lime juice and
¼ cup vegetable oil can be substituted.*

Pierce chicken several times with fork;
place in large resealable plastic bag or
bowl. Pour Mesquite Marinade with Lime
Juice over chicken; seal bag or cover
bowl. Refrigerate at least 30 minutes. Heat
1 tablespoon plus 1½ teaspoons oil in
large skillet. Add onion, bell pepper, Garlic
Powder with Parsley and hot pepper
sauce; sauté 5 to 7 minutes or until onion
is crisp-tender. Remove vegetable mixture
from skillet; set aside. Heat remaining
2 tablespoons oil in same skillet. Add
chicken; sauté 8 to 10 minutes or until
chicken is no longer pink in center,
stirring frequently. Return vegetable
mixture to skillet with tomato and
cilantro; heat through. Serve with tortillas
and lime wedges.          *Makes 4 to 6 servings*

*Tex-Mex Chicken Fajitas*

# Herb Marinated
## — Chicken Kabobs —

4 boneless skinless chicken breasts
2 small unpeeled zucchini, cut into
    ½-inch pieces
1 large red or green bell pepper, cut
    into ½-inch pieces
½ cup white vinegar
½ cup tomato juice
½ cup vegetable oil
2 tablespoons chopped onion
1 tablespoon brown sugar
2 cloves garlic, minced
1 teaspoon dried oregano leaves
1 teaspoon dried thyme leaves
1 teaspoon dried basil leaves
¼ teaspoon cayenne pepper
1 teaspoon salt
4 (10- to 12-inch) skewers*

*If using wooden skewers, soak in water
30 minutes before using to prevent burning.

Pound chicken slightly with meat mallet;
cut lengthwise into ½-inch strips. Place
chicken and vegetables in large bowl.
Combine all remaining ingredients,
except skewers, in jar with tight-fitting
lid; shake vigorously. Pour over chicken
and vegetables. Cover; refrigerate 1 hour.
Preheat broiler or prepare grill for low
coals. Drain chicken and vegetables,
reserving marinade in small saucepan.
Weave chicken strips accordion-fashion
onto skewers, alternating vegetables
between loops. Bring reserved marinade
to a boil; brush skewers with marinade.
Broil or grill 4 to 6 inches from heat 8 to
10 minutes or until chicken is no longer
pink in center, turning occasionally and
brushing with hot marinade.

*Makes 4 servings*

Favorite recipe from **Bob Evans Farms**®

# Mediterranean
## — Chicken Kabobs —

2 pounds boneless skinless chicken
    breasts or chicken tenders, cut
    into 1-inch pieces
1 small eggplant, peeled, cut into
    1-inch pieces
1 medium zucchini, cut crosswise into
    ½-inch slices
2 medium onions, each cut into
    8 wedges
16 medium mushrooms, stems
    removed
16 cherry tomatoes
1 cup chicken broth
⅔ cup balsamic vinegar
3 tablespoons olive oil or vegetable oil
2 tablespoons dried mint leaves
4 teaspoons dried basil leaves
1 tablespoon dried oregano leaves
2 teaspoons grated lemon peel
    Chopped fresh parsley (optional)
4 cups hot cooked couscous

Alternately thread chicken, eggplant,
zucchini, onions, mushrooms and
tomatoes onto 16 metal skewers; place in
large glass baking dish. Blend chicken
broth, vinegar, oil, mint, basil and oregano
in small bowl. Pour over kabobs; turn to
coat. Cover; refrigerate 2 hours.

Preheat broiler. Spray rack of broiler pan
with nonstick cooking spray. Place kabobs
on rack. Broil, 6 inches from heat, 10 to
15 minutes or until chicken is no longer
pink in center, turning occasionally. Or,
grill kabobs, covered, over medium-hot
coals, 10 to 15 minutes or until chicken is
no longer pink in center, turning
occasionally. Stir lemon peel and parsley
into couscous; serve with kabobs.

*Makes 8 servings*

# Kung Pao Chicken

1 pound boneless skinless chicken breasts, cut into 1-inch pieces
1 tablespoon cornstarch
2 teaspoons CRISCO® Oil
3 tablespoons chopped green onions with tops
2 cloves garlic, minced
¼ to ½ teaspoon crushed red pepper
¼ to ½ teaspoon ground ginger
2 tablespoons wine vinegar
2 tablespoons soy sauce
2 teaspoons sugar
⅓ cup unsalted dry roasted peanuts
4 cups hot cooked rice (cooked without salt or fat)

**1. Combine** chicken and cornstarch in small bowl. **Toss** to coat.

**2. Heat** Crisco Oil in large skillet or wok on medium-high heat. **Add** chicken. **Stir-fry** 5 to 7 minutes or until no longer pink in center. **Remove** from skillet.

**3. Add** onions, garlic, red pepper and ginger to skillet. **Stir-fry** 15 seconds. **Remove** from heat.

**4. Combine** vinegar, soy sauce and sugar in small bowl. **Stir** well. **Add** to skillet. **Return** chicken to skillet. **Stir** until chicken is well coated. **Stir** in nuts. **Heat** thoroughly, stirring occasionally. **Serve** over hot rice. **Garnish,** if desired.

*Makes 4 servings*

# Sesame Chicken and Vegetable Stir-Fry

1 tablespoon Oriental sesame oil
1 pound chicken tenders, cut into 1-inch pieces
2 cups broccoli flowerets
1 small red bell pepper, sliced
½ cup onion slices
½ cup snow peas
1 can (8 ounces) water chestnuts, sliced and drained
2 cloves garlic, minced
1 teaspoon five-spice powder
1 cup chicken broth
2 teaspoons cornstarch
2 cups hot cooked white rice

Heat oil in wok or large nonstick skillet over medium heat until hot. Add chicken; stir-fry 8 minutes or until chicken is no longer pink in center. Remove chicken from wok; set aside.

Add broccoli, pepper, onion, peas, water chestnuts and garlic to wok; stir-fry 5 to 8 minutes or until vegetables are crisp-tender. Sprinkle with five-spice powder; stir-fry 1 minute. Return chicken to wok. Add chicken broth; bring to a boil. Blend cornstarch and 2 tablespoons water in small bowl; stir into broth mixture. Boil 1 to 2 minutes, stirring constantly. Serve over rice.

*Makes 4 servings*

# Indian Chicken with Couscous

1 pound boneless skinless chicken breasts
2 teaspoons olive oil
1 cup chopped onion
1 cup chopped green bell pepper
1 teaspoon chili powder
1 teaspoon curry powder
½ teaspoon ground red pepper
1 can (14½ ounces) Mexican-style stewed tomatoes
⅓ cup golden raisins
1⅓ cups chicken broth
1⅓ cups uncooked quick-cooking couscous
Plain nonfat yogurt
¼ cup sliced green onions

Cut chicken into ¼-inch-thick slices; cut each slice into 1-inch-long strips. Heat oil in large nonstick skillet over medium-high heat until hot. Add chicken; cook and stir 5 minutes or until chicken is no longer pink in center. Remove from skillet.

Add onion, bell pepper, chili powder, curry powder and red pepper to same skillet; cook and stir 5 minutes or until vegetables are tender. Stir in chicken, tomatoes and raisins; bring to a boil. Cover; reduce heat to medium-low. Simmer 15 minutes. Uncover; simmer 5 minutes, stirring occasionally. Meanwhile, place chicken broth in small saucepan; bring to a boil over high heat. Stir in couscous; cover. Remove saucepan from heat; let stand 5 minutes. Serve chicken over couscous; top each serving with dollop of yogurt and sprinkle evenly with onions.

*Makes 4 servings*

# Spinach Pesto with Chicken and Pasta

2 cups packed DOLE® Fresh Spinach, torn
½ cup packed torn fresh basil
⅓ cup low-sodium chicken broth
¼ cup (1 ounce) grated Parmesan cheese
1 tablespoon olive or vegetable oil
2 garlic cloves
8 ounces uncooked fettucine or linguine
4 boneless skinless chicken breast halves
Vegetable cooking spray

• **Combine** spinach, basil, broth, cheese, oil and garlic in food processor or blender container. Process until mixture is finely chopped. Divide spinach pesto in half; set aside.

• **Cook** fettucine as package directs; drain.

• **Arrange** chicken on broiler pan sprayed with vegetable cooking spray. Broil 10 minutes; turn chicken over. Spread chicken with half of pesto. Broil 10 to 15 minutes more or until chicken is no longer pink in center.

• **Toss** fettucine with remaining pesto in large bowl. Serve with chicken.

*Makes 4 servings*

**Prep Time:** 20 minutes
**Cook Time:** 10 minutes

*Indian Chicken with Couscous*

# Chicken Paprikash

2 tablespoons CRISCO® Oil
1 broiler-fryer chicken, skin removed and cut into pieces (about 2½ pounds)
1 medium green bell pepper, chopped
1 medium onion, chopped
1 tablespoon plus 1¼ teaspoons paprika
2 cups chicken broth
2 to 3 parsley sprigs
1 container (16 ounces) nonfat sour cream alternative
1 tablespoon all-purpose flour
4 cups hot cooked noodles
  Salt and pepper (optional)

**1. Heat** Crisco Oil in large deep skillet over medium heat. **Add** chicken. **Cook** until browned. **Remove** from skillet.

**2. Add** green pepper and onion to skillet. **Cook** and stir until tender. **Stir** in paprika. **Cook** 1 minute.

**3. Return** chicken to skillet. **Add** broth and parsley. **Reduce** heat to low. **Cover.** **Simmer** 20 minutes or until chicken is no longer pink in center, adding water as necessary. **Remove** skillet from heat. **Remove** chicken from skillet.

**4. Combine** sour cream alternative and flour in small bowl. **Stir** into hot broth in skillet. **Place** small amount of mixture in food processor or blender. **Process** until smooth. **Pour** into small bowl. **Repeat** with remaining mixture. **Return** chicken and blended mixture to skillet. **Heat** thoroughly, stirring occasionally. **Serve** over hot noodles. **Season** with salt and pepper, if desired. *Makes 4 servings*

# - Picadillo Chicken -

1 broiler-fryer chicken, cut up (about 3½ pounds)
1½ tablespoons all-purpose flour
½ teaspoon salt
2 tablespoons vegetable oil
1 large onion, coarsely chopped
2 cloves garlic, minced
1 can (14½ ounces) stewed tomatoes
1 can (8 ounces) tomato sauce
⅓ cup raisins
⅓ cup sliced pickled jalapeños, drained
1 teaspoon ground cumin
¼ teaspoon cinnamon
⅓ cup toasted slivered almonds
  Hot cooked rice (optional)
1 cup (4 ounces) SARGENTO® Fancy Supreme® Shredded Cheese For Nachos & Tacos

Rinse chicken; pat dry. Dust with flour and sprinkle with salt. In large skillet, brown chicken skin-side down in hot oil over medium heat, about 5 minutes; turn. Add onion and garlic; cook 5 minutes more. Add stewed tomatoes, tomato sauce, raisins, jalapeños, cumin and cinnamon; heat to a boil. Reduce heat; cover and simmer 15 minutes. Uncover and simmer 5 to 10 minutes more or until chicken is no longer pink in center and sauce is thickened.* Stir in almonds; serve over rice. Sprinkle with Nachos & Tacos cheese. *Makes 6 servings*

*At this point, chicken may be covered and refrigerated up to 2 days before serving. Reheat before adding almonds.*

*Chicken Paprikash*

## Tex-Mex Drumsticks

¼ cup finely chopped pecans
¼ cup fine dry bread crumbs
1 tablespoon finely chopped parsley
1 teaspoon chili powder
1 package (1¼ pounds) PERDUE® Fresh Skinless Chicken Drumsticks
¼ cup taco-flavored or other salad dressing

**MICROWAVE DIRECTIONS:** On waxed paper, combine pecans, bread crumbs, parsley and chili powder. Brush drumsticks with dressing; roll in crumb mixture to coat all sides. Reserve remaining crumbs and dressing.

On microwave-safe roasting pan, arrange drumsticks in circular pattern, with meatier portions toward outside. Cover with waxed paper; microwave at MEDIUM-HIGH (70% power) 10 minutes per pound. Halfway through cooking time, turn drumsticks over. Remove waxed paper. Spoon reserved dressing over drumsticks; sprinkle with reserved crumb mixture. Cover with double thickness of paper towels. Continue to microwave, removing paper towels before last 2 minutes of cooking. Let stand, uncovered, 5 minutes before serving.

*Makes 4 servings*

## Hot 'n' Spicy Chicken Barbecue

½ cup A.1.® Steak Sauce
½ cup tomato sauce
¼ cup finely chopped onion
2 tablespoons cider vinegar
2 tablespoons maple syrup
1 tablespoon vegetable oil
2 teaspoons chili powder
½ teaspoon crushed red pepper flakes
1 (3-pound) chicken, cut up

In medium saucepan, combine steak sauce, tomato sauce, onion, vinegar, maple syrup, oil, chili powder and red pepper flakes. Over medium heat, heat mixture to a boil; reduce heat. Simmer for 5 to 7 minutes or until thickened; cool.

Grill chicken over medium heat for 30 to 40 minutes or until chicken is no longer pink, turning and basting frequently with prepared sauce. Serve hot.

*Makes 4 servings*

*Hot 'n' Spicy Chicken Barbecue*

# Spiced Orange Chicken with Lentils

3 tablespoons all-purpose flour
1 teaspoon ground coriander
1 teaspoon ground cumin
½ teaspoon salt
½ teaspoon dried mixed herbs (thyme, marjoram and rosemary)
¼ teaspoon freshly ground black pepper
8 chicken drumsticks
2 tablespoons FILIPPO BERIO® Olive Oil, divided
Finely grated peel and juice of 1 orange
1 large onion, finely chopped
2 cloves garlic, minced
2½ cups chicken broth
8 ounces dried lentils (about 1¼ cups), rinsed and drained
Salt and additional freshly ground black pepper
1 to 2 tablespoons honey
Orange wedges and chopped fresh parsley (optional)

In small plastic food storage bag, combine flour, coriander, cumin, salt, dried herbs and ¼ teaspoon pepper; shake until well mixed. Place 1 chicken drumstick at a time into bag. Seal bag; turn to coat evenly. In large skillet, heat 1 tablespoon olive oil over medium-high heat until hot. Add drumsticks; cook 5 minutes or until brown, turning occasionally. Stir orange peel and juice into skillet. Cover; reduce heat to low and simmer 20 minutes or until chicken is no longer pink in center and juices run clear.

Meanwhile, in another large skillet, heat remaining 1 tablespoon olive oil over medium heat until hot. Add onion and garlic; cook and stir 5 minutes or until onion is tender. Add chicken broth and lentils; bring to a boil. Cover; reduce heat to low and simmer 20 minutes or until lentils are tender and broth is absorbed. Season to taste with salt and black pepper.

Arrange lentils on serving plate; place drumsticks on top. Stir honey into chicken juices remaining in skillet. Heat thoroughly, stirring occasionally. Spoon over chicken and lentils. Garnish with orange wedges and parsley, if desired.

*Makes 4 servings*

*Spiced Orange Chicken with Lentils*

## Wingin' It on the Grill—Buffalo Style

2½ pounds chicken wings
½ cup FRANK'S® Original RedHot® Cayenne Pepper Sauce
⅓ cup butter or margarine, melted
   Prepared blue cheese salad dressing
   Celery sticks

Cut off wing tips from chicken wings; discard. Cut wings in half between remaining joint to make two pieces. Place wing pieces on grid. Grill over medium-high coals 30 minutes or until thoroughly cooked and crispy, turning often. Place in large bowl.

Combine RedHot sauce and butter. Pour over wings; toss well to coat evenly. Serve wings with blue cheese dressing and celery sticks. *Makes 6 servings*

**Prep Time:** 10 minutes
**Cook Time:** 30 minutes

**Shanghai Red Wings:** Cook wings as directed. Combine ¼ cup soy sauce, 3 tablespoons RedHot sauce, 3 tablespoons honey, 2 tablespoons peanut oil, 1 teaspoon grated peeled fresh ginger and 1 teaspoon minced garlic in small bowl; mix well. Pour over wings; toss well to coat evenly. Serve as directed.

**Cajun Wings:** Cook wings as directed. Combine ⅓ cup RedHot sauce, ⅓ cup ketchup, ¼ cup (½ stick) melted butter or margarine and 2 teaspoons Cajun seasoning blend in small bowl; mix well. Pour over wings; toss well to coat evenly. Serve as directed.

## Rosemary's Chicken

4 large boneless skinless chicken breast halves (about 1½ pounds)
¼ cup FRENCH'S® Classic Yellow® Mustard
¼ cup frozen orange juice concentrate, undiluted
2 tablespoons cider vinegar
2 teaspoons dried rosemary leaves, crushed
4 strips thick sliced bacon

Place chicken in large resealable plastic food storage bag or glass bowl. To prepare marinade, combine mustard, orange juice concentrate, vinegar and rosemary in small bowl. Pour over chicken. Seal bag or cover bowl and marinate in refrigerator 30 minutes. Wrap 1 strip bacon around each piece of chicken; secure with toothpicks.*

Place chicken on grid, reserving marinade. Grill over medium coals 25 minutes or until chicken is no longer pink in center, turning and basting often with marinade. (Do not baste during last 10 minutes of cooking.) Remove toothpicks before serving. Garnish as desired. *Makes 4 servings*

*\*Soak toothpicks in water 20 minutes to prevent burning.*

**Prep Time:** 15 minutes
**Marinate Time:** 30 minutes
**Cook Time:** 25 minutes

## Hawaiian Chicken

4 boneless skinless chicken breast
  halves (¾ to 1 pound)
½ to ¾ teaspoon LAWRY'S® Garlic Salt
½ to ¾ teaspoon LAWRY'S® Seasoned
  Pepper
2 tablespoons vegetable oil
½ cup thinly sliced onion
½ cup thinly sliced red or green bell
  pepper
1 cup pineapple juice
1 can (8 ounces) pineapple chunks,
  drained
¼ cup white vinegar
2 tablespoons plus 1½ teaspoons
  brown sugar
2 tablespoons cornstarch
2 tablespoons soy sauce
3 cups hot cooked rice

In shallow baking dish, place chicken.
Sprinkle with Garlic Salt and Seasoned
Pepper. Bake in 350°F oven 20 to 25
minutes or until no longer pink in center.
Meanwhile, in large skillet, heat oil. Add
onion and bell pepper; sauté until crisp-
tender. Stir in pineapple juice, pineapple
chunks, vinegar and brown sugar. In small
bowl, combine cornstarch and soy sauce;
add to skillet. Bring to a boil, stirring
constantly. Reduce heat to low; simmer
until thickened, stirring constantly. Serve
over chicken. *Makes 4 servings*

**Presentation:** Serve over hot cooked rice.

## Classic Chicken Marsala

2 tablespoons unsalted butter
1 tablespoon vegetable oil
4 boneless skinless chicken breast
  halves (about 1¼ pounds)
4 slices mozzarella cheese (1 ounce
  each)
12 capers, drained
4 flat anchovy fillets, drained
1 tablespoon chopped fresh parsley
1 clove garlic, minced
3 tablespoons Marsala wine
⅔ cup heavy or whipping cream
  Dash salt
  Dash ground black pepper
  Hot cooked pasta

Heat butter and oil in large skillet over
medium-high heat until melted and
bubbly. Add chicken; reduce heat to
medium. Cook, uncovered, 5 to 6 minutes
per side or until chicken is golden brown.
Remove chicken with slotted spoon
to work surface. Top each chicken breast
with 1 cheese slice, 3 capers and
1 anchovy fillet.

Return chicken to skillet. Sprinkle
with parsley. Cover; cook over low heat
3 minutes or until cheese is semi-melted
and chicken is no longer pink in center.
Remove chicken from skillet. Keep warm.

Add garlic to drippings remaining in
skillet; cook and stir over medium heat
30 seconds. Stir in wine; cook and stir
45 seconds, scraping up any brown bits in
skillet. Stir in cream. Cook and stir 3
minutes or until sauce thickens slightly.
Stir in salt and pepper. Spoon sauce over
chicken. Serve with pasta.

*Makes 4 servings*

## Tarragon Lemon Chicken

¼ cup all-purpose flour
  Salt and freshly ground black
    pepper
4 boneless skinless chicken breast
  halves
¼ cup FILIPPO BERIO® Olive Oil,
  divided
1 large onion, chopped
1 red bell pepper, seeded and cut into
  strips
2 ribs celery, thinly sliced
1 cup chicken broth
1 cup dry white wine
1 tablespoon chopped fresh tarragon
  *or* 1 teaspoon dried tarragon
    leaves
3 cloves garlic, crushed
  Finely grated peel and juice of
    1 lemon
  Salt and freshly ground black
    pepper
  Lemon slices and fresh tarragon
    sprigs (optional)

Preheat oven to 375°F. In small shallow bowl, combine flour with salt and black pepper to taste. Coat each chicken breast with flour mixture; reserve any remaining flour mixture. In large skillet, heat 2 tablespoons olive oil over medium heat until hot. Add onion, bell pepper and celery; cook and stir 5 minutes or until onion is tender. Remove onion mixture from skillet with slotted spoon; set aside.

Add remaining 2 tablespoons olive oil to skillet; heat over medium heat until hot. Add chicken; cook 5 minutes or until brown, turning occasionally. Add reserved flour mixture to skillet; mix well. Add

chicken broth, wine, tarragon, garlic, lemon peel and lemon juice; bring to a boil. Return onion mixture to skillet; mix well. Transfer mixture to large casserole. Cover with foil. Bake 40 minutes or until chicken is no longer pink in center and juices run clear. Garnish with lemon slices and tarragon, if desired.

*Makes 4 servings*

## Italian Chicken Breasts

1 pound BOB EVANS FARMS® Italian
  Roll Sausage
1 cup sliced fresh mushrooms
1 clove garlic, minced
3 (8-ounce) cans tomato sauce
1 (6-ounce) can tomato paste
1½ teaspoons Italian seasoning
4 boneless skinless chicken breast
  halves
1 cup (4 ounces) shredded mozzarella
  cheese
  Hot cooked pasta

Preheat oven to 350°F. Crumble sausage into large skillet. Cook over medium heat until browned, stirring occasionally. Remove sausage; set aside. Add mushrooms and garlic to drippings; cook and stir until tender. Stir in reserved sausage, tomato sauce, tomato paste and seasoning. Bring to a boil. Reduce heat to low; simmer 15 minutes to blend flavors. Meanwhile, arrange chicken in greased 11×7-inch baking dish. Pour tomato sauce mixture over chicken; cover with foil. Bake 40 minutes; uncover. Sprinkle with cheese; bake 5 minutes more. Serve over pasta.

*Makes 4 servings*

*Italian Chicken Breast*

# Chicken Scaloppine with Lemon-Caper Sauce

1 pound boneless skinless chicken breasts

3 tablespoons all-purpose flour, divided

¼ teaspoon ground black pepper

¼ teaspoon chili powder

½ cup chicken broth

1 tablespoon lemon juice

1 tablespoon drained capers

½ teaspoon olive oil, divided

Place chicken between 2 pieces of waxed paper; pound to ¼-inch thickness using flat side of meat mallet or rolling pin. Combine 2 tablespoons flour, pepper and chili powder in shallow plate. Dip chicken in flour mixture; lightly coat both sides.

Combine remaining 1 tablespoon flour, chicken broth, lemon juice and capers in small bowl. Spray large skillet with cooking spray; heat over medium-high heat until hot. Place chicken in skillet in single layer; cook 1½ minutes. Turn over; cook 1 to 1½ minutes or until chicken is no longer pink in center. Repeat with remaining chicken (brush pan with ¼ teaspoon oil each time you add pieces to prevent sticking). If cooking more than 2 batches, reduce heat to medium to prevent chicken from burning.

Pour broth mixture into skillet. Boil, uncovered, until thickened and reduced to about ¼ cup. Spoon sauce over chicken; serve immediately.

*Makes 4 servings*

# Southwest Chicken

1 package (6.8 ounces) RICE-A-RONI® Spanish Rice

½ cup chopped green bell pepper *or* 1 can (4 ounces) chopped green chilies, drained

1 can (14½ ounces) tomatoes, undrained, chopped

⅓ cup QUAKER® or AUNT JEMIMA® Yellow Corn Meal

1½ teaspoons chili powder

½ teaspoon garlic powder

4 boneless skinless chicken breast halves

2 eggs, beaten

3 tablespoons vegetable oil

¼ cup (1 ounce) shredded Cheddar or Monterey Jack cheese

**1.** Prepare Rice-A-Roni Mix as package directs, stirring in green pepper and tomatoes with water.

**2.** While Rice-A-Roni is simmering, combine corn meal, chili powder and garlic powder. Coat chicken with corn meal mixture; dip chicken into eggs, then coat again with corn meal mixture.

**3.** In second large skillet, heat oil over medium heat. Add chicken; cook 6 minutes on each side or until golden brown and no longer pink in center.

**4.** Serve rice topped with chicken; sprinkle with cheese. Cover; let stand a few minutes before serving.

*Makes 4 servings*

*Chicken Scaloppine with Lemon-Caper Sauce*

## Crunchy Cutlets
## — with Corn Salsa —

1 egg, beaten
1 cup plus 1 tablespoon water
1 pound boneless, skinless chicken
   breast halves, pounded to ¼-inch
   thickness
½ cup yellow cornmeal
½ teaspoon salt
2 tablespoons plus 1½ teaspoons olive
   or vegetable oil
2 green onions, sliced (about ¾ cup)
1 large red bell pepper, diced (about
   1 cup)
1 package (10 ounces) frozen whole
   kernel corn, partially thawed
1 envelope LIPTON® Recipe Secrets®
   Golden Onion or Golden Herb
   with Lemon Soup Mix
1 to 2 tablespoons chopped fresh
   cilantro (optional)

In small bowl, beat egg with 1 tablespoon water. Dip chicken in egg, then cornmeal combined with salt. In 12-inch skillet, heat 1 tablespoon oil over medium-high heat and cook half of the chicken 4 minutes or until chicken is no longer pink, turning once. Remove chicken to platter; keep warm. Repeat with remaining chicken and 1 tablespoon oil. Wipe out skillet. Heat remaining 1½ teaspoons oil in skillet over medium heat and cook green onions and red pepper 1 minute, stirring constantly. Add corn and golden onion soup mix blended with remaining 1 cup water. Bring to a boil. Reduce heat to low and simmer 7 minutes or until vegetables are tender and liquid is thickened. Stir in cilantro. To serve, spoon corn salsa over chicken. Serve, if desired, with a tomato salad.                          *Makes 4 servings*

## Oven-Crisped
## — Chicken Breasts —

8 boneless skinless chicken breast
   halves (about 2 pounds)
2 egg whites
½ cup skim milk
½ cup all-purpose flour
1 tablespoon paprika
1 teaspoon dried basil leaves
½ teaspoon salt
¼ teaspoon pepper
1 cup plain dry bread crumbs
¼ cup CRISCO® Oil

1. **Heat** oven to 425°F.

2. **Rinse** and dry chicken.

3. **Beat** egg whites in large shallow dish until frothy. **Beat** in milk.

4. **Combine** flour, paprika, basil, salt and pepper in large plastic food storage bag. **Place** bread crumbs in another large plastic food storage bag. **Shake** breast halves, one or two at a time, in flour mixture, then dip in egg white mixture. **Shake** in crumbs.

5. **Pour** Crisco Oil into 15¼×10¼×¾-inch jelly roll pan or other shallow pan. **Place** in 425°F oven for 3 or 4 minutes or until Crisco Oil is hot, but not smoking. **Add** chicken breasts in single layer.

6. **Bake** at 425°F for 10 minutes. **Turn** chicken over. **Sprinkle** with any remaining crumb mixture. **Bake** for 5 minutes or until chicken is no longer pink.                          *Makes 8 servings*

*Oven-Crisped Chicken Breast*

# Indonesian Grilled Turkey — with Saté Sauce —

2 disposable aluminum foil pans
    (9 inches each)
1 whole turkey breast (about
    5 pounds)
2 tablespoons FRENCH'S® 
    Worcestershire Sauce
2 tablespoons olive oil
2 teaspoons seasoned salt
½ teaspoon ground black pepper
    Saté Sauce (recipe follows)

To prepare grill, place doubled foil pans in center of grill under grilling rack. Arrange hot coals or lava rocks around foil pan. Fill pan with cold water. Place turkey on greased grid. Combine Worcestershire, oil and seasonings in small bowl; brush generously on turkey.

Grill, on covered grill, over medium-low to medium coals 1½ hours or until meat thermometer inserted into turkey reaches 170°F. Slice turkey. Serve with Saté Sauce.

*Makes 8 servings*

## Saté Sauce

½ cup chunky-style peanut butter
⅓ cup FRENCH'S® Worcestershire
    Sauce
¼ cup loosely packed fresh cilantro
    leaves
2 tablespoons FRANK'S® Original
    RedHot® Cayenne Pepper Sauce
2 tablespoons sugar
2 tablespoons water
1 tablespoon chopped peeled fresh
    ginger
2 cloves garlic, chopped

Place peanut butter, Worcestershire, cilantro, RedHot sauce, sugar, water, ginger and garlic in food processor or blender. Cover and process until smooth.

*Makes 1⅓ cups*

# — Turkey Shanghai —

    Nonstick cooking spray
12 ounces turkey breast tenderloin,
    thinly sliced
1 cup thinly sliced carrots
½ cup sliced green onions
3 cloves garlic, minced
4 cups chicken broth
6 ounces uncooked angel hair pasta
2 cups frozen French-style green
    beans
¼ cup plus 2 tablespoons stir-fry sauce
1 teaspoon Oriental sesame oil

Spray large nonstick skillet with cooking spray; heat over medium heat until hot. Add turkey and carrots; cook and stir 5 minutes or until turkey is no longer pink. Stir in onions and garlic; cook and stir 2 minutes. Add chicken broth to skillet; bring to a boil over high heat. Add pasta. Return to a boil. Reduce heat to low. Simmer, uncovered, 5 minutes, stirring frequently.

Add green beans to skillet. Simmer 2 to 3 minutes or until pasta is just tender, stirring occasionally. Remove from heat. Stir in stir-fry sauce and sesame oil. Let stand 5 minutes before serving. Garnish as desired.

*Makes 6 servings*

# Teriyaki Glazed Duckling with Spicy Apple Chutney

**1 frozen duckling, thawed and quartered**
**½ cup KIKKOMAN® Teriyaki Baste & Glaze**
**Spicy Apple Chutney (recipe follows)**

Rinse duckling quarters under cold water; pat dry with paper towels. Remove and discard excess fat from duckling; pierce skin liberally with fork. Place quarters, skin-side up, on grill 4 to 5 inches from hot coals in covered-style barbecue; cover. Cook 1 to 1¼ hours, or until duckling is no longer pink in center, brushing quarters generously with teriyaki baste & glaze during last 30 minutes of cooking time. Serve with Spicy Apple Chutney.           *Makes 4 servings*

## Spicy Apple Chutney

**1 pound cooking apples**
**1 cup chopped onion**
**1 cup sugar**
**½ cup raisins**
**½ cup water**
**⅓ cup KIKKOMAN® Teriyaki Marinade & Sauce**
**¼ cup vinegar**
**2 tablespoons minced fresh gingerroot**

Peel, core and coarsely chop apples. Combine apples with remaining ingredients in Dutch oven or large saucepan; bring to a boil over medium-high heat. Reduce heat to low; simmer, uncovered, 30 minutes, or until thickened, stirring occasionally.

*Makes 2 cups*

# Easy Chinese Roast Duck

**1 (4- to 5-pound) frozen duckling, thawed and quartered**
**3 tablespoons KIKKOMAN® Soy Sauce**
**1 tablespoon five-spice powder***
**1 tablespoon dry sherry**
**½ to ¾ teaspoon coarse ground black pepper**
**Hot cooked rice**

**If not available, combine 1 teaspoon fennel seeds, crushed, ½ teaspoon anise seeds, crushed and ½ teaspoon each ground cinnamon, cloves and ginger.*

Rinse duckling quarters; drain and dry thoroughly with paper towels. Discard excess fat. Pierce skin thoroughly with fork. Combine soy sauce, five-spice powder, sherry and pepper in large bowl. Add duckling quarters; rub with mixture and let stand 30 minutes. Place, skin-side up, on rack in shallow roasting pan. Bake in 350°F oven 1 hour and 10 minutes. Remove from oven; drain off pan drippings. Turn oven temperature to broil and position oven rack 4 to 5 inches from heat source. Broil quarters 2 to 3 minutes, or until skin is crisp. Serve with rice.

*Makes 4 servings*

# Chili Roasted Turkey Breast

1 envelope LIPTON® Recipe Secrets® Onion Soup Mix
¼ cup olive or vegetable oil
1½ teaspoons chili powder
1½ teaspoons fresh lime juice
½ teaspoon garlic powder with parsley
½ teaspoon ground cumin (optional)
¼ teaspoon dried oregano leaves, crushed
1 (5-pound) turkey breast with bone

Preheat oven to 350°F. In small bowl, blend all ingredients except turkey; let stand 5 minutes. In 13×9-inch baking or roasting pan, place turkey, meaty-side up. Insert meat thermometer into thickest part of breast, away from bone. Brush soup mixture onto turkey; tent with aluminum foil. Roast 1 hour, basting once. Remove aluminum foil and continue roasting 1 hour or until meat thermometer reaches 180°F. Let stand, tented with foil, 10 minutes

*Makes about 6 servings*

• *Also terrific with LIPTON® Recipe Secrets® Onion-Mushroom, Beefy Mushroom or Beefy Onion Soup Mix.*

# Butterflied Cornish Game Hens

2 Cornish game hens (about 3 pounds)*
Olive oil cooking spray
Seasoned salt
Ground black pepper
½ cup FRENCH'S® Dijon Mustard
Grilled vegetables (optional)

*You may substitute 3 pounds chicken parts (skinned, if desired) for the game hens.*

Remove neck and giblets from hens. Wash hens and pat dry. Place 1 hen, breast-side down, on cutting board. With kitchen shears or sharp knife, cut along one side of backbone, cutting as close to bone as possible. Cut down other side of backbone; remove backbone. Spread bird open and turn breast-side up, pressing to flatten. Repeat with remaining hen.

To keep drumsticks flat, make small slit through skin with point of knife between thigh and breast. Push end of leg through slit. Repeat on other side of bird and with remaining hen. Coat both sides of hens with cooking spray. Sprinkle with seasoned salt and pepper. Generously brush mustard on both sides of hens.

Place hens, skin-sides up, on oiled grid. Grill over medium-high coals 35 to 45 minutes until meat is no longer pink near bone and juices run clear, turning and basting often with remaining mustard. (Do not baste during last 10 minutes of cooking.) Serve with grilled vegetables, if desired. *Makes 4 servings*

*Butterflied Cornish Game Hens*

# CATCH OF THE DAY

*Sample the specialties of the sea—flavorful fish and succulent shellfish—cast in a variety of taste-tempting recipes that are sure to get you hooked on seafood.*

## Tuna Steaks with Shrimp Creole Sauce

4 tablespoons olive oil,
    divided
1 medium red onion,
    chopped
1 red or yellow bell pepper,
    seeded and chopped
2 ribs celery, sliced
2 cloves garlic, minced
1 can (14½ ounces) stewed
    tomatoes
¼ cup FRANK'S® Original
    RedHot® Cayenne Pepper
    Sauce
¼ cup tomato paste
½ teaspoon dried thyme
    leaves
1 bay leaf
½ pound medium-size raw
    shrimp, shelled and
    deveined
4 tuna, swordfish or codfish
    steaks, cut 1 inch thick
    (about 1½ pounds)
  Hot cooked rice (optional)

Heat *2 tablespoons* oil in medium skillet over medium-high heat. Add onion, pepper, celery and garlic; cook and stir 1 minute. Stir in tomatoes, RedHot sauce, tomato paste, thyme and bay leaf. Bring to a boil. Reduce heat to medium-low. Cook 5 minutes, stirring often. Add shrimp; cook 3 minutes or until shrimp turn pink. Remove and discard bay leaf. Set aside shrimp sauce.

Brush both sides of fish steaks with remaining *2 tablespoons* oil. Place steaks on grid. Grill over medium-high coals 10 minutes or until fish flakes easily with a fork,* turning once. Transfer to serving platter. Spoon shrimp sauce over fish. Serve with rice, if desired. Garnish as desired.    *Makes 4 servings*

*\*Tuna becomes dry and tough if overcooked. Cook tuna until it is opaque, but still feels somewhat soft in center. Watch carefully while grilling.*

**Prep Time:** 15 minutes
**Cook Time:** 20 minutes

*Tuna Steak with Shrimp Creole Sauce*

## Szechuan Tuna Steaks

4 tuna steaks (6 ounces each), cut 1 inch thick
¼ cup soy sauce
¼ cup dry sherry or sake
1 tablespoon Oriental sesame oil
1 teaspoon hot chili oil *or* ¼ teaspoon crushed red pepper
1 clove garlic, minced
3 tablespoons chopped fresh cilantro

Place tuna in single layer in large shallow glass dish. Combine soy sauce, sherry, sesame oil, hot chili oil and garlic in small bowl. Reserve ¼ cup soy sauce mixture at room temperature. Pour remaining soy sauce mixture over tuna. Cover and marinate in refrigerator 40 minutes, turning once.

Prepare grill. Drain tuna, discarding marinade. Place tuna on grid. Grill, uncovered, over medium-hot coals 6 minutes or until tuna is opaque, but still feels somewhat soft in center,* turning halfway through grilling time. Transfer tuna to carving board. Cut each tuna steak into thin slices; fan out slices onto serving plates. Drizzle tuna slices with reserved soy sauce mixture; sprinkle with cilantro.

*Makes 4 servings*

*Tuna becomes dry and tough if overcooked.*

## Tuna Cakes

1¼ cups bread crumbs, divided
1 can (12 ounces) STARKIST® Solid White or Chunk Light Tuna, drained and flaked
¾ cup shredded Cheddar cheese
¼ cup mayonnaise
1 egg, lightly beaten
⅓ cup bottled ranch dressing
½ cup finely chopped onion
½ cup finely chopped red or green bell pepper (optional)
2 tablespoons vegetable oil, divided

In large bowl, combine ½ cup bread crumbs with remaining ingredients except oil. Shape mixture into 8 patties, coating with remaining bread crumbs. In nonstick skillet, heat 1 tablespoon oil over medium heat; cook 4 cakes about 3 minutes per side. Repeat with remaining 1 tablespoon oil and 4 cakes.

*Makes 4 servings*

## Seafood Dijonnaise

1 pound salmon or halibut fillets
¾ cup LAWRY'S® Dijon & Honey Barbecue Sauce
½ medium onion, sliced
¼ cup toasted slivered almonds
Chopped fresh parsley or watercress (garnish)
Lemon slices (garnish)

Place fish in shallow glass baking dish; cover with Dijon & Honey Barbecue Sauce. Top with onion slices and almonds; cover. Bake in 350°F oven 20 minutes. Uncover; bake 5 minutes or until fish flakes easily with fork. *Makes 4 servings*

*Szechuan Tuna Steak*

## Salmon en Papillote

⅔ cup FRENCH'S® Dijon Mustard
½ cup (1 stick) butter or margarine, melted
¼ cup minced fresh dill weed *or* 1 tablespoon dried dill weed
3 cloves garlic, minced
4 salmon fillets (about 2 pounds), cut into 4×3×1½-inch portions
Salt
Ground black pepper
Vegetable cooking spray
2 cups very thin vegetable strips, such as bell peppers, carrots, leek, celery or fennel bulb
2 tablespoons capers, drained

**MICROWAVE DIRECTIONS:** Combine mustard, butter, dill weed and garlic in medium microwave-safe bowl. Cover loosely with vented plastic wrap. Microwave on HIGH 1 minute. Whisk sauce until smooth; set aside.

Sprinkle salmon with salt and black pepper. Cut four 12-inch circles of heavy-duty foil. Coat 1 side of foil with vegetable cooking spray. Place 1 piece salmon in center of each piece of foil. Spoon about 2 tablespoons mustard sauce over each piece of fish. Reserve remaining sauce. Top fish with vegetables and capers, dividing evenly. Fold foil in half over salmon and vegetables. Seal edges securely with tight double folds.

Place packets on grid. Cook over hot coals 15 to 20 minutes until fish flakes easily with a fork, opening foil packets carefully. Serve with reserved mustard sauce.
*Makes 4 servings*

## Mediterranean Cod

1 bag (16 ounces) BIRDS EYE® frozen Farm Fresh Mixtures Broccoli, Green Beans, Pearl Onions and Red Peppers
1 can (14½ ounces) stewed tomatoes
½ teaspoon dried basil
1 pound cod fillets, cut into serving pieces
½ cup orange juice, divided
2 tablespoons flour
¼ cup sliced black olives (optional)

• Combine vegetables, tomatoes and basil in large skillet. Bring to boil over medium-high heat.

• Place cod on vegetables. Pour ¼ cup orange juice over fish. Cover and cook 5 to 7 minutes or until fish is tender and flakes with fork.

• Remove cod and keep warm. Blend flour with remaining ¼ cup orange juice; stir into skillet. Cook until liquid is thickened and vegetables are coated.

• Serve fish with vegetables; sprinkle with olives. *Makes about 4 servings*

**Prep Time:** 5 minutes
**Cook Time:** 15 minutes

**Serving Suggestion:** Serve with rice or couscous.

*Mediterranean Cod*

## Catfish with Tropical Fruit Salsa

1 can (15¼ ounces) DOLE® Tropical Fruit Salad, drained
1 can (8 ounces) low-sodium whole kernel corn, drained
¼ cup chopped DOLE® Red or Green Onion
2 tablespoons diced mild green chilies
1 tablespoon chopped fresh cilantro or parsley
1 pound catfish or red snapper fillets
Vegetable cooking spray
2 tablespoons lime juice
½ teaspoon paprika

• **Chop** tropical fruit salad; stir together with corn, onion, chilies and cilantro in small bowl for salsa. Set aside.

• **Arrange** fish in single layer on broiler pan sprayed with vegetable cooking spray.

• **Broil** 4 minutes; turn fish over. Brush with lime juice; sprinkle with paprika. Broil 3 to 5 minutes more or until fish flakes easily with fork. Remove fish to serving platter. Serve with reserved tropical fruit salsa. Garnish with fresh cilantro sprigs and lime wedges, if desired.                *Makes 4 servings*

**Prep Time:** 10 minutes
**Broil Time:** 10 minutes

## Blackened Sea Bass

Hardwood charcoal*
2 teaspoons paprika
1 teaspoon garlic salt
1 teaspoon dried thyme leaves
¼ teaspoon ground white pepper
¼ teaspoon ground red pepper
¼ teaspoon ground black pepper
3 tablespoons butter or margarine
4 skinless sea bass or catfish fillets (4 to 6 ounces each)
Lemon halves
Fresh dill sprigs for garnish

*Hardwood charcoal takes somewhat longer than regular charcoal to become hot, but results in a hotter fire than regular charcoal. A hot fire is necessary to seal in the juices and cook fish quickly. If hardwood charcoal is not available, scatter dry hardwood, mesquite or hickory chunks over hot coals to create a hotter fire.*

Prepare grill. Meanwhile, combine paprika, garlic salt, thyme and peppers in small bowl; mix well. Set aside. Melt butter in small saucepan over medium heat. Pour melted butter into pie plate or shallow bowl. Cool slightly. Dip sea bass into melted butter, evenly coating both sides. Sprinkle both sides of sea bass evenly with paprika mixture. Place sea bass on grid. (Fire will flare up when sea bass is placed on grid, but will subside when grill is covered.) Grill, on covered grill, over hot coals 4 to 6 minutes or until sea bass is blackened and flakes easily with fork, turning halfway through grilling time. Serve with lemon halves. Garnish, if desired.                *Makes 4 servings*

*Catfish with Tropical Fruit Salsa*

## Fish with Hidden Valley Ranch® Tartar Sauce

1 cup (½ pint) sour cream
¼ cup chopped sweet pickles
1 package (1 ounce) HIDDEN VALLEY RANCH® Milk Recipe Original Ranch® Salad Dressing Mix
¾ cup dry bread crumbs
1½ pounds whitefish fillets (sole, flounder, snapper or turbot)
1 egg, beaten
  Vegetable oil
  French fried shoestring potatoes (optional)
  Lemon wedges (optional)

To make sauce, in small bowl, combine sour cream, pickles and 2 tablespoons of the salad dressing mix; cover and refrigerate. On large plate, combine bread crumbs and remaining salad dressing mix. Dip fillets in egg, then coat with bread crumb mixture. Fry fillets in 3 tablespoons oil until golden. (Add more oil to pan if necessary to prevent sticking.) Serve with chilled sauce. Serve with French fries and lemon wedges, if desired. *Makes 4 servings*

## Fish & Chips

¾ cup all-purpose flour
½ cup flat beer or lemon-lime carbonated beverage
  Vegetable oil
4 medium russet potatoes, each cut into 8 wedges
  Salt
1 egg, separated
1 pound cod fillets
  Malt vinegar (optional)

Combine flour, beer and 2 teaspoons oil in small bowl. Cover; refrigerate 1 to 2 hours. Pour 2 inches of oil into heavy skillet. Heat oil over medium heat until hot (about 365°F). Add as many potato wedges as will fit in single layer. Fry potato wedges 4 to 6 minutes or until outsides are brown, turning once. Drain on paper towels; sprinkle lightly with salt. Repeat with remaining potato wedges. (Allow temperature of oil to return to 365°F between batches.) Reserve oil to fry cod.

Stir egg yolk into flour mixture. Beat egg white with electric mixer at high speed in bowl until soft peaks form. Fold egg white into flour mixture; set aside. Rinse fish and pat dry with paper towels. Cut fish into 8 pieces. Dip 4 fish pieces into batter; fry 4 to 6 minutes or until batter is crispy and brown and fish flakes easily when tested with fork, turning once. Drain on paper towels. Repeat with remaining fish pieces. (Allow temperature of oil to return to 365°F between batches.) Serve immediately with potato wedges. Sprinkle fish with malt vinegar, if desired. *Makes 4 servings*

## Southern Fried Catfish with —— Hush Puppies ——

**Hush Puppy Batter (recipe follows)**
**4 catfish fillets (about 1½ pounds)**
**½ cup yellow cornmeal**
**3 tablespoons all-purpose flour**
**1½ teaspoons salt**
**¼ teaspoon ground red pepper**
**Vegetable oil for frying**
**Fresh parsley sprigs for garnish**

Prepare Hush Puppy Batter; set aside. Rinse catfish and pat dry with paper towels. Combine cornmeal, flour, salt and red pepper in shallow dish. Dip fish in cornmeal mixture. Heat 1 inch of oil in large, heavy saucepan over medium heat until hot (about 375°F).

Fry fish, a few pieces at a time, 4 to 5 minutes or until golden brown and fish flakes easily when tested with fork. Adjust heat to maintain temperature. (Allow temperature of oil to return to 375°F between each batch.) Drain fish on paper towels.

To make Hush Puppies, drop tablespoonfuls of batter into hot oil. Fry, a few pieces at a time, 2 minutes or until golden brown. Garnish, if desired.

*Makes 4 servings*

### Hush Puppy Batter

**1½ cups yellow cornmeal**
**½ cup all-purpose flour**
**2 teaspoons baking powder**
**½ teaspoon salt**
**1 cup milk**
**1 small onion, minced**
**1 egg, slightly beaten**

Combine cornmeal, flour, baking powder and salt in medium bowl. Add milk, onion and egg. Stir until blended. Allow batter to stand 5 to 10 minutes before frying.

*Makes about 24 hush puppies*

## Fillets Stuffed —— with Crabmeat ——

**1 envelope LIPTON® Recipe Secrets® Savory Herb with Garlic Soup Mix**
**1 package (6 ounces) frozen crabmeat, thawed and well drained**
**½ cup fresh bread crumbs**
**½ cup water**
**2 teaspoons lemon juice**
**4 fish fillets (about 1 pound)**
**1 tablespoon margarine or butter, melted**

Preheat oven to 350°F. In medium bowl, combine savory herb with garlic soup mix, crabmeat, bread crumbs, water and lemon juice.

Top fillets evenly with crabmeat mixture; roll up and secure with wooden toothpicks. Place in 2-quart oblong baking dish. Brush fish with margarine and bake 25 minutes or until fish flakes. Remove toothpicks before serving.

*Makes 4 servings*

**Menu Suggestion:** Serve with hot cooked white rice tossed with sliced almonds and orange wedges for dessert.

•*Also terrific with LIPTON® Recipe Secrets® Golden Herb with Lemon or Golden Onion Soup Mix.*

# — Soleful Roulettes —

1 package (6¼ ounces) long-grain and wild rice mix
1 package (3 ounces) cream cheese, softened
2 tablespoons milk
32 medium fresh spinach leaves
4 sole fillets (about 1 pound)
Salt
Ground black pepper
¼ cup dry white wine
½ cup water

Cook rice mix according to package directions. Place 2 cups cooked rice in large bowl. Cover and refrigerate remaining rice and save for another use. Combine cream cheese and milk in medium bowl. Stir into rice; set aside.

Place spinach in heatproof bowl. Pour very hot water (not boiling) over spinach to wilt leaves slightly. Rinse sole and pat dry with paper towels. Sprinkle both sides of each fillet with salt and pepper. Cover each fillet with spinach leaves. Divide rice mixture evenly and spread over top of each spinach-lined fillet. Roll up and secure with wooden toothpicks.

Combine wine and water in large, heavy saucepan. Stand fillets upright on rolled edges in saucepan; cover. Simmer over low heat. (*Do not boil.* This will cause fish to break apart.) Simmer 10 minutes or until fish flakes easily when tested with fork.

*Makes 4 servings*

# Grilled Prawns with Salsa Vera Cruz

1 can (14½ ounces) DEL MONTE® Mexican Recipe Stewed Tomatoes
1 orange, peeled and chopped
¼ cup sliced green onions
¼ cup chopped cilantro or parsley
1 tablespoon olive oil
1 to 2 teaspoons minced jalapeño pepper
1 small clove garlic, crushed
1 pound medium shrimp, peeled and deveined
Hot cooked white rice

Drain tomatoes, reserving liquid; chop tomatoes. In medium bowl, combine tomatoes, reserved liquid, orange, green onions, cilantro, oil, jalapeño and garlic. Season to taste with salt and pepper, if desired. Thread shrimp onto skewers; season with salt and pepper, if desired. Brush grill with oil. Cook shrimp over hot coals about 3 minutes per side or until shrimp just turn opaque pink. Top with salsa mixture and serve over rice, if desired.

*Makes 4 servings*

**Prep Time:** 27 minutes
**Cooking Time:** 6 minutes

**Helpful Hint:** Thoroughly rinse shrimp in cold water before cooking.

*Soleful Roulette*

## Shrimp Monterey

2 tablespoons butter or margarine
2 large cloves garlic, minced
2 pounds medium shrimp, shelled and deveined
¼ teaspoon ground red pepper
½ cup dry white wine
2 cups (8 ounces) SARGENTO® Classic Supreme® Shredded Monterey Jack Cheese
2 tablespoons chopped fresh parsley

In large skillet, melt butter; add garlic. Cook over medium heat 1 minute. Add shrimp and red pepper; cook about 4 minutes, stirring often, until shrimp turn pink. Using slotted spoon, remove shrimp to 11×7-inch baking dish.* Add wine to skillet; bring to a boil. Cook about 5 minutes over high heat, stirring constantly, until liquid is reduced by half. Pour reduced liquid over shrimp in baking dish. Combine Monterey Jack cheese and parsley; spoon over shrimp. Bake in preheated 350°F oven about 10 minutes or until cheese is melted.

*Makes 6 servings*

*\*Shrimp may also be placed in six individual serving casseroles. Continue as directed.*

## Butterflied Shrimp Parmesan

1½ pounds large shrimp
1 cup (4 ounces) shredded ALPINE LACE® Fat Free Pasteurized Process Skim Milk Cheese Product—For Parmesan Lovers
¼ cup Italian seasoned dry bread crumbs
2 tablespoons unsalted butter substitute
¾ cup chopped red bell pepper
½ cup thinly sliced green onions
1 tablespoon minced garlic
⅛ teaspoon crushed red pepper flakes or to taste
⅓ cup minced fresh parsley
6 tablespoons 2% low fat milk

**1.** Peel the shrimp, leaving the tails on. Then butterfly each shrimp by cutting it along the outer curved edge almost all the way through. Open the shrimp up like a book and remove the dark vein. In a small bowl, toss the cheese with the bread crumbs and set aside.

**2.** In a large nonstick skillet, melt the butter over medium-high heat. Add the bell pepper, green onions, garlic and red pepper flakes and cook for 5 minutes or until tender. Add the shrimp and sauté for 5 minutes or just until the shrimp turn pink and opaque. Uncover and stir in the parsley.

**3.** In a small saucepan, bring the milk just to a boil, then stir into the shrimp mixture. Stir in the cheese mixture and cook until the cheese is melted. Serve immediately. *Makes 4 servings*

*Butterflied Shrimp Parmesan*

## Lemon-Garlic Shrimp

1 package (6.2 ounces) RICE-A-RONI® With ⅓ Less Salt Broccoli Au Gratin
1 tablespoon margarine or butter
1 pound medium shrimp, shelled, deveined or large scallops, halved
1 medium red or green bell pepper, cut into short thin strips
2 cloves garlic, minced
½ teaspoon Italian seasoning
½ cup reduced-sodium or regular chicken broth
1 tablespoon lemon juice
1 tablespoon cornstarch
3 medium green onions, cut into ½-inch pieces
1 teaspoon grated lemon peel

**1.** Prepare Rice-A-Roni Mix as package directs.

**2.** While Rice-A-Roni is simmering, heat margarine in second large skillet or wok over medium-high heat. Add shrimp, red pepper, garlic and Italian seasoning. Stir-fry 3 to 4 minutes or until shrimp is opaque.

**3.** Combine chicken broth, lemon juice and cornstarch in small bowl, mixing until smooth. Add broth mixture and onions to skillet. Cook and stir 2 to 3 minutes or until sauce thickens.

**4.** Stir ½ teaspoon lemon peel into rice. Serve rice topped with shrimp mixture; sprinkle with remaining ½ teaspoon lemon peel.       *Makes 4 servings*

## Spicy Broiled Shrimp

¼ cup butter or margarine
2 tablespoons vegetable oil
1 bay leaf, crushed
2½ teaspoons LAWRY'S® Seasoned Salt
¾ to 1 teaspoon hot pepper sauce
1 teaspoon dried rosemary, crushed
¾ teaspoon LAWRY'S® Garlic Powder with Parsley
¼ teaspoon dried basil, crushed
¼ teaspoon dried oregano, crushed
1½ pounds large shrimp, peeled and deveined

In small saucepan, melt butter over low heat. Add all remaining ingredients except shrimp; cook, uncovered, 5 minutes. Rinse shrimp; pat dry with paper towels. Place on broiler pan. Brush generously with melted butter mixture. Broil, 5 inches from heat source, 5 minutes or until shrimp turn pink, turning and brushing frequently with melted butter mixture. Garnish as desired.

*Makes 4 servings*

**Presentation:** Spoon any remaining melted butter mixture over cooked shrimp. Serve with lemon wedges and warm bread. This recipe is also great served over hot cooked rice.

*Spicy Broiled Shrimp*

# Grilled Bacon — Wrapped Shrimp —

¼ cup water
¼ cup soy sauce
3 tablespoons sugar
2 tablespoons red wine vinegar
1 tablespoon Worcestershire sauce
1 (½-inch) piece fresh ginger, peeled and grated
2 cloves garlic, minced
¼ teaspoon cayenne pepper
16 uncooked large shrimp, peeled and deveined
16 slices bacon
4 (8- to 10-inch) skewers*

*If using wooden skewers, soak in water 30 minutes before using to prevent burning.*

To prepare marinade, combine first 8 ingredients in large nonaluminum saucepan. Cook and stir over medium heat 10 minutes for flavors to blend. Cool to lukewarm. Place shrimp in marinade; cover and refrigerate 2 hours, stirring occasionally.

Prepare grill for medium coals or preheat broiler. Remove shrimp, reserving marinade. Cook bacon in large skillet over medium heat just until tender; drain on paper towels. (Do not overcook.) Wrap 1 slice bacon around each shrimp. Thread four shrimp onto each skewer. Grill or broil 4 to 6 inches from heat 6 to 10 minutes or until shrimp turn pink and opaque, brushing with reserved marinade and turning occasionally. Serve hot. Refrigerate leftovers.        *Makes 4 servings*

Favorite recipe from **Bob Evans Farms**®

# Maryland Crab Cakes

1¼ pounds lump crabmeat, picked over and flaked
¾ cup plain dry bread crumbs, divided
1 cup (4 ounces) shredded ALPINE LACE® Reduced Fat Baby Swiss Cheese
⅓ cup finely chopped green onions
¼ cup plain low fat yogurt
¼ cup minced fresh parsley
2 tablespoons fresh lemon juice
1 teaspoon minced garlic
½ teaspoon hot red pepper sauce
¼ cup egg substitute *or* 1 large egg, beaten
   Butter-flavor nonstick cooking spray
2 large lemons, thinly sliced

**1.** In a large bowl, lightly toss the crab with ¼ cup of the bread crumbs, the cheese, green onions, yogurt, parsley, lemon juice, garlic and hot pepper sauce. Gently stir in the egg substitute.

**2.** Form the mixture into twelve 3-inch patties, using about ¼ cup of crab mixture for each. Spray both sides of the patties with the cooking spray. On wax paper, spread out the remaining ½ cup of bread crumbs. Coat each patty with the crumb mixture, pressing lightly, then refrigerate for 1 hour.

**3.** Preheat the oven to 400°F. Spray a baking sheet with the cooking spray. Place the crab cakes on the baking sheet and bake for 20 minutes or until golden brown and crispy, turning once halfway through. Serve immediately with the lemon slices.        *Makes 6 servings*

## Shrimp on the Barbie

1 pound large shrimp, shelled and deveined
1 *each* red and yellow bell pepper, seeded and cut into 1-inch chunks
4 slices lime (optional)
½ cup prepared smoky-flavor barbecue sauce
2 tablespoons FRENCH'S® Worcestershire Sauce
2 tablespoons FRANK'S® Original RedHot® Cayenne Pepper Sauce
1 clove garlic, minced

Thread shrimp, peppers and lime, if desired, alternately onto metal skewers. Combine barbecue sauce, Worcestershire, RedHot sauce and garlic in small bowl; mix well. Brush on skewers. Place skewers on grid, reserving sauce mixture. Grill over hot coals 15 minutes or until shrimp turn pink, turning and basting often with sauce mixture. (Do not baste during last 5 minutes of cooking.) Serve warm. *Makes 4 servings*

**Prep Time:** 10 minutes
**Cook Time:** 15 minutes

## Garlic Clams

2 pounds littleneck clams
2 teaspoons olive oil
2 tablespoons finely chopped onion
2 tablespoons chopped garlic
½ cup dry white wine
¼ cup chopped red bell pepper
2 tablespoons lemon juice
1 tablespoon chopped fresh parsley

Tap clams; discard any that remain open. Scrub clams; soak clams in mixture of ½ cup salt to 1 gallon water 20 minutes. Drain water; repeat 2 more times. Heat oil in large saucepan over medium-high heat until hot. Add onion and garlic; cook and stir about 3 minutes. Add clams, wine, bell pepper and lemon juice. Cover; simmer 3 to 10 minutes or until clams open. Transfer clams as they open to large bowl; cover. Discard any clams that do not open. Increase heat to high. Add parsley; boil until liquid reduces to ⅓ cup. Pour over clams; serve immediately.

*Makes 4 servings*

## Lobster with Burned Butter Sauce

8 tablespoons butter (1 stick)
2 tablespoons chopped fresh parsley
1 tablespoon cider vinegar
1 tablespoon capers
2 live lobsters*

*Purchase live lobsters as close to the time of cooking as possible. Store in refrigerator.*

Fill 8-quart stockpot with enough water to cover lobsters. Cover stockpot; bring water to a boil over high heat. Meanwhile, to make Burned Butter Sauce, melt butter in medium saucepan over medium heat. Cook and stir butter until it turns dark chocolate brown. Remove from heat. Add parsley, vinegar and capers. Pour into 2 individual ramekins; set aside. Holding each lobster by its back, submerge head first into boiling water. Cover; return to a boil. Cook lobsters 10 minutes for 1 pound, 12 minutes for 1¼ pounds or 18 minutes for 2 pounds. Serve lobster with Burned Butter Sauce. *Makes 2 servings*

## Lemon Sesame Scallops

1 pound sea scallops
8 ounces whole wheat spaghetti
3 tablespoons sesame oil, divided
¼ cup chicken broth or clam juice
½ teaspoon grated lemon peel
3 tablespoons lemon juice
2 tablespoons oyster sauce
1 tablespoon soy sauce
1 tablespoon cornstarch
1 tablespoon vegetable oil
2 carrots, thinly sliced
1 yellow bell pepper, thinly sliced
4 slices peeled fresh ginger
1 clove garlic, minced
6 ounces fresh snow peas, trimmed *or*
    1 (6-ounce) package frozen snow
    peas, thawed
2 green onions, thinly sliced
1 tablespoon sesame seeds, toasted

Rinse scallops and pat dry with paper towels. Cook spaghetti according to package directions. Drain in colander. Place spaghetti in large bowl; toss with 2 tablespoons sesame oil. Cover to keep warm.

Combine broth, lemon peel, lemon juice, oyster sauce, soy sauce and cornstarch in 1-cup glass measure; set aside.

Heat remaining 1 tablespoon sesame oil and vegetable oil in large skillet or wok over medium heat. Add carrots and bell pepper; stir-fry 4 to 5 minutes or until crisp-tender. Transfer to large bowl; set aside.

Add ginger and garlic to skillet. Stir-fry 1 minute over medium high-heat. Add scallops; stir-fry 1 minute. Add snow peas and onions; stir-fry 2 to 3 minutes or until peas turn bright green and scallops turn opaque. Remove slices of ginger; discard. Transfer scallop mixture to bowl with vegetable mixture, leaving any liquid in skillet. Stir broth mixture; add to liquid in skillet. Cook and stir 5 minutes or until thickened.

Return scallop mixture to skillet; cook 1 minute. Serve immediately over warm spaghetti; sprinkle with sesame seeds.

*Makes 4 servings*

## Scallop Kabobs

1 pound large sea scallops
1 green bell pepper, seeded and cut
    into 1-inch chunks
1 cup small mushrooms, wiped clean
1 cup cubed fresh pineapple
¼ cup FRENCH'S® Bold'n Spicy®
    Mustard
¼ cup FRENCH'S® Worcestershire
    Sauce
¼ cup (½ stick) butter or margarine,
    melted

Thread scallops, pepper, mushrooms and pineapple alternately onto metal skewers. Combine remaining ingredients; brush onto skewers.

Place skewers on oiled grid. Grill over hot coals 10 minutes or until scallops are opaque, turning and basting once with mustard mixture. Serve warm.

*Makes 4 servings*

**Prep Time:** 15 minutes
**Cook Time:** 10 minutes

*Lemon Sesame Scallops*

# ONE-DISH MEALS

*Dig into these delicious, updated versions of all-time favorite one-dish meals—savory pot pies, cheesy enchiladas, creamy casseroles and in-a-minute skillet dishes. Many are great for casual, make-ahead meals, while some of the more sophisticated dishes are perfect for entertaining.*

## Skillet Chicken Pot Pie

1 can (10¾ ounces) fat-free reduced-sodium cream of chicken soup

1¼ cups skim milk, divided

1 package (10 ounces) frozen mixed vegetables

2 cups diced cooked chicken

½ teaspoon ground black pepper

1 cup buttermilk biscuit baking mix

¼ teaspoon summer savory or parsley

Heat soup, 1 cup milk, vegetables, chicken and pepper in medium skillet over medium heat until mixture comes to a boil.

Combine biscuit mix and summer savory in small bowl. Stir in 3 to 4 tablespoons milk just until soft dough is formed. Drop dough by tablespoonfuls onto chicken mixture to make 6 dumplings. Partially cover and simmer 12 minutes or until dumplings are cooked through, spooning liquid from pot pie over dumplings once or twice during cooking. Garnish with additional summer savory, if desired.   *Makes 6 servings*

*Skillet Chicken Pot Pie*

## Chicken Enchiladas

1¾ cups fat free sour cream
½ cup chopped green onions
⅓ cup minced fresh cilantro
1 tablespoon minced fresh jalapeño chili pepper
1 teaspoon ground cumin
1 tablespoon vegetable oil
12 ounces boneless skinless chicken breasts, cut into 3×1-inch strips
1 teaspoon minced garlic
8 flour tortillas (8 inches)
1 cup (4 ounces) shredded ALPINE LACE® Reduced Fat Cheddar Cheese
1 cup bottled chunky salsa (medium or hot)
1 small ripe tomato, chopped
Sprigs of cilantro (optional)

**1.** Preheat the oven to 350°F. Spray a 13×9×3-inch baking dish with nonstick cooking spray.

**2.** In a small bowl, mix together the sour cream, green onions, cilantro, jalapeño pepper and cumin.

**3.** Spray a large nonstick skillet with the cooking spray, pour in the oil and heat over medium-high heat. Add the chicken and garlic and sauté for 4 minutes or until the juices run clear when the chicken is pierced with a fork.

**4.** Divide the chicken strips among the 8 tortillas, placing them down the center of the tortillas. Top with the sour cream mixture, then roll them up and place them, seam side down, in the baking dish.

**5.** Sprinkle with the cheese, cover with foil and bake for 30 minutes or until bubbly. Spoon the salsa in a strip down the center and sprinkle the tomato over the salsa. Garnish with the sprigs of cilantro, if you wish. Serve hot!

*Makes 8 servings*

## Chicken and Vegetable Risotto

Nonstick olive oil cooking spray
2 cups sliced mushrooms
½ cup chopped onion
4 cloves garlic, minced
¼ cup finely chopped fresh parsley
3 to 4 tablespoons finely chopped fresh basil
6 cups chicken broth
1½ cups uncooked arborio rice
1 pound chicken tenders, cut into ½-inch pieces, cooked
2 cups broccoli flowerets, cooked crisp-tender
4 plum tomatoes, seeded, chopped
½ teaspoon salt
½ teaspoon ground black pepper
2 tablespoons grated Parmesan cheese

Spray large nonstick saucepan with cooking spray. Add mushrooms, onion and garlic; cook and stir about 5 minutes or until tender. Add parsley and basil; cook and stir 1 minute. Place chicken broth in medium saucepan; bring to a boil over high heat.

Add rice to mushroom mixture; cook and stir over medium heat 1 to 2 minutes. Stir ½ cup hot chicken broth into saucepan; cook, stirring constantly, until broth is absorbed. Stir remaining hot chicken broth into rice mixture, ½ cup at a time, stirring constantly until all broth is absorbed before adding next ½ cup.

Add chicken, broccoli, tomatoes, salt and pepper. Cook and stir 2 to 3 minutes or until heated through. Sprinkle with cheese.

*Makes 4 servings*

## Classic Arroz Con Pollo

2 tablespoons olive oil
1 cut-up chicken
2 cups uncooked rice
1 cup chopped onion
2 bell peppers (red and green), chopped
1 clove garlic, minced
1½ teaspoons salt, divided
1½ teaspoons dried basil
4 cups chicken broth
1 tablespoon lime juice
⅛ teaspoon ground saffron *or*
    ½ teaspoon ground turmeric
1 bay leaf
2 cups chopped tomatoes
½ teaspoon ground black pepper
1 cup fresh or frozen green peas

Heat oil in large Dutch oven until hot. Add chicken; cook 10 minutes or until brown, turning occasionally. Remove chicken; keep warm. Add rice, onion, bell peppers, garlic, ¾ teaspoon salt and dried basil to pan; cook and stir 5 minutes. Add broth, lime juice, saffron and bay leaf.

Bring to a boil; stir in tomatoes. Arrange chicken on top and sprinkle with remaining ¾ teaspoon salt and black pepper. Cover; reduce heat to low. Cook 20 minutes more. Stir in peas; cover and cook 10 minutes or until juices run clear, not pink. Remove bay leaf.

*Makes 8 servings*

## Mexicali Baked Chicken

Nonstick cooking spray
4 skinless chicken legs
½ cup halved sliced onion
3 cloves garlic, finely chopped
1 cup sliced cooked potato
1 cup vegetable juice cocktail
½ cup sliced green bell pepper, halved
½ cup drained canned diced tomatoes
¼ cup chicken broth
2 bay leaves
1 teaspoon paprika
½ teaspoon ground cumin
¼ teaspoon salt
¼ teaspoon ground black pepper

Preheat oven to 325°F. Spray large skillet with cooking spray. Heat over medium heat until hot. Add chicken legs, onion and garlic. Cook 5 minutes or until chicken is browned, turning occasionally. Add remaining ingredients to skillet. Cook 5 minutes, stirring occasionally. Spoon into 1-quart casserole. Bake, covered, 45 minutes or until chicken is no longer pink in center. Remove and discard bay leaves.

*Makes 4 servings*

## Coq au Vin

1 pint pearl onions
4 slices thick-cut bacon
1 cup sliced button mushrooms
1 tablespoon peanut oil
1 whole frying chicken (3 to
    4 pounds), cut into serving pieces
3 tablespoons all-purpose flour
¼ cup tomato paste
1 can (about 14 ounces) chicken broth
1 cup dry red wine
1 clove garlic, minced
1 tablespoon fresh thyme *or*
    1 teaspoon dried thyme leaves
½ teaspoon salt
⅛ teaspoon ground black pepper
    Fresh thyme and sage for garnish

Bring 1 quart water to a boil in 2-quart saucepan over high heat. Add onions; boil 2 minutes. Drain onions; plunge into cold water to stop cooking. Cut off stem ends of onions; remove skins. Discard skins.

Preheat oven to 350°F. Cut bacon into ½-inch pieces. Cook in Dutch oven over medium heat until brown and crispy. Remove bacon from Dutch oven; drain on paper towels.

Add onions to bacon drippings; cook 7 minutes or until golden, stirring occasionally. Reduce heat to low. Cook, covered, 5 minutes. Remove onions to bowl; set aside. Heat bacon drippings over medium-high heat. Add mushrooms. Cook and stir 3 to 4 minutes or until tender. Add mushrooms to onions. Add peanut oil to bacon drippings. Add chicken; cook 5 minutes per side or until browned. Remove chicken from Dutch oven; set aside.

Remove all but 2 tablespoons drippings from Dutch oven. Add flour; cook and stir 1 minute. Stir in tomato paste; cook 1 minute. Add broth, wine, garlic, thyme, salt and pepper; bring to a boil. Add chicken, onions, mushrooms and bacon. Cover; bake 45 minutes to 1 hour or until chicken is tender. Garnish, if desired.

*Makes 4 servings*

## Chicken Provençal

3 tablespoons low fat plain yogurt
2 tablespoons mayonnaise
½ small clove garlic, minced
1 (3-pound) broiler-fryer chicken,
    cut up and skinned
½ teaspoon dried thyme
1 tablespoon vegetable oil
1 can (14½ ounces) DEL MONTE®
    Original Recipe Stewed Tomatoes
1 can (8 ounces) DEL MONTE® Tomato
    Sauce
2 small zucchini, sliced

In small bowl, combine yogurt, mayonnaise and garlic; set aside. Sprinkle chicken with thyme. Season with salt and pepper, if desired. In large skillet, brown chicken in oil over medium-high heat; drain. Add tomatoes and tomato sauce; cover and simmer about 20 minutes or until chicken is no longer pink in center, stirring occasionally. Add zucchini during last 5 minutes. Serve with garlic sauce.

*Makes 4 to 6 servings*

**Prep Time:** 5 minutes
**Cook Time:** 30 minutes

*Coq au Vin*

# Turkey Cottage Pie

¼ cup margarine or butter
¼ cup all-purpose flour
1 envelope LIPTON® Recipe Secrets®
  Golden Onion or Savory Herb
  with Garlic Soup Mix
2 cups water
2 cups cut-up cooked turkey or
  chicken
1 package (10 ounces) frozen mixed
  vegetables, thawed
1¼ cups shredded Swiss or Cheddar
  cheese (about 5 ounces)
5 cups hot mashed potatoes

Preheat oven to 375°F. In large saucepan, melt margarine over medium heat. Add flour; cook stirring constantly, 5 minutes or until golden. Stir in golden onion soup mix thoroughly blended with water. Bring to a boil over high heat. Reduce heat to low and simmer 15 minutes or until thickened. Stir in turkey, vegetables and 1 cup cheese. Turn into lightly greased 2-quart casserole; top with hot potatoes, then remaining ¼ cup cheese. Bake 30 minutes or until bubbling.

*Makes about 8 servings*

**Menu Suggestion:** Serve this all-in-one meal with baked apples or apple pie.

# Tasty Turkey Pot Pie

½ cup MIRACLE WHIP® Salad Dressing
2 tablespoons flour
1 teaspoon instant chicken bouillon
⅛ teaspoon pepper
¾ cup milk
1½ cups chopped cooked turkey or
  chicken
1 (10-ounce) package frozen mixed
  vegetables, thawed, drained
1 (4-ounce) can refrigerated crescent
  rolls

**COMBINE** salad dressing, flour, bouillon and pepper in medium saucepan. Gradually add milk.

**COOK,** stirring constantly, over low heat until thickened. Add turkey and vegetables; heat thoroughly, stirring occasionally.

**SPOON** into 8-inch square baking dish. Unroll dough into two rectangles. Press perforations together to seal. Place rectangles side-by-side to form square; press edges together to form seam. Cover turkey mixture with dough.

**BAKE** at 375°F 15 to 20 minutes or until browned.     *Makes 4 to 6 servings*

**Preparation Time:** 15 minutes
**Baking Time:** 20 minutes

*Turkey Cottage Pie*

## Texas-Style Deep Dish Chili Pie

1 tablespoon vegetable oil
1 pound beef stew meat, cut into
    ½-inch cubes
2 cans (14½ ounces each) Mexican-
    style stewed tomatoes, undrained
1 medium green bell pepper, diced
1 package (1.25 ounces) LAWRY'S®
    Taco Spices & Seasonings
1 tablespoon yellow cornmeal
1 can (15¼ ounces) kidney beans,
    drained
1 package (15 ounces) refrigerated pie
    crusts
½ cup (2 ounces) shredded Cheddar
    cheese, divided

In Dutch oven, heat oil and brown beef;
drain fat. Add stewed tomatoes, bell
pepper, Taco Spices & Seasonings and
cornmeal. Bring to a boil; reduce heat and
simmer, uncovered, 20 minutes. Add
kidney beans. In 10-inch pie plate, unfold
1 crust and fill with chili mixture and
½ of cheese. Top with remaining crust,
fluting edges. Bake, uncovered, in 350°F
oven 30 minutes. Sprinkle remaining
cheese over crust, return to oven and
bake 10 minutes longer.

*Makes 6 servings*

## Southwestern Meat Loaf

1 envelope LIPTON® Recipe Secrets®
    Onion Soup Mix
2 pounds ground beef
2 cups crushed cornflakes or bran
    flakes cereal (about 3 ounces)
1½ cups frozen or drained canned
    whole kernel corn
1 small green bell pepper, chopped
¾ cup water
⅓ cup ketchup
2 eggs

Preheat oven to 350°F. In large bowl,
combine all ingredients. In 13×9-inch
baking or roasting pan, shape into loaf.
Bake 1 hour or until done. Let stand 10
minutes before serving. Serve, if desired,
with salsa.          *Makes about 8 servings*

•*Also terrific with LIPTON® Recipe Secrets®
Onion-Mushroom or Beefy Onion Soup Mix.*

*Southwestern Meat Loaf*

# Countdown Casserole

1 jar (8 ounces) pasteurized process
   cheese spread
¾ cup milk
2 cups (12 ounces) cubed cooked
   roast beef
1 bag (16 ounces) frozen vegetable
   combination (broccoli, corn, red
   pepper), thawed and drained
4 cups frozen hash brown potatoes,
   thawed
1 can (2.8 ounces) FRENCH'S® French
   Fried Onions
½ teaspoon seasoned salt
¼ teaspoon freshly ground black
   pepper
½ cup (2 ounces) shredded Cheddar
   cheese

Preheat oven to 375°F. Spoon cheese
spread into 12×8-inch baking dish; place
in oven just until cheese melts, about
5 minutes. Using fork, stir milk into
melted cheese until well blended. Stir in
beef, vegetables, potatoes, ½ *can* French
Fried Onions and the seasonings. Bake,
covered, at 375°F 30 minutes or until
heated through. Top with Cheddar
cheese; sprinkle *remaining* onions down
center. Bake, uncovered, 3 minutes or
until onions are golden brown.

*Makes 4 to 6 servings*

# Heartland Shepherd's Pie

¾ pound ground beef
1 medium onion, chopped
1 can (14½ ounces) DEL MONTE®
   Original Recipe Stewed Tomatoes
1 can (8 ounces) DEL MONTE® Tomato
   Sauce
1 can (14½ ounces) DEL MONTE®
   Mixed Vegetables, drained
   Instant mashed potato flakes plus
   ingredients to prepare (enough
   for 6 servings)
3 cloves garlic, minced

Preheat oven to 375°F. In large skillet,
brown meat and onion over medium-high
heat; drain. Add tomatoes and tomato
sauce; cook over high heat until
thickened, stirring frequently. Stir in
mixed vegetables. Season with salt and
pepper, if desired. Spoon into 2-quart
baking dish; set aside. Prepare 6 servings
mashed potatoes according to package
directions, first cooking garlic in specified
amount of butter. Top meat mixture with
potatoes. Bake 20 minutes or until heated
through. Garnish with chopped parsley, if
desired.    *Makes 4 to 6 servings*

**Prep Time:** 5 minutes
**Cook Time:** 30 minutes

*Countdown Casserole*

# Pork with Couscous & Root Vegetables

1 teaspoon vegetable oil
½ pound pork tenderloin, thinly sliced
2 sweet potatoes, peeled, chopped
2 medium turnips, peeled, chopped
1 carrot, sliced
3 cloves garlic, finely chopped
1 can (about 15 ounces) garbanzo beans (chick-peas), rinsed and drained
1 cup fat-free reduced-sodium vegetable broth
½ cup pitted prunes, cut into thirds
1 teaspoon ground cumin
½ teaspoon ground cinnamon
¼ teaspoon ground allspice
¼ teaspoon ground nutmeg
¼ teaspoon ground black pepper
1 cup uncooked quick-cooking couscous, cooked
2 tablespoons dried currants

Heat oil in large nonstick skillet over medium-high heat until hot. Add pork, sweet potatoes, turnips, carrot and garlic. Cook and stir 5 minutes. Stir in beans, vegetable broth, prunes, cumin, cinnamon, allspice, nutmeg and pepper. Cover; bring to a boil over high heat. Reduce heat to medium-low. Simmer 30 minutes. Serve pork and vegetables on couscous. Top each serving evenly with currants. Garnish with sprigs of thyme, if desired.

*Makes 4 servings*

# Pastitso

8 ounces uncooked elbow macaroni
½ cup cholesterol-free egg substitute
¼ teaspoon ground nutmeg
¾ pound lean ground lamb, beef or turkey
½ cup chopped onion
1 clove garlic, minced
1 can (8 ounces) tomato sauce
¾ teaspoon dried mint leaves
½ teaspoon dried oregano leaves
½ teaspoon ground black pepper
⅛ teaspoon ground cinnamon
2 teaspoons reduced-calorie margarine
3 tablespoons all-purpose flour
1½ cups skim milk
2 tablespoons grated Parmesan cheese

Cook pasta according to package directions. Drain and transfer to medium bowl; stir in egg substitute and nutmeg.

Lightly spray bottom of 9-inch square baking dish with nonstick cooking spray. Spread pasta mixture onto bottom of baking dish. Set aside.

Preheat oven to 350°F. Cook lamb, onion and garlic in large nonstick skillet over medium heat until lamb is no longer pink. Stir in tomato sauce, mint, oregano, pepper and cinnamon. Reduce heat to low and simmer 10 minutes; spread over pasta.

Melt margarine in small nonstick saucepan over medium heat. Add flour. Stir constantly for 1 minute. Whisk in milk. Cook, stirring constantly, until thickened, about 6 minutes; spread over meat mixture. Sprinkle with cheese. Bake 30 to 40 minutes or until set.

*Makes 6 servings*

# Sausage & Noodle Casserole

1 pound BOB EVANS FARMS® Original Recipe Roll Sausage
1 cup chopped onion
¼ cup chopped green bell pepper
1 (10-ounce) package frozen peas
1 (10¾-ounce) can condensed cream of chicken soup
1 (8-ounce) package egg noodles, cooked according to package directions and drained
Salt and black pepper to taste
1 (2.8-ounce) can French fried onions, crushed

Preheat oven to 350°F. Crumble sausage into large skillet. Add chopped onion and green pepper. Cook over medium heat until meat is browned and vegetables are tender, stirring occasionally. Drain off any drippings. Cook peas according to package directions. Drain, reserving liquid in 2-cup glass measuring cup; set aside. Add enough water to pea liquid to obtain 1⅓ cups liquid. Combine liquid and soup in large bowl; stir in sausage mixture, noodles, reserved peas, salt and black pepper. Mix well. Spoon mixture into greased 2½-quart baking dish. Sprinkle with French fried onions. Bake 30 minutes or until bubbly. Serve hot. Refrigerate leftovers.  *Makes 6 servings*

# Quick Bean Cassoulet

1½ cups diagonally cut carrot slices
3 cloves garlic, minced
2 tablespoons margarine
2 (15½-ounce) cans Great Northern white beans, rinsed, drained
¾ pound smoked sausage slices, halved
1 cup dry white wine or chicken broth
¾ teaspoon rubbed sage
¾ pound VELVEETA® Pasteurized Process Cheese Spread, cubed
1 large tomato, chopped
½ cup fresh bread crumbs
¼ cup chopped parsley

SAUTÉ carrots and garlic in 1 tablespoon margarine in Dutch oven 5 to 7 minutes or until carrots are crisp-tender.

STIR in beans, sausage, wine and sage. Bring to boil. Reduce heat to low. Cover; simmer 5 minutes.

ADD process cheese spread and tomato; stir until process cheese spread is melted. Stir in 3 tablespoons parsley. Spoon into 2-quart casserole or serving bowl.

MELT remaining margarine. Add to combined remaining parsley and bread crumbs; toss lightly. Sprinkle over cassoulet. Garnish with fresh sage.

*Makes 6 servings*

# Greek White Bean Risotto

1 tablespoon low-sodium chicken-
  flavor bouillon granules
  Nonstick cooking spray
3 cloves garlic, minced
1½ cups uncooked arborio rice
2 teaspoons dried oregano leaves
⅓ cup finely chopped solid-pack
  sun-dried tomatoes
1 cup rinsed, drained canned
  cannellini beans (white kidney
  beans)
¾ cup (3 ounces) crumbled feta cheese
⅓ cup shredded Parmesan cheese
1 teaspoon lemon juice
½ teaspoon ground black pepper

Combine 5½ cups water and bouillon granules in large saucepan; cover. Bring to a simmer over medium-low heat.

Spray large saucepan with nonstick cooking spray; heat over medium heat until hot. Add garlic; cook and stir 1 minute. Add rice and oregano; reduce heat to medium-low. Stir 1 cup hot chicken broth into rice mixture; cook until broth is absorbed, stirring constantly. Stir ½ cup hot chicken broth into rice mixture, stirring constantly until broth is absorbed. Stir tomatoes into rice mixture.

Stir remaining hot chicken broth into rice mixture, ½ cup at a time, stirring constantly until all broth is absorbed before adding next ½ cup. (Total cooking time for chicken broth absorption is 35 to 40 minutes or until rice is just tender but still firm to the bite.)

Stir beans into rice mixture; cook 1 minute, stirring constantly. Remove from heat. Stir in cheeses, lemon juice and pepper. Cover; let stand 5 minutes. Stir once. Serve with breadsticks, if desired. Garnish as desired.   *Makes 5 servings*

# Favorite Mac 'n Cheese

2 cups (7 ounces) elbow macaroni,
  cooked and drained
¼ cup chopped green pepper
¼ cup chopped red pepper
¼ cup chopped onion
2 tablespoons margarine
1 pound VELVEETA® Pasteurized
  Process Cheese Spread, cubed
½ cup milk
  Kraft® 100% Grated Parmesan
  (optional)

**PREHEAT** oven to 350°F.

**COOK** and stir vegetables in margarine until vegetables are crisp-tender. Reduce heat to low.

**ADD** process cheese spread and milk; stir until process cheese spread is melted. Stir in macaroni; spoon into 2-quart casserole.

**BAKE** 15 minutes. Sprinkle with KRAFT® 100% Grated Parmesan Cheese, if desired.

*Makes 6 servings*

**Prep Time:** 15 minutes
**Cook Time:** 15 minutes

*Greek White Bean Risotto*

# Double Spinach Bake

8 ounces uncooked spinach fettuccine
Nonstick cooking spray
1 cup fresh mushroom slices
1 green onion with top, finely chopped
1 clove garlic, minced
4 to 5 cups fresh spinach, coarsely chopped *or* 1 package (10 ounces) frozen spinach, thawed and drained
1 tablespoon water
1 container (15 ounces) nonfat ricotta cheese
¼ cup skim milk
1 egg
½ teaspoon ground nutmeg
½ teaspoon ground black pepper
¼ cup (1 ounce) shredded reduced-fat Swiss cheese

Preheat oven to 350°F. Cook pasta according to package directions. Drain and set aside. Spray medium skillet with cooking spray. Add mushrooms, onion and garlic. Cook and stir over medium heat until mushrooms are tender. Add spinach and water. Cover; cook until spinach is wilted, about 3 minutes.

Combine ricotta cheese, milk, egg, nutmeg and black pepper in large bowl. Gently stir in noodles and vegetables; toss to coat evenly.

Lightly coat shallow 11×7-inch baking dish with cooking spray. Spread noodle mixture into casserole. Sprinkle with Swiss cheese. Bake 25 to 30 minutes or until knife inserted halfway into center comes out clean. *Makes 6 servings*

# Vegetable & Pasta Paella

Nonstick cooking spray
1 cup chopped onion
¾ cup chopped green bell pepper
2 cloves garlic, minced
1½ cups sliced portobello mushrooms or any variety mushrooms
2 cups fat-free reduced-sodium chicken broth
1 can (14½ ounces) Mexican-style stewed tomatoes, undrained
1 teaspoon chili powder
1 teaspoon paprika
½ teaspoon ground cumin
⅛ teaspoon ground black pepper
¾ cup uncooked orzo pasta
1 can (about 15 ounces) garbanzo beans (chick-peas), rinsed and drained
1 cup frozen green peas, thawed

Spray large nonstick skillet with cooking spray; heat over medium heat until hot. Add onion, bell pepper and garlic; cook and stir 5 minutes or until vegetables are tender. Add mushrooms; cook and stir 1 minute.

Add chicken broth, tomatoes, chili powder, paprika, cumin and black pepper to skillet; bring to a boil over high heat, stirring occasionally. Stir in pasta. Cover; reduce heat to medium-low. Simmer, 15 minutes, stirring occasionally.

Add beans and peas to skillet; bring to a boil over high heat. Reduce heat to low. Simmer, uncovered, 5 minutes, stirring frequently. Serve immediately. Garnish with sprigs of rosemary and thyme, if desired. *Makes 6 servings*

*Double Spinach Bake*

## Red Chili Tortilla Torte

2 cans (16 ounces) pinto beans or black beans, rinsed and drained
¼ cup low-salt chicken broth
1 tablespoon vegetable oil
2 large onions, sliced
2 red bell peppers, cut into ¼-inch strips
2 zucchini, thinly sliced
2 cloves garlic, minced
1 cup whole kernel corn
1 teaspoon ground cumin
½ teaspoon salt
¼ teaspoon cayenne pepper
6 (8-inch) flour tortillas
2 cups NEWMAN'S OWN® All Natural Salsa
2 cups (8 ounces) shredded Monterey Jack cheese

In food processor, combine pinto beans and chicken broth. Process until smooth; set aside. Heat oil in large nonstick skillet over medium heat. Add onions, bell peppers, zucchini and garlic; sauté until tender, 10 to 12 minutes. Add corn, cumin, salt and cayenne pepper; cook about 2 minutes. Heat oven to 375°F. Grease 8-inch round baking dish. Spread ½ cup of pinto bean mixture on one flour tortilla; place on bottom of baking dish. Spoon 1 cup of the onion mixture on top of beans. Spoon ⅓ cup of Newman's Own® All Natural Salsa on top of onion mixture; top with ⅓ cup of cheese. Repeat with remaining ingredients, ending with cheese. Bake until heated through, about 45 minutes. Let stand 10 minutes; cut into wedges to serve.

*Makes 8 to 10 servings*

## Brazilian Corn and Shrimp Moqueca Casserole

2 tablespoons olive oil
½ cup chopped onion
¼ cup chopped green bell pepper
¼ cup tomato sauce
2 tablespoons chopped parsley
½ teaspoon TABASCO® pepper sauce
1 pound medium shrimp, peeled, deveined
Salt to taste
2 tablespoons all-purpose flour
1 cup milk
1 can (16 ounces) cream-style corn
Grated Parmesan cheese

In large oven-proof skillet over medium-high heat, heat oil. Add onion, bell pepper, tomato sauce, parsley and TABASCO sauce. Cook, stirring occasionally, for 5 minutes. Add shrimp and salt. Cover and reduce heat to low. Simmer for 2 to 3 minutes. Preheat oven to 375°F. Sprinkle flour over shrimp mixture; stir. Add milk gradually, stirring after each addition. Cook over medium heat until mixture thickens. Remove from heat. Pour corn over mixture; do not stir. Sprinkle with Parmesan cheese. Bake for 30 minutes or until browned.

*Makes 4 servings*

# Company Crab

1 pound blue crabmeat, fresh, frozen or pasteurized
1 can (15 ounces) artichoke hearts, drained
1 can (4 ounces) sliced mushrooms, drained
2 tablespoons butter or margarine
2½ tablespoons all-purpose flour
½ teaspoon salt
⅛ teaspoon ground red pepper
1 cup half-and-half
2 tablespoons dry sherry
2 tablespoons crushed cornflakes
1 tablespoon grated Parmesan cheese
Paprika

Thaw crabmeat if frozen. Remove any pieces of shell or cartilage. Cut artichoke hearts in half. Place artichokes in well-greased, shallow 1½-quart casserole. Add crabmeat and mushrooms; cover and set aside.

Melt butter over medium heat in small saucepan. Stir in flour, salt and ground red pepper. Gradually stir in half-and-half. Continue cooking until sauce thickens, stirring constantly. Stir in sherry. Pour sauce over crabmeat. Combine cornflakes and cheese in small bowl; sprinkle over casserole. Sprinkle with paprika. Bake in preheated 450°F oven 12 to 15 minutes or until bubbly. *Makes 6 servings*

Favorite recipe from **Florida Department of Agriculture and Consumer Services, Bureau of Seafood and Aquaculture**

# Scandinavian Salmon-Cheddar Pie

3 large eggs
¼ cup milk
3 tablespoons chopped parsley, divided
2 tablespoons butter, melted
2 tablespoons minced green onion
1 tablespoon plus 1 teaspoon lemon juice
1 teaspoon Worcestershire sauce
½ teaspoon dry mustard
2 cups (8 ounces) shredded Wisconsin Cheddar cheese
½ pound fresh cooked, flaked salmon *or* 1 can (6½ ounces) salmon, drained, deboned and flaked
1 (9-inch) pie shell, baked and cooled
¾ cup dairy sour cream
¼ cup finely chopped cucumber
1 teaspoon dill weed
⅛ teaspoon ground white pepper

Heat oven to 425°F. Beat eggs in large bowl; add milk, 2 tablespoons parsley, butter, green onion, 1 tablespoon lemon juice, Worcestershire sauce and mustard; mix well. Fold in cheese and salmon; pour into cooled pie shell. Bake 20 to 25 minutes or until just set and crust is golden brown. Let stand 10 minutes before serving. Combine sour cream, cucumber, remaining 1 tablespoon parsley, dill, remaining 1 teaspoon lemon juice and pepper; mix well. Dollop each serving with sour cream mixture.

*Makes 6 servings*

Favorite recipe from **Wisconsin Milk Marketing Board**

173

# ENDLESS PASTABILITIES

*Longing for creative ways to serve pasta? Look no further—offered here are oodles of ways to use noodles. Sample your favorites stuffed with savory fillings, dressed in mouthwatering sauces or flavored with Italian, Oriental or Mexican seasonings.*

## Sweet Potato Ravioli with Asiago Cheese Sauce

¾ **pound sweet potatoes**
2 **tablespoons plain yogurt**
1 **teaspoon minced fresh chives**
1 **tablespoon plus ¼ teaspoon minced fresh sage, divided**
24 **wonton wrappers**
1 **tablespoon margarine**
1 **tablespoon plus 2 teaspoons all-purpose flour**
½ **cup skim milk**
½ **cup chicken broth**
½ **cup (2 ounces) shredded Asiago or Cheddar cheese**
¼ **teaspoon ground nutmeg**
¼ **teaspoon ground white pepper**
⅛ **teaspoon ground cinnamon**

Preheat oven to 350°F. Bake sweet potatoes 40 to 45 minutes or until tender. Cool completely. Peel potatoes and mash pulp. Stir in yogurt, chives and ¼ teaspoon sage. Place wonton wrappers on counter. Spoon 1 rounded teaspoon potato mixture in center of each wonton. Spread filling flat, leaving ½-inch border. Brush edges lightly with water. Fold wontons in half diagonally, pressing lightly to seal. Place filled wontons on baking sheet; cover loosely.

Bring 1½ quarts water to a boil in large saucepan. Reduce heat to medium. Add a few ravioli at a time. *(Do not overcrowd.)* Cook 3 to 4 minutes or until tender. Transfer to platter. Melt margarine in small saucepan over medium heat. Stir in flour; cook 1 minute, stirring constantly. Gradually stir in milk and chicken broth. Cook and stir until slightly thickened. Stir in cheese, nutmeg, white pepper and cinnamon. Serve ravioli on sauce. Sprinkle with remaining sage.

*Makes 8 servings*

*Sweet Potato Ravioli with Asiago Cheese Sauce*

## Cheese Ravioli with Spinach Pesto and Chicken

Spinach Pesto (recipe follows)
2 (9-ounce) packages refrigerated
   low-fat ravioli
Nonstick cooking spray
¾ cup matchstick-size carrot strips
¾ cup thinly sliced celery
½ cup chopped onion (about 1 small)
2 cloves garlic, minced
1 can (14½ ounces) no-salt-added
   stewed tomatoes
1½ pounds chicken tenders, cut
   crosswise into halves
¼ cup dry white wine
2 teaspoons dried rosemary leaves
¼ teaspoon salt
⅛ teaspoon ground black pepper

Prepare Spinach Pesto; set aside. Prepare ravioli according to package directions; drain and keep warm. Spray large nonstick skillet with cooking spray; heat over medium heat. Add carrots, celery, onion and garlic; cook and stir about 5 minutes or until crisp-tender. Add tomatoes, chicken, wine, rosemary, salt and pepper; heat to a boil. Reduce heat to low and simmer, uncovered, about 10 minutes or until chicken is no longer pink in center. Arrange ravioli on serving plates; spoon chicken and vegetable mixture over ravioli. Top with Spinach Pesto. *Makes 8 servings*

## Spinach Pesto

2 cups packed fresh spinach leaves
2 tablespoons grated Romano cheese
2 tablespoons olive oil or vegetable oil
1 to 2 tablespoons lemon juice
1 tablespoon dried basil leaves
3 cloves garlic

Process all ingredients in food processor until smooth. *Makes about 1 cup*

## Ravioli with Tomatoes and Zucchini

2 packages (9 ounces each) fresh or
   frozen cheese ravioli or tortellini
¾ pound hot Italian sausage, crumbled
1 can (14½ ounces) DEL MONTE®
   Diced Tomatoes
1 medium zucchini, thinly sliced and
   quartered
1 teaspoon basil, crushed
½ cup ricotta cheese *or* 2 tablespoons
   grated Parmesan cheese

**1.** In 8-quart pot, cook pasta according to package directions; drain. Keep hot.

**2.** Meanwhile, in 6-quart pot, brown sausage over medium-high heat or until no longer pink in center; drain.

**3.** Add tomatoes, zucchini and basil. Cook, uncovered, over medium-high heat about 8 minutes or until zucchini is just tender-crisp, stirring occasionally. Season with pepper, if desired.

**4.** Spoon sauce over hot pasta. Top with ricotta cheese. *Makes 4 servings*

*Ravioli with Tomatoes and Zucchini*

## Cheese-Sauced Manicotti

8 manicotti shells
1 cup chopped onion
¼ cup water
2 cloves garlic, minced
3 tablespoons all-purpose flour
1⅔ cups skim milk, divided
¾ cup shredded part-skim mozzarella cheese
1 teaspoon dried Italian seasoning
¼ teaspoon ground black pepper
1 package (10 ounces) frozen chopped spinach, thawed and well drained
1 cup nonfat ricotta cheese
½ cup 1% low-fat cottage cheese
½ teaspoon dried marjoram leaves
1 medium tomato, sliced

Prepare manicotti according to package directions; drain. Rinse under cold water; drain. Meanwhile, preheat oven to 350°F. Coat 13×9-inch baking dish with nonstick cooking spray.

To make sauce, combine onion, water and garlic in medium saucepan. Bring to a boil over high heat. Reduce heat to medium-low. Cover; simmer 3 to 4 minutes or until onion is tender. Blend flour and ⅓ cup milk in small bowl until smooth. Stir into onion mixture. Stir in remaining 1⅓ cups milk. Cook and stir over medium heat until mixture boils and thickens. Cook and stir 1 minute. Add mozzarella cheese, Italian seasoning and pepper. Cook and stir until cheese melts.

Combine spinach, ricotta cheese, cottage cheese, ⅓ cup sauce and marjoram in medium bowl. Spoon ⅓ cup spinach mixture into each manicotti shell. Place in prepared baking dish. Pour remaining sauce over top. Cover; bake 30 to 35 minutes or until heated through. Arrange tomato slices on top. Bake, uncovered, 4 to 5 minutes or until tomato is heated through. *Makes 4 servings*

## Stuffed Pasta Shells

4 ounces (about 18) large pasta shells, cooked and drained
2 cups finely chopped cooked ham or turkey
1 cup ricotta cheese
½ cup MIRACLE WHIP® Salad Dressing
¼ cup chopped red onion
2 tablespoons cold water
¼ cup (1 ounce) KRAFT® 100% Grated Parmesan Cheese
¼ cup dry bread crumbs
1 to 2 tablespoons chopped fresh parsley
1 tablespoon margarine, melted

**HEAT** oven to 350°F.

**COMBINE** ham, ricotta cheese, salad dressing and onion; mix lightly.

**FILL** shells with ham mixture; place, filled-side up, in shallow baking dish.

**ADD** 2 tablespoons cold water to dish; cover with foil. Bake 30 minutes or until thoroughly heated.

**COMBINE** Parmesan cheese, crumbs, parsley and margarine; sprinkle over shells. Continue baking, uncovered, 5 minutes. Serve with your favorite accompaniments. *Makes 6 servings*

## Mexican Stuffed Shells

1 pound ground beef
1 jar (12 ounces) mild or medium
   picante sauce
1 can (8 ounces) tomato sauce
½ cup water
1 can (4 ounces) chopped green
   chilies, drained
1 cup (4 ounces) shredded Monterey
   Jack cheese
1 can (2.8 ounces) FRENCH'S® French
   Fried Onions
12 large pasta shells, cooked in
   unsalted water and drained

Preheat oven to 350°F. In large skillet, brown ground beef; drain. In small bowl, combine picante sauce, tomato sauce and water. Stir *½ cup* sauce mixture into skillet along with chilies, *½ cup* cheese and *½ can* French Fried Onions; mix well. Spread half the remaining sauce mixture onto bottom of 10-inch round baking dish. Stuff cooked shells with beef mixture. Arrange shells in baking dish; top with remaining sauce. Bake, covered, at 350°F for 30 minutes or until heated through. Top with *remaining* onions and *½ cup* cheese; bake, uncovered, 5 minutes or until cheese is melted.

*Makes 6 servings*

## Four-Cheese Lasagna

½ pound ground beef
½ cup chopped onion
⅓ cup chopped celery
1 clove garlic, minced
1½ teaspoons dried basil leaves
¼ teaspoon dried oregano leaves
¼ teaspoon salt
⅛ teaspoon ground black pepper
1 package (3 ounces) cream cheese,
   cubed
⅓ cup light cream or milk
½ cup dry white wine
½ cup (2 ounces) shredded Wisconsin
   Cheddar or Gouda cheese
1 egg, slightly beaten
1 cup cream-style cottage cheese
6 ounces lasagna noodles, cooked and
   drained
6 ounces sliced Wisconsin mozzarella
   cheese

In large skillet, brown meat with onion, celery and garlic; drain. Stir in basil, oregano, salt and pepper. Reduce heat to low. Add cream cheese and cream. Cook, stirring frequently, until cream cheese is melted. Stir in wine. Gradually add Cheddar cheese, stirring until cheese is almost melted. Remove from heat. In small bowl, combine egg and cottage cheese. Into greased 10×6-inch baking dish, layer half *each* of the noodles, meat sauce, cottage cheese mixture and mozzarella cheese; repeat layers. Bake, uncovered, at 375°F, 30 to 35 minutes or until hot and bubbly.   *Makes 6 servings*

Favorite recipe from **Wisconsin Milk Marketing Board**

## Cheesy Chicken Roll-Ups

¼ cup butter
1 medium onion, finely chopped
4 ounces fresh mushrooms, sliced
3 boneless skinless chicken breast halves, cut into bite-size pieces
¾ cup dry white wine
½ teaspoon dried tarragon leaves
½ teaspoon salt
½ teaspoon ground black pepper
6 lasagna noodles, cooked, drained, each cut lengthwise into halves
1 package (8 ounces) cream cheese, cubed, softened
½ cup heavy cream
½ cup dairy sour cream
1½ cups (6 ounces) shredded Swiss cheese, divided
1 cup (4 ounces) shredded Muenster cheese, divided
3 tablespoons toasted sliced almonds
Chopped fresh parsley

Melt butter in large skillet over medium-high heat. Add onion and mushrooms; cook and stir until tender. Add chicken, wine, tarragon, salt and pepper; bring to a boil. Reduce heat to low; simmer 10 minutes, stirring occasionally.

Preheat oven to 325°F. Form each lasagna noodle half into a circle; place in 13×9-inch baking dish. Using slotted spoon, fill center of lasagna rings with chicken. To wine mixture remaining in skillet, add cream cheese, heavy cream, sour cream, ¾ cup Swiss cheese and ½ cup Muenster cheese. Heat until cheeses melt, stirring frequently.

*(Do not boil.)* Pour over lasagna rings. Sprinkle with remaining cheeses and almonds. Bake 35 minutes or until hot and bubbly; sprinkle with parsley. Garnish as desired. *Makes 6 servings*

Favorite recipe from **Southeast United Dairy Industry Association, Inc.**

## Tomato Pesto Lasagna

8 ounces lasagna noodles (2 inches wide)
1 pound crumbled sausage or ground beef
1 can (14½ ounces) DEL MONTE® Pasta Style Chunky Tomatoes
1 can (6 ounces) DEL MONTE® Tomato Paste
8 ounces ricotta cheese
1 package (4 ounces) pesto sauce*
2 cups shredded mozzarella cheese
Grated Parmesan cheese (optional)

*Available frozen or refrigerated at the supermarket.*

Cook noodles according to package directions; rinse, drain and separate noodles. In large skillet, brown meat; drain. Stir in tomatoes, tomato paste and ¾ cup water; mix well. In 2-quart or 9-inch square baking dish, layer one third meat sauce, then half *each* of noodles (cut noodles to fit, if necessary), ricotta, pesto and mozzarella cheese; repeat layers, ending with meat sauce. Top with grated Parmesan cheese, if desired. Bake at 350°F, 30 minutes or until heated through. *Makes 6 servings*

*Cheesy Chicken Roll-Ups*

## Cheese Tortellini with Tuna

1 tuna steak* (about 6 ounces)
1 package (9 ounces) refrigerated reduced-fat cheese tortellini
Nonstick cooking spray
1 cup finely chopped red bell pepper
1 cup finely chopped green bell pepper
¼ cup finely chopped onion
¾ teaspoon fennel seeds, crushed
½ cup evaporated skim milk
2 teaspoons all-purpose flour
½ teaspoon dry mustard
½ teaspoon ground black pepper

*Or, substitute 1 can (6 ounces) tuna packed in water, drained, for tuna steak. Omit step 1.

**1.** Grill or broil tuna 4 inches from heat source until fish just begins to flake, about 7 to 9 minutes, turning once. Remove and discard skin. Cut tuna into chunks; set aside.

**2.** Cook pasta according to package directions. Drain; set aside.

**3.** Spray large nonstick skillet with cooking spray. Add bell peppers, onion and fennel seeds; cook over medium heat until crisp-tender. Whisk together milk, flour, mustard and black pepper in small bowl until smooth; add to skillet. Cook until thickened, stirring constantly. Stir in tuna and pasta; reduce heat to low and simmer until heated through, about 3 minutes. Serve immediately.

*Makes about 4 servings*

## Sweet & Sour Tortellini

1 package (7 to 12 ounces) cheese-filled tortellini
½ pound boneless tender beef steak (sirloin, rib eye or top loin)
2 teaspoons cornstarch
2 teaspoons KIKKOMAN® Soy Sauce
1 small clove garlic, minced
½ cup KIKKOMAN® Sweet & Sour Sauce
⅓ cup chicken broth
1 tablespoon sugar
2 tablespoons dry sherry
2 tablespoons vegetable oil, divided
1 medium onion, chunked
1 small red pepper, chunked
1 small green pepper, chunked

Cook tortellini according to package directions, omitting salt; drain. Cut meat into thin bite-size pieces. Combine cornstarch, soy sauce and garlic in small bowl; stir in meat. Let stand 15 minutes. Meanwhile, combine sweet & sour sauce, chicken broth, sugar and sherry; set aside. Heat 1 tablespoon oil in hot wok or large skillet over high heat. Add meat mixture; stir-fry 1 minute. Remove from wok. Heat remaining 1 tablespoon oil in wok. Add onion and peppers; stir-fry 3 minutes. Add meat mixture, sweet & sour sauce mixture and tortellini. Heat thoroughly, stirring occasionally. *Makes 4 servings*

*Cheese Tortellini with Tuna*

## Sweety Meaty Sauce for Ziti

2 tablespoons CHEF PAUL PRUDHOMME'S Poultry Magic®, divided
1 pound ground turkey
2 tablespoons olive oil
2 tablespoons margarine
1 cup chopped onion
1 cup chopped green pepper
2 cups canned crushed tomatoes
1 cup tomato puree
¾ cup finely chopped carrots
1½ cups chicken stock or water, divided
1 tablespoon granulated sugar
½ teaspoon salt
1 tablespoon dark brown sugar (optional)
12 ounces ziti pasta, cooked and drained

Mix 1 tablespoon plus 2 teaspoons Poultry Magic® with turkey, working it in well with your hands; set aside.

Heat oil and margarine in 3½-quart saucepan over medium-high heat 1 minute or until margarine has melted and mixture begins to sizzle. Add turkey; cook, stirring occasionally to separate chunks, until turkey is no longer pink, about 6 minutes. Add onion and green pepper; cook and stir 3 to 4 minutes or until tender. Add the remaining 1 teaspoon Poultry Magic®, tomatoes, tomato puree, carrots, ½ cup stock, granulated sugar and salt; mix well. (If you like a sweeter sauce, add brown sugar.) Cook, stirring occasionally, 3 to 4 minutes or until mixture comes to a boil. Reduce heat to low; cover. Simmer 30 minutes, stirring occasionally. Stir in remaining 1 cup stock; cover. Simmer an additional 20 minutes or until sauce has thickened and has changed from bright red to dark red in color, stirring occasionally. Remove from heat. Serve on hot pasta.

*Makes 4 servings*

## Garden Primavera Pasta

6 ounces bow tie pasta
1 jar (6 ounces) marinated artichoke hearts
2 cloves garlic, minced
½ teaspoon dried rosemary, crushed
1 green pepper, cut into thin strips
1 large carrot, cut into 3-inch julienne strips
1 medium zucchini, cut into 3-inch julienne strips
1 can (14½ ounces) DEL MONTE® Pasta Style Chunky Tomatoes
12 small pitted ripe olives (optional)

Cook pasta according to package directions; drain. Drain artichokes, reserving marinade. Toss pasta in 3 tablespoons artichoke marinade; set aside. Cut artichoke hearts into halves. In large skillet, cook garlic and rosemary in 1 tablespoon artichoke marinade. Add remaining ingredients, except pasta and artichokes. Cook, uncovered, over medium-high heat 4 to 5 minutes or until vegetables are tender-crisp and sauce is thickened. Add artichoke hearts. Spoon over pasta. Serve with grated Parmesan cheese, if desired. *Makes 4 servings*

**Prep Time:** 15 minutes
**Cook Time:** 10 minutes

*Garden Primavera Pasta*

## Shrimp and Snow — Peas with Fusilli —

6 ounces uncooked fusilli
 Nonstick cooking spray
2 cloves garlic, minced
¼ teaspoon crushed red pepper
12 ounces medium shrimp, peeled and
 deveined
2 cups snow peas
1 can (8 ounces) sliced water
 chestnuts, drained
⅓ cup sliced green onions
3 tablespoons lime juice
2 tablespoons finely chopped fresh
 cilantro
2 tablespoons olive oil
1 tablespoon reduced-sodium soy
 sauce
1½ teaspoons Mexican seasoning

Cook pasta according to package directions. Drain; set aside.

Spray large nonstick skillet with cooking spray; heat over medium heat until hot. Add garlic and red pepper; stir-fry 1 minute. Add shrimp; stir-fry 5 minutes or until shrimp are opaque. Remove shrimp from skillet.

Add snow peas and 2 tablespoons water to skillet; cook, covered, 1 minute. Uncover; cook and stir 2 minutes or until snow peas are crisp-tender. Remove snow peas from skillet. Combine pasta, shrimp, snow peas, water chestnuts and green onions in large bowl. Blend lime juice, cilantro, oil, soy sauce and Mexican seasoning in small bowl. Drizzle over pasta mixture; toss to coat. Garnish as desired. *Makes 6 servings*

## Orzo Pasta with ——— Shrimp ———

8 ounces uncooked orzo pasta
3 tablespoons plus ½ teaspoon
 FILIPPO BERIO® Olive Oil, divided
3 cloves garlic, minced
1¼ pounds small shrimp, peeled
1½ medium tomatoes, chopped
2 tablespoons chopped fresh cilantro
2 tablespoons chopped fresh Italian
 parsley
 Juice of 1 lemon
2 ounces feta cheese, crumbled
 Salt and freshly ground black
 pepper

Cook pasta according to package directions until al dente (tender but still firm). Drain. Toss with ½ teaspoon olive oil; set aside. Heat remaining 3 tablespoons olive oil in large skillet over medium heat until hot. Add garlic; cook and stir 2 to 3 minutes or until golden. Add shrimp; cook and stir 3 to 5 minutes or until shrimp are opaque (do not overcook). Stir in pasta. Add tomatoes, cilantro, parsley and lemon juice. Sprinkle with feta cheese. Season to taste with salt and pepper. *Makes 4 servings*

*Shrimp and Snow Peas with Fusilli*

## Angel Hair al Fresco

¾ cup skim milk
1 tablespoon margarine or butter
1 package (4.8 ounces) PASTA RONI™ Angel Hair Pasta with Herbs
1 can (6⅛ ounces) white tuna in water, drained, flaked *or* 1½ cups chopped cooked chicken
2 medium tomatoes, chopped
⅓ cup sliced green onions
¼ cup dry white wine or water
¼ cup slivered almonds, toasted (optional)
1 tablespoon chopped fresh basil *or* 1 teaspoon dried basil

**1.** In 3-quart saucepan, combine 1⅓ cups water, skim milk and margarine. Bring just to a boil.

**2.** Stir in pasta, contents of seasoning packet, tuna, tomatoes, onions, wine, almonds and basil. Return to a boil; reduce heat to medium.

**3.** Boil, uncovered, stirring frequently, 6 to 8 minutes. Sauce will be thin, but will thicken upon standing.

**4.** Let stand 3 minutes or until desired consistency. Stir before serving.

*Makes 4 servings*

## Capellini Orange Almondine

1 pound Angel Hair Pasta (Capellini) or your favorite long, thin pasta shape
2 tablespoons margarine, divided
½ cup orange spreadable fruit or orange marmalade
½ cup toasted almonds
¼ cup whole milk
1 (6-ounce) can mandarin oranges, drained

Prepare pasta according to package directions; drain. Place in large serving bowl. Melt 1 tablespoon margarine and orange fruit spread in small saucepan over medium heat. Pour over pasta; toss to coat. Brown almonds in remaining 1 tablespoon margarine. Add milk and mandarin oranges to pasta; toss to combine. *Makes 6 to 8 servings*

Favorite recipe from **National Pasta Association**

## Bow Tie Pasta with Garlic Vegetables

3 medium carrots, thinly sliced
2 small zucchini, thinly sliced
¼ cup margarine
1 large onion, chopped
4 garlic cloves, minced
½ cup chicken broth
½ cup heavy cream
½ teaspoon salt
½ teaspoon dried leaf tarragon
¼ teaspoon ground black pepper
2 cups hot, cooked, drained bow tie pasta

Place carrots and zucchini in medium saucepan. Add water to cover. Cook, uncovered, 3 minutes or until crisp-tender. Drain; set aside. Melt margarine in same saucepan. Add onion and garlic; cook until tender. Gradually stir in broth, cream, salt, tarragon and pepper; simmer 5 minutes or until sauce is slightly thickened. Add vegetables; heat thoroughly, stirring occasionally. Add pasta to sauce; toss lightly. Serve immediately. *Makes 4 servings*

## Linguine Carbonara

12 ounces uncooked linguine
6 slices bacon, cut into 1-inch pieces
1 box (10 ounces) BIRDS EYE® frozen Deluxe Baby Whole Carrots
1 cup BIRDS EYE® frozen Green Peas
½ cup milk
½ teaspoon dried oregano
½ teaspoon garlic powder
⅓ cup grated Parmesan cheese

• Cook pasta according to package directions; drain.

• Meanwhile, cook bacon in large skillet until golden brown. Drain bacon, reserving 2 tablespoons drippings in skillet.

• Add vegetables, milk, oregano, garlic powder and bacon; cook and stir over medium heat 5 minutes. Add linguine; heat through. Add cheese; toss to coat. Add salt and pepper to taste.

*Makes 4 to 6 servings*

## Shrimp Fettucine

4 ounces egg or spinach fettucine
½ pound medium shrimp, peeled and deveined
1 clove garlic, minced
1 tablespoon olive oil
1 can (14½ ounces) DEL MONTE® Pasta Style Chunky Tomatoes
½ cup whipping cream
¼ cup sliced green onions

Cook pasta according to package directions; drain. In large skillet, cook shrimp and garlic in oil over medium-high heat until shrimp are pink and opaque. Stir in tomatoes; simmer 5 minutes. Blend in cream and green onions; heat through. *Do not boil.* Serve over hot pasta.

*Makes 3 to 4 servings*

## Pasta with Tuna Sauce

½ cup MIRACLE WHIP® Salad Dressing, divided
2 cups assorted cut-up vegetables
1 package (7 ounces) spaghetti, cooked, drained
1 can (6⅛ ounces) tuna, drained, flaked
¼ teaspoon dill weed

**HEAT** 2 tablespoons of the dressing in large skillet on medium-high heat. Add vegetables; cook and stir 4 to 6 minutes or until tender-crisp.

**STIR** in remaining dressing, spaghetti, tuna and dill. Cook 3 minutes or until thoroughly heated. *Makes 4 servings*

# Fettuccine Alfredo with Shiitake Mushrooms

    1 tablespoon olive or vegetable oil
    2 medium cloves garlic, finely
        chopped
    1 cup sliced shiitake or white
        mushrooms
    2 tablespoons dry white wine
    1 tablespoon finely chopped fresh
        basil leaves*
 1½ cups milk
    1 cup canned crushed tomatoes
    ½ cup water
    2 tablespoons butter or margarine
    1 package LIPTON® Noodles & Sauce—
        Alfredo
      Dash pepper

*Substitution: Use ½ teaspoon dried basil leaves, crushed.*

In 10-inch skillet, heat oil over medium heat. Add garlic; cook and stir 30 seconds. Add mushrooms, wine and basil; cook and stir 2 minutes or until mushrooms are tender. Stir in remaining ingredients. Bring to a boil; simmer 8 minutes or until noodles are tender, stirring occasionally. Garnish, if desired, with additional basil leaves and cherry tomatoes.

*Makes about 2 servings*

# Pad Thai

    3 tablespoons ketchup
    3 tablespoons fish sauce
    2 tablespoons packed brown sugar
    1 tablespoon lime juice
    1 jalapeño pepper, seeded, minced
    1 teaspoon curry powder
    2 tablespoons peanut oil, divided
    1 pound medium shrimp, peeled
    3 cloves garlic, minced
    3 eggs, lightly beaten
    8 ounces flat rice noodles, cooked
    2 cups fresh bean sprouts, divided
    ⅔ cup chopped peanuts
    3 green onions, thinly sliced
    1 carrot, shredded
    ¾ cup shredded red cabbage
    ½ cup cilantro, coarsely chopped
    1 lime, cut into wedges

Combine ¼ cup water, ketchup, fish sauce, sugar, lime juice, chili and curry powder in medium bowl; set aside. Heat wok over high heat. Add 1 tablespoon oil. Add shrimp; stir-fry 2 minutes or until shrimp turn opaque. Remove from wok. Reduce heat to medium. Add remaining oil to wok. Add garlic; stir-fry 20 seconds or until golden. Add eggs; cook 2 minutes or just until set, stirring every 30 seconds to scramble. Stir in ketchup mixture. Increase heat to high. Add noodles; stir to coat with sauce. Cook 2 minutes, stirring often, until noodles are tender. (Add water, 1 tablespoon at a time, if sauce is absorbed and noodles are still dry.) Add cooked shrimp, 1½ cups sprouts, peanuts and onions; cook and stir until heated through. Transfer to large serving platter. Serve with remaining sprouts, carrot, cabbage and cilantro. Squeeze lime over noodles before eating. *Makes 4 servings*

*Pad Thai*

## Soba Stir-Fry

8 ounces uncooked soba noodles
   (Japanese buckwheat pasta)
1 tablespoon olive oil
2 cups sliced fresh shiitake
   mushrooms
1 medium red bell pepper, cut into
   thin strips
2 whole dried red peppers *or*
   ¼ teaspoon crushed red pepper
1 clove garlic, minced
2 cups shredded napa cabbage
2 teaspoons cornstarch
½ cup fat-free reduced-sodium chicken
   broth
2 tablespoons reduced-sodium tamari
   or soy sauce
1 tablespoon rice wine or dry sherry
1 package (14 ounces) firm tofu,
   drained and cut into 1-inch cubes
2 green onions, thinly sliced

Cook noodles according to package directions. Drain and set aside. Heat oil in large nonstick skillet or wok over medium heat. Add mushrooms, bell pepper, dried peppers and garlic. Cook 3 minutes or until mushrooms are tender. Add cabbage. Cover. Cook 2 minutes or until cabbage is wilted.

Combine cornstarch, chicken broth, tamari and rice wine in small bowl. Stir sauce into vegetable mixture. Cook 2 minutes or until sauce is bubbly. Stir in noodles and tofu; toss gently until heated through. Sprinkle with green onions. Serve immediately.          *Makes 4 servings*

## Sesame Peanut Noodles with Green Onions

1 tablespoon peanut or vegetable oil
1 teaspoon finely chopped garlic
¼ cup peanut butter
1 teaspoon soy sauce
2¼ cups water
1 package LIPTON® Noodles & Sauce—
   Chicken Flavor
½ cup sliced green onions
2 tablespoons sesame seeds, toasted

In medium saucepan, heat oil and cook garlic over medium heat 30 seconds. Stir in peanut butter and soy sauce; cook until melted. Add water and bring to a boil. Stir in noodles & sauce—chicken flavor, then simmer, stirring frequently, 10 minutes or until noodles are tender. Stir in green onions and 1 tablespoon sesame seeds. To serve, sprinkle with remaining 1 tablespoon sesame seeds.

*Makes about 4 servings*

**MICROWAVE DIRECTIONS:** In 1½-quart microwave-safe casserole, microwave oil with garlic, uncovered, at HIGH (Full Power) 20 seconds. Stir in peanut butter and soy sauce and microwave 30 seconds or until melted; stir. Add water and noodles & sauce—chicken flavor; microwave 12 minutes or until noodles are tender. Stir in green onions and 1 tablespoon sesame seeds. Sprinkle with remaining 1 tablespoon sesame seeds and serve immediately.

*Soba Stir-Fry*

# ON THE SIDE

*Complement every meal with these simple-to-make serve-withs that spotlight the best of Mother Nature—vegetables, rice and pasta. Whether you need a dish suitable for a family supper or an elegant dinner, these innovative recipes will round out any meal.*

## Cold Asparagus with Lemon-Mustard Dressing

12 fresh asparagus spears
2 tablespoons fat-free mayonnaise
1 tablespoon sweet brown mustard
1 tablespoon fresh lemon juice
1 teaspoon grated lemon peel, divided

Steam asparagus until crisp-tender and bright green; immediately drain and run under cold water. Cover; refrigerate until chilled. Combine mayonnaise, mustard and lemon juice in small bowl; blend well. Stir in ½ teaspoon lemon peel; set aside.

Divide asparagus between 2 plates. Spoon 2 tablespoons dressing over each serving; sprinkle each with ¼ teaspoon lemon peel. Garnish with carrot strips and edible flowers, such as pansies, violets or nasturtiums, if desired. *Makes 2 servings*

*Cold Asparagus with Lemon-Mustard Dressing*

## Broccoli with Sesame Vinaigrette

1 teaspoon butter or margarine
1 teaspoon sesame seeds
1 pound fresh broccoli
2 tablespoons plus 1½ teaspoons
    white wine vinegar
1 tablespoon water
2 teaspoons olive or sesame oil
½ teaspoon LAWRY'S® Seasoned Salt
½ teaspoon LAWRY'S® Seasoned
    Pepper

**Microwave Directions:** On shallow microwave-safe plate, place butter and sesame seeds. Cover with plastic wrap. Microwave on HIGH 1 minute or until seeds are toasted; set aside. Trim off large ends of broccoli stalks; discard. Place trimmed broccoli in shallow microwave-safe dish; cover. Microwave on HIGH 7 minutes or until broccoli is crisp-tender. Place broccoli on serving platter; keep warm. Combine sesame seeds, vinegar, water, oil, Seasoned Salt and Seasoned Pepper; drizzle over broccoli. Garnish as desired.                    *Makes 4 servings*

**Presentation:** Serve with any grilled meat or poultry.

## Brussels Sprouts with Almonds and Dijon Mustard

1 box (10 ounces) BIRDS EYE® frozen
    Brussels Sprouts
1½ tablespoons sliced almonds (toasted,
    if desired)
1½ teaspoons butter or margarine,
    melted
1½ teaspoons Dijon mustard

•Cook Brussels sprouts according to package directions.

•Combine with remaining ingredients; mix well. Serve hot with salt and pepper to taste.                    *Makes 3 to 4 servings*

## Sweet-Sour Red Cabbage

1 tablespoon butter or margarine
½ cup wine vinegar
¼ cup honey
1 teaspoon salt
1 medium head red cabbage,
    shredded (8 cups)
2 apples, cored and diced

Melt butter in large nonstick skillet or stainless steel saucepan over medium heat. Stir in vinegar, honey and salt. Add cabbage and apples; toss well. Reduce heat to low; cover and simmer 45 to 50 minutes.                    *Makes 4 to 6 servings*

*Broccoli with Sesame Vinaigrette*

## Honey Glazed Carrots and Parsnips

½ pound carrots, peeled, thinly sliced
½ pound parsnips, peeled, thinly sliced
¼ cup chopped fresh parsley
2 tablespoons honey

Steam carrots and parsnips 3 to 4 minutes until crisp-tender. Rinse under cold running water; drain and set aside. Just before serving, combine carrots, parsnips, parsley and honey in large saucepan or skillet. Cook over medium heat just until heated through. Garnish with fresh Italian parsley, if desired. Serve immediately.

*Makes 6 servings*

## Grilled Corn-on-the-Cob

¼ pound butter or margarine, softened
1 tablespoon KIKKOMAN® Soy Sauce
½ teaspoon dried tarragon leaves, crumbled
6 ears fresh corn

Thoroughly blend butter, soy sauce and tarragon leaves. Husk corn. Lay each ear on piece of foil large enough to wrap around it; spread ears generously with seasoned butter. Wrap foil around corn; seal edges. Place on grill 3 inches from hot coals; cook 20 to 30 minutes or until corn is tender, turning over frequently. (Or, place wrapped corn on baking sheet. Bake in 325°F oven 30 minutes.) Serve immediately. *Makes 6 servings*

## Green Bean Rice Almondine

2 tablespoons reduced-calorie margarine
½ cup finely chopped onion
1¼ cups fat-free reduced-sodium chicken broth
½ teaspoon lemon pepper seasoning
1 cup diagonally sliced green beans
1¼ cups uncooked instant white rice
3 tablespoons sliced almonds, toasted

Melt margarine in medium saucepan over medium heat; add onion. Cook and stir 5 minutes or until onion is tender. Add chicken broth and lemon pepper seasoning; bring to a boil over high heat. Add beans; cover. Reduce heat to low. Simmer 7 minutes or until beans are tender, stirring occasionally.

Stir rice into saucepan; cover. Remove from heat. Let stand 5 minutes or until liquid is absorbed and rice is tender. Fluff rice mixture with fork. Stir in almonds; blend well. Serve immediately. Garnish as desired. *Makes 6 servings*

*Green Bean Rice Almondine*

## Country Corn Pudding

2 cups milk
½ cup yellow cornmeal
¼ cup (½ stick) butter or margarine, melted
1 tablespoon sugar
½ teaspoon salt
4 large eggs, beaten
2 tablespoons FRANK'S® Original RedHot® Cayenne Pepper Sauce
1 can (11 ounces) Mexican-style corn, drained
1 can (2.8 ounces) FRENCH'S® French Fried Onions, divided
1 cup (4 ounces) shredded Cheddar cheese
½ teaspoon baking powder
Salsa (optional)

**MICROWAVE DIRECTIONS:** Whisk together milk, cornmeal, butter, sugar and salt in 3-quart microwave-safe bowl. Cover with vented plastic wrap and microwave on HIGH 8 minutes or until mixture is very thick and almost all of the liquid is absorbed, whisking twice. (Mixture should mound when dropped from a spoon.)

Combine eggs, RedHot sauce, corn, *½ can* French Fried Onions, cheese and baking powder in medium bowl. Stir egg mixture into cornmeal mixture; microwave, uncovered, on MEDIUM (50% power) 5 minutes or until knife inserted in center comes out clean. Sprinkle with *remaining* French Fried Onions. Microwave on MEDIUM 1 minute or until onions are golden. Serve with salsa, if desired.

*Makes 6 servings*

**Prep Time:** 10 minutes
**Cook Time:** 20 minutes

## Lemon-Nutmeg Spinach

1 box (10 ounces) BIRDS EYE® frozen Chopped or Whole Leaf Spinach
1½ tablespoons butter or margarine, melted
2 teaspoons lemon juice
⅛ teaspoon ground nutmeg

• Cook spinach according to package directions; drain well.

• Combine with remaining ingredients.

• Serve hot with salt and pepper to taste.

*Makes 3 to 4 servings*

**Prep Time:** 3 to 4 minutes
**Cook Time:** 6 to 7 minutes

## Honey Nut Squash

2 acorn squash (about 6 ounces each)
¼ cup honey
2 tablespoons butter or margarine, melted
2 tablespoons chopped walnuts
2 tablespoons raisins
2 teaspoons Worcestershire sauce

Cut acorn squash lengthwise into halves; do not remove seeds. Place cut side up in baking pan or on baking sheet. Bake at 400°F 30 to 45 minutes or until tender. Remove seeds and fibers.

Combine honey, butter, walnuts, raisins and Worcestershire sauce; spoon into squash. Bake 5 to 10 minutes more or until lightly glazed.

*Makes 4 servings*

Favorite recipe from **National Honey Board**

## Easy Dilled Succotash

1½ cups frozen lima beans
1 small onion, finely chopped
1½ cups frozen whole kernel corn
1 teaspoon salt
1 teaspoon sugar
1 teaspoon dried dill weed

Bring ½ cup water in medium saucepan to a boil over high heat. Add beans and onion; cover. Reduce heat to low. Simmer 8 minutes.

Stir corn into bean mixture; cover. Simmer 5 minutes or until vegetables are tender. Drain bean mixture; discard liquid. Place bean mixture in serving bowl; stir in salt, sugar and dill until well blended. Garnish as desired.                *Makes 4 servings*

## Baked Tomatoes

4 medium tomatoes
½ cup dry bread crumbs
1 tablespoon chopped fresh basil *or*
    1 teaspoon dried basil leaves
½ teaspoon salt
½ teaspoon dried oregano leaves
¼ teaspoon freshly ground black
    pepper
1 clove garlic, minced (optional)
2 tablespoons FILIPPO BERIO®
    Olive Oil

Preheat oven to 375°F. Cut off stems and a thin slice from bottom of each tomato. Cut each tomato in half crosswise. Place in shallow casserole, cut side up. In small bowl, combine bread crumbs, basil, salt, oregano, pepper and garlic, if desired. Stir in olive oil. Spoon evenly over tomatoes. Bake 15 to 20 minutes or until lightly browned.                *Makes 8 servings*

## South-of-the-Border Vegetable Kabobs

5 cloves garlic, peeled
½ cup A.1.® BOLD Steak Sauce
¼ cup FLEISCHMANN'S® margarine,
    melted
1 tablespoon finely chopped fresh
    cilantro
¾ teaspoon ground cumin
¼ teaspoon coarsely ground black
    pepper
⅛ teaspoon ground red pepper
3 ears corn, cut crosswise into
    1½-inch-thick slices, blanched
3 medium plum tomatoes, cut into
    ½-inch-thick slices
1 small zucchini, cut lengthwise into
    thin slices
1 cup baby carrots, blanched

Mince 1 garlic clove; halve remaining garlic cloves and set aside. In small bowl, combine steak sauce, margarine, cilantro, minced garlic, cumin and peppers; set aside.

Alternately thread vegetables and halved garlic cloves onto 6 (10-inch) metal skewers. Grill kabobs over medium heat for 7 to 9 minutes or until done, turning and basting often with steak sauce mixture. Remove vegetables and garlic from skewers; serve immediately.

*Makes 6 servings*

## Savory Grilled Potatoes in Foil

½ cup MIRACLE WHIP® Salad Dressing
3 garlic cloves, minced
½ teaspoon paprika
¼ teaspoon *each* salt, pepper
3 baking potatoes, cut into ¼-inch slices
1 large onion, sliced

**MIX** salad dressing and seasonings in large bowl until well blended. Stir in potatoes and onion to coat.

**DIVIDE** potato mixture evenly among six 12-inch square pieces of heavy-duty foil. Seal each to form packet.

**PLACE** foil packets on grill over medium-hot coals (coals will have slight glow). Grill, covered, 25 to 30 minutes or until potatoes are tender. *Makes 6 servings*

## Lipton® California Mashed Potatoes

2 pounds all-purpose potatoes, peeled, if desired, and cut into chunks
Water
2 tablespoons chopped fresh parsley (optional)
1 envelope LIPTON® Recipe Secrets® Onion Soup Mix
¾ cup milk, heated to boiling
½ cup sour cream

In 3-quart saucepan, cover potatoes with water. Bring to a boil over high heat.

Reduce heat to low and simmer uncovered 20 minutes or until potatoes are very tender; drain. Return potatoes to saucepan. Mash potatoes; stir in parsley and onion soup mix blended with hot milk and sour cream.

*Makes about 8 servings*

## Santa Fe Potato Cakes

3 cups cooked instant mashed potato flakes or leftover unbuttered mashed potatoes
1 can (4 ounces) diced green chilies, drained
⅔ cup cornmeal, divided
3 green onions, sliced
⅓ cup (about 1½ ounces) shredded Cheddar cheese
2 eggs, beaten
2 tablespoons chopped fresh cilantro
1 teaspoon chili powder
½ teaspoon LAWRY'S® Seasoned Salt
½ teaspoon LAWRY'S® Seasoned Pepper
2 tablespoons olive oil, divided

In large bowl, combine potatoes, chilies, ½ cup cornmeal, onions, cheese, eggs, cilantro, chili powder, Seasoned Salt and Seasoned Pepper; shape into eight patties. Sprinkle both sides with remaining cornmeal; set aside. In large nonstick skillet, heat 1 tablespoon oil over medium heat. Add four patties; cook 5 to 7 minutes or until golden brown, turning once. Remove from skillet; keep warm. Repeat with remaining oil and patties. Garnish as desired. *Makes 4 servings*

*Savory Grilled Potatoes in Foil*

## — Arroz Mexicana —

1 medium onion, chopped
2 cloves garlic, crushed
½ teaspoon dried oregano, crushed
1 tablespoon vegetable oil
¾ cup uncooked long-grain white rice
1 can (14½ ounces) DEL MONTE®
    Mexican Recipe Stewed Tomatoes
1 green pepper, chopped

In large skillet, cook onion, garlic and oregano in oil until onion is tender. Stir in rice; cook until rice is golden, stirring frequently. Drain tomatoes reserving liquid; pour liquid into measuring cup. Add water to measure 1½ cups. Stir into rice mixture; bring to boil. Reduce heat; cover and simmer over medium heat 15 minutes or until rice is tender. Stir in tomatoes and green pepper; cook 5 minutes. Garnish with chopped parsley, if desired.                *Makes 4 to 6 servings*

## California-Style — Wild Rice Pilaf —

1 cup uncooked brown and wild rice
    mix or other wild rice blend
1 package (9 ounces) DOLE®
    California Style Vegetables*
1 teaspoon dried basil leaves, crushed

*Cut cauliflower into smaller pieces, if desired.*

•**Cook** rice as package directs, stirring in vegetables, seasoning packet and basil during last 3 minutes of cooking time.

•**Drain** excess liquid from vegetable-rice mixture. Spoon into serving dish. Garnish with fresh herbs, if desired.

*Makes 6 servings*

## Spiced Mushroom Pecan Rice — Timbales —

Nonstick cooking spray
1 cup finely chopped shiitake or other
    mushrooms
¾ cup apple juice
1 (3-inch) cinnamon stick, broken in
    half
¼ teaspoon salt
3 whole allspice
¾ cup uncooked white basmati rice
¼ cup toasted pecans
3 tablespoons minced fresh chives or
    green onions

Spray 5 (5-ounce) custard cups or molds with cooking spray; set aside.

Spray heavy medium saucepan with cooking spray; heat over medium-high heat until hot. Add mushrooms; cook and stir 5 minutes or until tender. Stir ¾ cup water, apple juice, cinnamon sticks, salt and allspice into saucepan; bring to a boil over high heat. Stir in rice; cover. Reduce heat to medium-low. Simmer 15 to 20 minutes or until liquid is absorbed and rice is tender. Remove saucepan from heat. Remove cinnamon sticks and allspice; discard. Stir pecans and chives into saucepan.

Spoon rice mixture evenly into prepared cups; pack down with back of spoon. Let stand 5 minutes; unmold onto serving plates. Serve immediately. Garnish as desired.                *Makes 5 servings*

*Spiced Mushroom Pecan Rice Timbales*

## Spinach Parmesan Risotto

3⅔ cups fat-free reduced-sodium
    chicken broth
½ teaspoon ground white pepper
    Nonstick cooking spray
1 cup uncooked arborio rice
1½ cups chopped fresh spinach
½ cup fresh or frozen green peas
1 tablespoon minced fresh dill *or*
    1 teaspoon dried dill weed
½ cup grated Parmesan cheese
1 teaspoon grated lemon peel

Combine chicken broth and pepper in medium saucepan; cover. Bring to a simmer over medium-low heat. Keep broth simmering by adjusting heat.

Spray large saucepan with cooking spray; heat over medium-low heat until hot. Add rice; cook and stir 1 minute. Stir ⅔ cup hot chicken broth into saucepan; cook, stirring constantly until broth is absorbed.

Stir remaining hot chicken broth into rice mixture, ½ cup at a time, stirring constantly until all broth is absorbed before adding next ½ cup. When last ½ cup chicken broth is added, stir spinach, peas and dill into saucepan. Cook, stirring gently until all broth is absorbed and rice is just tender but still firm to the bite. (Total cooking time for chicken broth absorption is about 35 to 40 minutes.)

Remove saucepan from heat; stir in cheese and lemon peel. Garnish as desired. *Makes 6 servings*

## Grandma's Old Fashioned Sausage Stuffing

1 pound BOB EVANS FARMS® Original
    Recipe or Sage Roll Sausage
4 large apples, such as Red Delicious,
    McIntosh or Granny Smith
½ chopped celery
2 teaspoons salt
8 cups dried toasted fresh or prepared
    seasoned bread cubes
1 small minced onion (optional)
½ cup milk
    Canned chicken broth (optional)

Crumble sausage into medium skillet. Cook over medium heat until lightly browned, stirring occasionally. Place sausage and drippings in large bowl. Core, peel and chop apples into ½-inch pieces. Add apples and all remaining ingredients, except broth, if desired, to sausage mixture; blend thoroughly. Bake mixture loosely stuffed in bird or place stuffing in greased 13×9-inch baking dish. Add turkey drippings and/or broth to adjust moistness and bake 30 to 45 minutes in 350°F oven. Leftover stuffing should be removed from bird and stored in the refrigerator separately. Reheat thoroughly before serving.

*Makes 10 servings, enough for a
12- to 15-pound turkey*

## — Black Bean Pilaf —

**1 tablespoon olive oil**
**1 can (15 to 16 ounces) black beans, drained and rinsed**
**1 medium onion, sliced**
**½ cup drained, chopped sun-dried tomatoes in oil**
**¼ teaspoon salt**
**¼ teaspoon ground black pepper**
**3 cups cooked brown rice (cooked in chicken broth)**

Heat oil in large skillet over medium-high heat until hot. Add beans, onion, tomatoes, salt and pepper; cook 3 to 5 minutes or until heated through. Stir in rice; heat thoroughly. Serve immediately.

*Makes 6 servings*

## — Spicy Cornbread —

**1 pound BOB EVANS FARMS® Original Recipe Roll Sausage**
**3 green onions with tops, chopped**
**1½ cups biscuit mix**
**1 cup cornmeal**
**1 cup grated longhorn cheese**
**⅔ cup milk**
**½ cup thick and chunky picante sauce**
**1 egg, slightly beaten**
**2 teaspoons hot pepper sauce or to taste**
**1 jalapeño pepper, seeded and chopped (optional)**

Preheat oven to 400°F. Crumble sausage into large skillet. Add onions. Cook over medium heat until sausage is browned, stirring occasionally. Drain off any drippings. Place sausage mixture in large bowl; add remaining ingredients, mixing well with wooden spoon. Spread mixture evenly into greased 11×7-inch baking dish. Bake 20 minutes. Cool on wire rack 20 minutes before cutting into squares. Serve warm or at room temperature. Refrigerate leftovers. *Makes 12 servings*

## Boston Baked Beans

**3 tablespoons KIKKOMAN® Lite Teriyaki Marinade & Sauce**
**3 tablespoons molasses**
**2 tablespoons packed brown sugar**
**½ teaspoon instant minced onion**
**¼ teaspoon dry mustard**
**1 can (31 ounces) pork and beans, rinsed and drained**
**⅛ teaspoon liquid smoke**

Combine lite teriyaki sauce, molasses, brown sugar, onion and mustard in medium saucepan. Carefully stir in pork and beans. Bring to boil over medium-high heat. Reduce heat to low; simmer, uncovered, 5 minutes, gently stirring after 3 minutes. Blend in liquid smoke; simmer 30 seconds longer.

*Makes 4 to 6 servings*

## Pasta with Onion and Goat Cheese

2 teaspoons olive oil
4 cups thinly sliced sweet onions
3 ounces goat cheese
¼ cup skim milk
6 ounces uncooked baby bow tie or other small pasta
1 clove garlic, minced
2 tablespoons dry white wine *or* ⅓-less-salt chicken broth
1½ teaspoons chopped fresh sage *or* ½ teaspoon dried sage leaves
½ teaspoon salt
¼ teaspoon ground black pepper
2 tablespoons chopped toasted walnuts

Heat oil in large nonstick skillet over medium heat. Add onions and cook slowly until golden and caramelized, about 20 to 25 minutes, stirring occasionally.

Combine goat cheese and milk in small bowl; mix until well blended. Set aside.

Cook pasta according to package directions, omitting salt. Drain and set aside.

Add garlic to onions in skillet; cook until tender, about 3 minutes. Add wine, sage, salt and pepper; cook until liquid is evaporated. Remove from heat; add pasta and goat cheese mixture, stirring to melt cheese. Sprinkle with walnuts.

*Makes 8 servings*

## Lemon Broccoli Pasta

Nonstick cooking spray
3 tablespoons sliced green onions
1 clove garlic, minced
2 cups fat-free reduced-sodium chicken broth
1½ teaspoons grated lemon peel
⅛ teaspoon ground black pepper
2 cups fresh or frozen broccoli flowerets
3 ounces uncooked angel hair pasta
⅓ cup low-fat sour cream
2 tablespoons grated Parmesan cheese

Generously spray large nonstick saucepan with cooking spray; heat over medium heat until hot. Add green onions and garlic; cook and stir 3 minutes or until onions are tender.

Stir chicken broth, lemon peel and pepper into saucepan; bring to a boil over high heat. Stir in broccoli and pasta; return to a boil. Reduce heat to low. Simmer, uncovered, 6 to 7 minutes, stirring frequently or until pasta is tender. Remove saucepan from heat. Stir in sour cream until well blended. Let stand 5 minutes. Top with cheese before serving. Garnish as desired. *Makes 6 servings*

*Pasta with Onion and Goat Cheese*

# DELI DELIGHTS & PREMIUM PIZZAS

*Perk up midday munching with this delicious collection of all-American favorites. Star-studded sandwiches and burgers will chase away the lunchtime blues, while festive tacos, burritos and pizzas are just the things to liven up casual meals.*

## The Californian

3 tablespoons reduced-fat
    cream cheese, softened
1 tablespoon chutney
4 slices pumpernickel bread
4 lettuce leaves
¾ pound thinly sliced
    chicken breast (from
    deli)
1⅓ cups alfalfa sprouts
1 medium mango, peeled
    and sliced
1 pear, cored and sliced
4 strawberries

Combine cream cheese and chutney in small bowl; spread about 1 tablespoon mixture on each bread slice. Place 1 lettuce leaf on top of each cream cheese mixture. Divide chicken evenly into 4 servings; place on lettuce. Arrange alfalfa sprouts on chicken; arrange mango and pear slices on sprouts. Garnish each open-faced sandwich with a strawberry. *Makes 4 servings*

# Tarragon Chicken
## - Salad Sandwiches -

1¼ pounds boneless skinless chicken
    breasts, cooked
1 cup thinly sliced celery
1 cup seedless red or green grapes,
    cut into halves
½ cup raisins
½ cup plain nonfat yogurt
¼ cup reduced-fat mayonnaise or salad
    dressing
2 tablespoons finely chopped shallots
    or onion
2 tablespoons minced fresh tarragon
    *or* 1 teaspoon dried tarragon
    leaves
½ teaspoon salt
⅛ teaspoon ground white pepper
6 washed lettuce leaves
6 sandwich rolls, split

Cut chicken into scant ½-inch pieces. Combine chicken, celery, grapes and raisins in large bowl. Combine yogurt, mayonnaise, shallots, tarragon, salt and pepper in small bowl. Add to chicken mixture; mix lightly. Place 1 lettuce leaf in each roll. Divide chicken mixture evenly into 6 servings; spoon into rolls.

*Makes 6 servings*

# Meatball
## —— Grinders ——

1 pound ground chicken
½ cup fresh whole wheat or white
    bread crumbs (1 slice bread)
1 egg white
3 tablespoons finely chopped fresh
    parsley
2 cloves garlic, minced
¼ teaspoon salt
⅛ teaspoon ground black pepper
    Nonstick cooking spray
¼ cup chopped onion
1 can (8 ounces) whole tomatoes,
    drained and coarsely chopped
1 can (4 ounces) no-salt-added tomato
    sauce
1 teaspoon dried Italian seasoning
4 small hard rolls, split
2 tablespoons grated Parmesan cheese

Combine chicken, bread crumbs, egg white, parsley, garlic, salt and pepper in medium bowl. Form mixture into 12 to 16 meatballs. Spray medium nonstick skillet with cooking spray; heat over medium heat until hot. Add meatballs; cook and stir about 5 minutes or until browned on all sides. Remove meatballs from skillet.

Add onion to skillet; cook and stir 2 to 3 minutes. Stir in tomatoes, tomato sauce and Italian seasoning; bring to a boil over high heat. Reduce heat to low; simmer, covered, 15 minutes. Return meatballs to skillet; simmer, covered, 15 minutes.

Place 3 to 4 meatballs in each roll. Divide sauce evenly into 4 servings; spoon over meatballs. Sprinkle with cheese.

*Makes 4 servings*

*Tarragon Chicken Salad Sandwich*

## Spicy Sesame Turkey Sandwich

½ cup mayonnaise

1½ teaspoons LAWRY'S® Pinch of Herbs, divided

1½ teaspoons LAWRY'S® Lemon Pepper, divided

1 teaspoon sesame oil

1 teaspoon fresh lemon juice

4 or 5 turkey cutlets (about 1¼ pounds)

½ cup all-purpose flour

2 tablespoons toasted sesame seeds

¼ to ½ teaspoon cayenne pepper

¼ cup milk

¼ cup vegetable oil

6 whole wheat buns, toasted

1 tomato, cut into 6 slices

6 sprigs watercress

In small bowl, combine mayonnaise, ½ teaspoon Pinch of Herbs, ½ teaspoon Lemon Pepper, sesame oil and lemon juice; cover. Refrigerate until ready to serve. Cut turkey into six equal portions. In large resealable plastic bag, combine flour, sesame seeds, cayenne pepper, remaining Pinch of Herbs and remaining Lemon Pepper. Dip each turkey cutlet into milk. Add turkey, a few pieces at a time, to plastic bag; seal bag. Shake until well coated. In large, heavy skillet, heat oil over medium heat. Add turkey; cook 5 to 8 minutes or until no longer pink in center, turning over after 3 minutes. Spread cut sides of buns with mayonnaise mixture. Top bottom half of each bun with turkey; cover with tomato, watercress and top half of bun.

*Makes 6 servings*

## Turkey Muffuletta

1 jar (5 ounces) pimiento-stuffed green olives, drained and chopped

1 can (3¼ ounces) pitted ripe olives, drained and chopped

3 tablespoons minced fresh parsley

2 tablespoons olive oil

1 tablespoon drained capers

1½ teaspoons minced garlic

½ teaspoon dried oregano leaves, crushed

1 loaf (1 pound) round Italian or French bread

1 package (8 ounces) turkey salami slices

1 package (4 ounces) thinly sliced Provolone cheese

In medium bowl, combine olives, parsley, oil, capers, garlic and oregano.

With serrated bread knife, slice bread in half horizontally. Hollow out each bread half, leaving ¾-inch shell. Reserve removed bread for other uses.

Spread half the olive mixture onto bottom half of bread shell. Evenly arrange half the turkey salami over olive mixture. Top with cheese and remaining turkey salami.

Spread remaining olive mixture onto top half of bread shell. Carefully invert top bread shell over bottom bread shell; press down firmly. Wrap bread shell in aluminum foil. Refrigerate overnight. To serve, cut bread shell into 8 wedges.

*Makes 8 servings*

Favorite recipe from **National Turkey Federation**

*Spicy Sesame Turkey Sandwich*

# Philadelphia Cheese Steak Sandwiches

2 cups sliced red or green bell
    peppers (about 2 medium)
1 small onion, thinly sliced
1 tablespoon vegetable oil
½ cup A.1.® BOLD Steak Sauce
1 teaspoon prepared horseradish
8 ounces thinly sliced beef sandwich
    steaks
4 ounces thinly sliced mozzarella
    cheese
4 long sandwich rolls, split

In medium saucepan, over medium heat, sauté peppers and onion slices in oil until tender. Stir in steak sauce and horseradish; keep warm.

In lightly greased medium skillet, over medium-high heat, cook sandwich steaks until desired doneness. Portion beef, pepper mixture and cheese on roll bottoms.

Broil sandwich bottoms 4 inches from heat source for 3 to 5 minutes or until cheese melts; replace tops. Serve immediately.           *Makes 4 sandwiches*

# Tuna Melt

1 can (12 ounces) STARKIST® Solid
    White or Chunk Light Tuna,
    drained and flaked
⅓ cup mayonnaise
1½ tablespoons sweet pickle relish
1½ tablespoons chopped onion
½ tablespoon mustard
3 English muffins, split and toasted
6 tomato slices, halved
6 slices American, Cheddar, Swiss or
    Monterey Jack cheese
Fresh fruit (optional)

In medium bowl, combine tuna, mayonnaise, pickle relish, onion and mustard; mix well. Spread about ⅓ cup on each muffin half. Top with tomato slice and cheese slice. Broil 4 to 5 minutes or until cheese melts. Serve with fresh fruit, if desired.           *Makes 6 servings*

**Prep Time:** 15 minutes

**Hint:** For a festive look, cut each slice of cheese into strips. Arrange in a decorative pattern over sandwiches.

*Philadelphia Cheese Steak Sandwich*

## Black Gold Burgers

¾ **cup finely chopped onion**
6 **large cloves garlic, minced (about 3 tablespoons)**
2 **tablespoons FLEISCHMANN'S®️ margarine**
1 **tablespoon sugar**
¾ **cup A.1.®️ BOLD Steak Sauce**
1½ **pounds ground beef**
6 **hamburger rolls, split**

In medium skillet, over medium heat, cook and stir onion and garlic in margarine until tender but not brown; stir in sugar. Reduce heat to low; cook for 10 minutes. Stir in steak sauce; keep warm.

Shape ground beef into 6 patties. Grill burgers over medium heat for 5 minutes on each side or until done. Place burgers on roll bottoms; top each with 3 tablespoons sauce and roll top. Serve immediately; garnish as desired.

*Makes 6 servings*

## — Lahaina Burgers —

1¼ **pounds lean ground beef**
¼ **cup plus 1 tablespoon KIKKOMAN®️ Lite Teriyaki Marinade & Sauce, divided**
4 **green onions and tops, chopped**
1 **teaspoon minced fresh gingerroot**
1 **large clove garlic, minced**
1 **egg, slightly beaten**
1 **slice bread, torn into small pieces**
1 **can (8 ounces) sliced pineapple, drained**

Thoroughly combine beef, ¼ cup lite teriyaki sauce, green onions, ginger, garlic, egg and bread; shape into 4 patties. Place on grill 4 to 5 inches from hot coals. Cook 3 minutes; turn over. Cook 3 minutes longer (for rare), or to desired doneness. During last 2 minutes of cooking time, place pineapple slices on grill. Cook 1 minute. Turn over and brush with remaining 1 tablespoon lite teriyaki sauce. Cook 1 minute longer. (Or, place patties on rack of broiler pan. Broil 4 minutes; turn over. Broil 3 minutes longer (for rare), or to desired doneness. During last 2 minutes of cooking time, place pineapple slices on broiler pan. Broil 1 minute. Turn over and brush with remaining 1 tablespoon lite teriyaki sauce. Broil 1 minute longer.) Top patties with pineapple just before serving.

*Makes 4 servings*

## Meatless Sloppy Joes

**Nonstick cooking spray**
2 **cups thinly sliced onions**
2 **cups chopped green bell peppers**
2 **cloves garlic, finely chopped**
2 **tablespoons ketchup**
1 **tablespoon prepared mustard**
1 **can (about 15 ounces) kidney beans, rinsed, drained and mashed**
1 **can (8 ounces) tomato sauce**
1 **teaspoon chili powder**
**Cider vinegar**
4 **sandwich rolls, split**

Spray large nonstick skillet with cooking spray. Heat over medium-high heat until hot. Add onions, peppers and garlic. Cook and stir 5 minutes or until vegetables are tender. Stir in ketchup and mustard.

Add beans, tomato sauce and chili powder to skillet. Reduce heat to medium-low. Cook and stir 5 minutes or until thickened, adding up to ⅓ cup cider vinegar if mixture is too dry. Spoon bean mixture evenly into sandwich rolls. Garnish as desired. *Makes 4 servings*

## Kahlúa® Picadillo Filling

¼ cup raisins, finely chopped
4 tablespoons KAHLÚA®, divided
⅓ cup finely chopped onion
1 tablespoon vegetable oil
½ cup canned green chilies, drained and finely chopped
2 tablespoons vinegar, divided
1 teaspoon salt
⅛ teaspoon pepper
1 pound lean ground chuck
1 can (16 ounces) whole peeled tomatoes, chopped and undrained
⅓ cup pine nuts or slivered almonds (optional)

Combine raisins and 3 tablespoons Kahlúa®; set aside. In large nonstick skillet, cook and stir onion in oil over medium heat until transparent. Add chilies, 1 tablespoon vinegar, salt and pepper. Add ground chuck and raisin mixture; mix thoroughly. Lightly brown beef mixture, breaking up meat as it cooks. Add tomatoes with juice and

remaining 1 tablespoon *each* Kahlúa® and vinegar. Bring to a boil; simmer until thickened, about 15 minutes. Stir in nuts, if desired. *Makes about 3¼ cups*

**Serving Suggestions:** Use Kahlúa® Picadillo Filling for tacos, tostadas, enchiladas or your favorite Mexican casseroles. For parties, serve with dishes of grated cheese, green onions, chopped fresh tomatoes, shredded lettuce, guacamole, sour cream, and taco and tostada shells.

## Tacos

1 pound BOB EVANS FARMS® Original Recipe or Zesty Hot Roll Sausage
1 (8-ounce) jar taco sauce
1 package taco shells (10 to 12 count)
2 cups (8 ounces) shredded Cheddar cheese
1 large onion, chopped
2 tomatoes, chopped
¼ head iceberg lettuce, shredded
Fresh cilantro sprigs and bell pepper triangles (optional)

Preheat oven to 350°F. Crumble sausage into medium skillet; cook over medium-high heat until browned, stirring occasionally. Drain off any drippings. Stir in taco sauce. Bring to a boil. Reduce heat to low; simmer 5 minutes. Meanwhile, bake taco shells until warm and crisp. To assemble tacos, place 2 tablespoons sausage mixture in each taco shell and top evenly with cheese, onion, tomatoes and lettuce. Garnish with cilantro and pepper triangles, if desired. Serve hot. Refrigerate any leftover filling.

*Makes 10 to 12 servings*

## Grilled Pizza

**2 loaves (1 pound each) frozen bread dough, thawed***

**Olive oil**

**K.C. MASTERPIECE® Barbecue Sauce or pizza sauce**

**Seasonings: finely chopped garlic and fresh or dried herbs**

**Toppings: any combination of slivered ham, shredded barbecued chicken and grilled vegetables, such as thinly sliced mushrooms, zucchini, yellow squash, bell peppers, eggplant, pineapple chunks or tomatoes**

**Salt and black pepper**

**Cheese: any combination of shredded mozzarella, provolone or Monterey Jack, grated Parmesan or crumbled feta**

*\*Substitute your favorite pizza crust recipe. Dough for 1 large pizza will make 4 individual ones.*

Divide each loaf of dough into 4 balls. Roll on cornmeal-coated or lightly floured surface and pat out dough to ¼-inch thickness to make small circles. Brush each circle with oil.

Arrange hot KINGSFORD® Briquets on one side of the grill. Oil hot grid to help prevent sticking. Vegetables, such as mushrooms, zucchini, yellow squash, bell peppers and eggplant need to be grilled until tender before being used as toppings.

Place 4 circles directly above medium Kingsford® Briquets. (The dough will not fall through the grid.) Grill circles, on an uncovered grill, until dough starts to bubble in spots on the top and the bottom gets lightly browned. Turn over using tongs. Continue to grill until the other side is lightly browned, then move the crusts to the cool part of the grill.

Brush each crust lightly with barbecue sauce; top with garlic and herbs, then top with meat or vegetables. Season with salt and pepper, then top with cheese. Cover pizzas and grill, about 5 minutes until cheese melts, bottom of crust is crisp and pizza looks done. Repeat with remaining dough. *Makes 8 individual pizzas*

## Ya Gotta Empanada

**1 package (4.4 to 6.8 ounces) Spanish rice mix, prepared according to package directions**

**1 cup shredded cooked chicken**

**1 cup (4 ounces) shredded Cheddar cheese**

**½ cup sliced green onions**

**¼ cup chopped black olives**

**1 package (15 ounces) refrigerated pie crust**

Combine rice, chicken, cheese, onions and olives in large bowl. Spoon half of rice mixture on half of each pie crust. Fold crust over filling. Seal and crimp edges. Place on baking sheet. Bake at 400°F 20 to 22 minutes or until golden brown. Cut each empanada in half. Serve immediately. *Makes 4 servings*

Favorite recipe from **USA Rice Council**

*Grilled Pizzas*

## Chicago Deep-Dish Beef Pizza

1 package (¼ ounce) active dry yeast
¾ cup warm water (105° to 115°F)
1 teaspoon sugar
1 teaspoon salt, divided
2 tablespoons olive oil
2 to 2¼ cups quick-mixing flour
  Cornmeal
½ to 1 pound lean ground round
2 cloves garlic, peeled and crushed
3 cups shredded JARLSBERG or
  JARLSBERG LITE™ Cheese, divided
1½ to 2 cups canned tomato sauce
1 small green pepper, sliced
1 can (4 ounces) sliced mushrooms,
  drained

In large bowl, dissolve yeast in water. Stir in sugar, ¾ teaspoon salt and olive oil. Add 1 cup flour and beat until smooth. Mix in remaining flour until dough forms. Turn out onto lightly floured surface; knead 1 minute.

Grease heavy 10½- to 12-inch skillet with ovenproof handle or 13×9-inch metal baking pan. Sprinkle lightly with cornmeal. Roll dough out 1½ inches larger than skillet; press onto bottom and up side. Cover; let rise 30 minutes.

Preheat oven to 425°F. Heat small skillet over medium heat until hot. Crumble ground round into skillet. Add garlic and remaining ¼ teaspoon salt; cook 7 minutes or until no longer pink, stirring to separate meat. Drain well. Sprinkle 2 cups cheese over bottom of crust. Top with beef mixture; drizzle with tomato sauce. Arrange green pepper and mushrooms on tomato sauce. Sprinkle

with remaining 1 cup cheese. Bake 20 to 25 minutes or until cheese is melted and crust is lightly browned. Let stand on wire rack 10 minutes.      *Makes 6 servings*

## Funky Buffalo-Style Chicken Pizza

2 large prebaked pizza crust shells
  (12 inches each)
1 cup prepared pizza sauce or
  barbecue sauce
½ cup thinly sliced celery
3 cups sliced cooked chicken*
6 tablespoons FRANK'S® Original
  RedHot® Cayenne Pepper Sauce
2 tablespoons butter or margarine,
  melted
2 cups (8 ounces) shredded
  mozzarella cheese
⅔ cup (3 ounces) crumbled
  Gorgonzola or blue cheese

*To cook chicken, grill 1 pound boneless skinless chicken over hot coals 10 minutes or until no longer pink in center, turning once.*

Place pizza shells on disposable foil pizza pans or on heavy-duty foil. Spread shells with pizza sauce and sprinkle with celery, dividing evenly. Place chicken in large bowl. Add RedHot sauce and butter; toss well to coat evenly. Arrange chicken evenly on top of pizzas. Sprinkle with the cheeses.

Place pizzas on barbecue grill grid. Cook pizzas over medium-high coals 15 minutes or until crust is crispy and cheese melts. To serve, cut into wedges.

*Makes 8 servings*

## — Baja Pizza Pouch —

1 pound bulk hot pork sausage
½ pound lean ground beef
1 can (12 ounces) refried beans
1 teaspoon ground cumin
¼ teaspoon garlic powder
1 package (16 ounces) hot roll mix
1 can (14.5 ounces) crushed Italian-
   flavored tomatoes
2 cups (8 ounces) shredded Wisconsin
   Monterey Jack cheese
1 cup (4 ounces) shredded Wisconsin
   Cheddar cheese
   Butter, melted
1 cup guacamole (optional)

Heat large skillet over medium heat until hot. Crumble pork sausage and ground beef into skillet. Cook, stirring to separate meat, until no longer pink. Drain off fat. Add beans, cumin and garlic powder; heat through. Oil two baking sheets. Preheat oven to 400°F. Prepare hot roll mix according to package directions for pizza crust. Divide dough into eight pieces. Form each piece into a ball. On lightly floured surface, roll each ball into a 7-inch circle. Place circles on prepared baking sheets. Spread ½ cup meat mixture on half of each to within ½ inch of edge. Layer each with 2 tablespoons crushed tomatoes, ¼ cup Monterey Jack cheese and 2 tablespoons Cheddar cheese. Moisten edges with water and fold over to enclose fillings, pressing edges firmly together with fork. Brush with melted butter. Cut slit in each pouch. Bake 18 minutes or until golden brown. Serve with guacamole, if desired.

*Makes 8 calzones*

Favorite recipe from **Wisconsin Milk Marketing Board**

## Vegetable Pizza with Oat Bran Crust

1 cup QUAKER® Oat Bran™ Hot
   Cereal, uncooked
1 cup all-purpose flour
1 teaspoon baking powder
¾ cup skim milk
3 tablespoons vegetable oil
1 tablespoon QUAKER® Oat Bran™
   Hot Cereal, uncooked
1 can (8 ounces) low-sodium tomato
   sauce
1 cup sliced mushrooms (about
   3 ounces)
1 medium green, red or yellow bell
   pepper or combination, cut into
   rings
½ cup chopped onion
1¼ cups (5 ounces) shredded part-skim
   mozzarella cheese
½ teaspoon oregano leaves or Italian
   seasoning, crushed

Combine 1 cup oat bran, flour and baking powder. Add milk and oil; mix well. Let stand 10 minutes.

Heat oven to 425°F. Lightly spray 12-inch round pizza pan with vegetable oil cooking spray or oil lightly. Sprinkle with 1 tablespoon oat bran. With lightly oiled fingers, pat dough out evenly; shape edge to form rim. Bake 18 to 20 minutes. Spread sauce evenly over partially baked crust. Top with vegetables; sprinkle with cheese and oregano. Bake an additional 12 to 15 minutes or until golden brown. Cut into 8 wedges. *Makes 4 servings*

# BREAKFAST & BRUNCH

*Waking up to a fabulous morning meal won't be a once-in-a-blue-moon occasion after tasting these delicious dishes.*

## Breakfast Burritos with Baked Citrus Fruit

4 green onions, thinly sliced, divided
1¼ cups cholesterol-free egg substitute
2 tablespoons diced mild green chilies
½ cup (2 ounces) shredded reduced-fat Monterey Jack or Cheddar cheese
¼ cup lightly packed fresh cilantro
4 (7-inch) flour tortillas
¼ cup salsa
¼ cup low-fat sour cream
Baked Citrus Fruit, prepared (recipe follows)

Spray large nonstick skillet with cooking spray. Set aside ¼ cup green onions. Add remaining onions, egg substitute and chilies to skillet. Cook, stirring occasionally, about 4 minutes or until eggs are just set. Stir in cheese and cilantro. Cook to desired doneness. Stack tortillas; wrap in paper towels. Microwave at HIGH about 1 minute. Place one quarter of eggs in center of each tortilla. Fold sides over fillings to enclose. Top with salsa, sour cream and reserved green onions. Serve with Baked Citrus Fruit.     *Makes 4 servings*

### Baked Citrus Fruit

2 oranges, peeled and sliced
1 grapefruit, peeled and sliced
1½ tablespoons brown sugar
½ teaspoon ground cinnamon

Preheat oven to 400°F. Arrange fruit on baking sheet, overlapping slices. Combine sugar and cinnamon; sprinkle over fruit. Bake until fruit is hot.

*Makes 4 servings*

*Breakfast Burritos with Baked Citrus Fruit*

# Blintzes with — Raspberry Sauce —

**Raspberry Sauce (recipe follows)**
**1 (16-ounce) container low-fat cottage cheese (1% milk fat)**
**3 tablespoons EGG BEATERS® Healthy Real Egg Product**
**½ teaspoon sugar**
**10 prepared Crepes (recipe follows)**

Prepare Raspberry Sauce. Set aside. In small bowl, combine cottage cheese, Egg Beaters® and sugar; spread about 2 tablespoonfuls mixture down center of each crepe. Fold crepes into thirds; fold top and bottom of each crepe to meet in center, forming blintzes. In lightly greased nonstick skillet, over medium heat, place blintzes seam-side down; cook 4 minutes or until golden brown. Turn over; cook 4 more minutes or until golden brown. Top with Raspberry Sauce and garnish as desired. *Makes 10 servings*

**Raspberry Sauce:** In blender or food processor, purée 1 (16-ounce) package thawed frozen raspberries; strain. Stir in 2 tablespoons sugar.

## Crepes

**1 cup all-purpose flour**
**1 cup skim milk**
**½ cup EGG BEATERS® Healthy Real Egg Product**
**1 tablespoon FLEISCHMANN'S® Margarine, melted**

In medium bowl, blend flour, milk, Egg Beaters® and margarine; let stand 30 minutes.

Heat lightly greased 8-inch nonstick skillet or crepe pan over medium-high heat. Pour in scant ¼ cup batter, tilting pan to cover bottom. Cook 1 to 2 minutes; turn crepe over and cook 30 seconds to 1 minute more. Place on waxed paper. Stir batter and repeat to make a total of 10 crepes.

# Huevos — Rancheros —

**2 tablespoons olive oil**
**1 green bell pepper, chopped**
**½ cup chopped onion**
**1 tomato, peeled, chopped**
**1 can (8 ounces) tomato sauce**
**½ cup water**
**1 clove garlic, minced**
**1 teaspoon dried oregano leaves**
**1 teaspoon TABASCO® pepper sauce**
**½ teaspoon salt**
**6 eggs**
**6 (7-inch) flour tortillas or English muffins**

In large skillet, heat oil. Add green pepper and onion; cook until tender. Add tomato, tomato sauce, water, garlic, oregano, TABASCO sauce and salt. Simmer, covered, for 20 minutes. Uncover. Break eggs, one at a time, into cup and slip into sauce. Cover and simmer over low heat until eggs are set, about 5 minutes. Serve eggs on tortillas or toasted English muffins topped with sauce.

*Makes 6 servings*

## Eggs Benedict Mousseline

6 ounces (1 carton) ALPINE LACE® Fat Free Cream Cheese with Garden Vegetables
¼ cup 2% low fat milk
1 tablespoon unsalted butter substitute
1 tablespoon fresh lemon juice
Dash cayenne pepper
2 regular-size English muffins, split
4 thin slices (½ ounce each) ALPINE LACE® Boneless Cooked Ham, divided
1 teaspoon white vinegar
4 large eggs

**1.** Preheat the broiler. In a medium-size saucepan, heat the cheese, milk and butter over medium heat until the cheese is melted; whisk in the lemon juice and pepper. Keep warm.

**2.** On a baking sheet, arrange the 4 muffin halves, split sides up. Broil for 1 minute or until golden brown; keep warm. In a large nonstick skillet, cook the ham over medium heat for 2 minutes. Place one slice of ham on each muffin half.

**3.** Wipe out the skillet. Fill the skillet two-thirds full with water. Add the vinegar and bring to a simmer over medium heat. Break each egg into a saucer, then slide it into the water. Spoon the water gently over the eggs for 3 minutes or until they are cooked the way you like them. Using a slotted spoon, place 1 egg on each muffin; ladle some sauce over the top and serve. *Makes 4 servings*

## Chilies Rellenos Casserole

3 eggs, separated
¾ cup all-purpose flour
¾ cup milk
½ teaspoon salt
1 tablespoon butter or margarine
½ cup chopped onion
2 cans (7 ounces each) whole green chilies, drained
8 slices (1 ounce each) Monterey Jack cheese, cut into halves
Garnishes: sour cream, sliced green onions, pitted ripe olive slices, guacamole and salsa

Preheat oven to 350°F.

Combine egg yolks, flour, milk and salt in blender or food processor container; process until smooth. Pour into bowl; set aside.

Melt butter in small skillet over medium heat. Add onion; cook until tender.

Pat chilies dry with paper towels. Slit each chili lengthwise and carefully remove seeds. Place 2 halves of cheese and 1 tablespoon onion in each chili; reshape chilies to cover cheese. Place chilies in single layer in greased 13×9-inch baking dish.

In small clean bowl, beat egg whites until soft peaks form; fold into yolk mixture. Pour over chilies. Bake 20 to 25 minutes or until topping is puffed and knife inserted in center comes out clean. Broil 4 inches below heat 30 seconds or until topping is golden brown. Serve with desired garnishes. *Makes 4 servings*

# Make-Ahead Breakfast Casserole

2½ cups seasoned croutons
1 pound BOB EVANS FARMS® Original Recipe Roll Sausage
4 eggs
2¼ cups milk
1 (10½-ounce) can condensed cream of mushroom soup
1 (10-ounce) package frozen chopped spinach, thawed and squeezed dry
1 (4-ounce) can mushrooms, drained and chopped
1 cup (4 ounces) shredded sharp Cheddar cheese
1 cup (4 ounces) shredded Monterey Jack cheese
¼ teaspoon dry mustard
Fresh herb sprigs and carrot strips (optional)
Picante sauce or salsa (optional)

Spread croutons onto bottom of greased 13×9-inch baking dish. Crumble sausage into medium skillet. Cook over medium heat until browned, stirring occasionally. Drain off any drippings. Spread over croutons. Whisk eggs and milk in large bowl until blended. Stir in soup, spinach, mushrooms, cheeses and mustard. Pour egg mixture over sausage and croutons. Refrigerate overnight. Preheat oven to 325°F. Bake egg mixture 50 to 55 minutes or until set and lightly browned on top. Garnish with herb sprigs and carrot, if desired. Serve hot with picante sauce, if desired. Refrigerate leftovers.

*Makes 10 to 12 servings*

# Egg Blossoms

4 sheets filo pastry
2 tablespoons butter, melted
4 teaspoons grated Parmesan cheese
4 eggs
4 teaspoons minced green onion
Salt and freshly ground pepper
Tomato Sauce, prepared (recipe follows)

Preheat oven to 350°F. Grease 4 (2½-inch) muffin cups.

Brush 1 sheet of filo with butter. Top with another sheet; brush with butter. Cut stack into 6 (4-inch) squares. Repeat with remaining 2 sheets. Stack 3 squares together, rotating so corners do not overlap. Press into greased muffin cup. Repeat with remaining squares.

Sprinkle 1 teaspoon cheese into each filo-lined cup. Break 1 egg into each cup. Sprinkle onion over eggs. Season with salt and pepper. Bake 15 to 20 minutes or until pastry is golden and eggs are set. Serve with Tomato Sauce.

*Makes 4 servings*

## Tomato Sauce

1 can (16 ounces) whole tomatoes, undrained, chopped
1 clove garlic, minced
½ cup chopped onion
1 tablespoon white wine vinegar
¼ teaspoon dried oregano leaves
½ teaspoon salt

Combine tomatoes, garlic, onion, vinegar, oregano and salt in medium saucepan. Cook, stirring occasionally, over medium heat until onion is tender about 20 minutes. Serve warm.

*Make-Ahead Breakfast Casserole*

# — Seafood Crepes —

Basic Crepes (recipe follows)
3 tablespoons butter or margarine
⅓ cup finely chopped shallots or
    sweet onion
2 tablespoons dry vermouth
3 tablespoons all-purpose flour
1½ cups plus 2 tablespoons milk,
    divided
¼ to ½ teaspoon hot pepper sauce
    (optional)
8 ounces cooked, peeled and deveined
    shrimp, coarsely chopped
    (1½ cups)
8 ounces lump crabmeat or imitation
    crabmeat, shredded (1½ cups)
2 tablespoons snipped fresh chives or
    green onion tops
3 tablespoons freshly grated
    Parmesan cheese
Fresh chives and red onion for
    garnish

Prepare Basic Crepes. Preheat oven to 350°F. Melt butter over medium heat in medium saucepan. Add shallots; cook and stir 5 minutes or until tender. Add vermouth; cook 1 minute. Add flour; cook and stir 1 minute. Gradually stir in 1½ cups milk and hot pepper sauce. Bring to a boil, stirring frequently. Reduce heat to low; cook and stir 1 minute or until mixture thickens. Remove from heat; stir in shrimp and crabmeat. Measure ½ cup seafood mixture; reserve.

To assemble crepes, spoon about ¼ cup seafood mixture down center of each crepe. Roll up crepes jelly-roll style. Place seam sides down in well-greased 13×9-inch baking dish. Stir chives and remaining 2 tablespoons milk into reserved seafood mixture. Spoon seafood mixture down center of crepes; sprinkle cheese evenly over tops. Bake uncovered 15 to 20 minutes or until heated through. Garnish, if desired. Serve immediately.

*Makes 6 servings*

## Basic Crepes

1½ cups milk
1 cup all-purpose flour
2 eggs
¼ cup butter or margarine, melted and
    cooled, divided
¼ teaspoon salt

Combine milk, flour, eggs, 2 tablespoons butter and salt in food processor; process using on/off pulsing action until smooth. Let stand at room temperature 30 minutes. Heat ½ teaspoon butter in 7- or 8-inch crepe pan or skillet over medium heat.

Process crepe batter until blended. Pour ¼ cup batter into hot pan; immediately rotate pan back and forth to swirl batter over entire surface. Cook 1 to 2 minutes or until brown around edge and top is dry. Carefully turn crepe with spatula and cook 30 seconds. Transfer crepe to waxed paper. Repeat with remaining batter and butter.

*Makes about 1 dozen*

*Seafood Crepes*

## Asparagus-Swiss Soufflé

¼ cup unsalted butter substitute
½ cup chopped yellow onion
¼ cup all-purpose flour
½ teaspoon salt
¼ teaspoon cayenne pepper
1 cup 2% low fat milk
1 cup (4 ounces) shredded ALPINE LACE® Reduced Fat Baby Swiss Cheese
1 cup egg substitute *or* 4 large eggs
1 cup coarsely chopped fresh asparagus pieces, cooked or frozen asparagus pieces, thawed and drained
3 large egg whites

**1.** Preheat the oven to 325°F. Spray a 1½-quart soufflé dish with nonstick cooking spray.

**2.** In a large saucepan, melt the butter over medium heat, add the onion and sauté for 5 minutes or until tender. Stir in the flour, salt and pepper and cook for 2 minutes or until bubbly. Add the milk and cook, stirring constantly, for 5 minutes or until the sauce thickens. Add the cheese and stir until melted.

**3.** In a small bowl, whisk the egg substitute (or the whole eggs). Whisk in a little of the hot cheese sauce, then return this egg mixture to the saucepan and whisk until well blended. Remove from the heat and fold in the drained asparagus.

**4.** In a medium-size bowl, using an electric mixer set on high, beat the egg whites until stiff peaks form. Fold the hot cheese sauce into the whites, then spoon into the soufflé dish.

**5.** Place the soufflé on a baking sheet and bake for 50 minutes or until golden brown and puffy.  *Makes 8 servings*

## Light Farmhouse Frittata

⅓ cup thinly sliced yellow bell pepper
⅓ cup thinly sliced red bell pepper
⅓ cup thinly sliced green bell pepper
⅓ cup chopped green onions
⅓ cup chopped walnuts
8 egg whites
2 egg yolks
2 tablespoons plain nonfat yogurt
1 tablespoon grated Asiago or Parmesan cheese

Preheat oven to 350°F. Cook and stir peppers, green onions and walnuts in *ovenproof* skillet. Beat egg whites and yolks in large bowl; stir in yogurt and pour mixture over vegetables in skillet. Stir; cook over medium heat until eggs begin to set. Sprinkle cheese over top and bake 8 to 10 minutes or until eggs are well set. Cut into wedges to serve.

*Makes 4 servings*

Favorite recipe from **Walnut Marketing Board**

*Asparagus-Swiss Soufflé*

## Sausage Vegetable Frittata

5 eggs
¼ cup milk
2 tablespoons grated Parmesan cheese
½ teaspoon dried oregano leaves
½ teaspoon black pepper
1 (10-ounce) package BOB EVANS FARMS® Skinless Link Sausage
2 tablespoons butter or margarine
1 small zucchini, sliced (about 1 cup)
½ cup shredded carrots
⅓ cup sliced green onions with tops
¾ cup (6 ounces) shredded Swiss cheese
Carrot curls (optional)

Whisk eggs in medium bowl; stir in milk, Parmesan cheese, oregano and pepper. Set aside. Cook sausage in large skillet over medium heat until browned, turning occasionally. Drain off any drippings. Remove sausage from skillet and cut into ½-inch lengths. Melt butter in same skillet. Add zucchini, shredded carrots and onions; cook and stir over medium heat until tender. Top with sausage, then Swiss cheese. Pour egg mixture over vegetable mixture. Stir gently to combine. Cook, without stirring, over low heat 8 to 10 minutes or until center is almost set. Remove from heat. Let stand 5 minutes before cutting into wedges; serve hot. Garnish with carrot curls, if desired. Refrigerate leftovers.

*Makes 4 to 6 servings*

## Double Onion Quiche

3 cups thinly sliced yellow onions
3 tablespoons butter or margarine
1 cup thinly sliced green onions
3 eggs
1 cup heavy cream
½ cup grated Parmesan cheese
¼ teaspoon hot pepper sauce
1 package (1 ounce) HIDDEN VALLEY RANCH® Milk Recipe Original Ranch® Salad Dressing Mix
1 (9-inch) deep-dish pastry shell, baked, cooled
Fresh oregano sprig for garnish

Preheat oven to 350°F. In medium skillet, cook and stir yellow onions in butter, stirring occasionally, about 10 minutes. Add green onions; cook 5 minutes. Remove from heat; cool.

In large bowl, whisk eggs until frothy. Whisk in cream, cheese, pepper sauce and salad dressing mix. Stir in cooled onion mixture. Pour egg and onion mixture into cooled pastry shell. Bake 35 to 40 minutes until top is browned and knife inserted in center comes out clean. Cool on wire rack 10 minutes before slicing. Garnish with oregano.

*Makes 8 servings*

*Sausage Vegetable Frittata*

## Broccoli & Cheese Quiche

2 cups zwieback crumbs
½ teaspoon ground nutmeg
⅓ cup honey
2 cups fresh broccoli florets or frozen broccoli florets, thawed and drained
½ tablespoon unsalted butter substitute
1 cup chopped yellow onion
1 cup (4 ounces) ALPINE LACE® Reduced Fat Baby Swiss Cheese
1 cup (4 ounces) ALPINE LACE® Reduced Fat Colby Cheese
1 cup chopped red bell pepper
¾ cup egg substitute *or* 3 large eggs
2 large egg whites
¾ cup 2% low fat milk
½ teaspoon salt
½ teaspoon dry mustard
¼ teaspoon freshly ground white pepper

**1.** Preheat the oven to 400°F. Spray a 10-inch pie plate with nonstick cooking spray. To make the crumb crust: Toss the crumbs and nutmeg with the honey until the crumbs are thoroughly coated. Press onto the bottom and up the side of the pie plate.

**2.** To make the filling: Coarsely chop the broccoli. Half-fill a medium-size saucepan with water and bring to a boil over medium-high heat. Add the broccoli and cook, uncovered, for 5 minutes or just until crisp-tender. Drain.

**3.** In a small nonstick skillet, melt the butter over medium-high heat. Add the onion and sauté for 5 minutes or until tender. Layer both of the cheeses, then the onion, bell pepper and broccoli in the crust.

**4.** In a medium-size bowl, whisk the egg substitute (or the whole eggs), the egg whites, milk, salt, mustard and pepper together until blended. Pour evenly over the vegetables in the crust.

**5.** Bake for 10 minutes. *Reduce the oven temperature to 350°F.* Bake 20 minutes longer or until golden brown and puffy and a knife inserted in the center comes out clean.
*Makes 8 servings*

## Spinach Cheese Strata

6 slices whole wheat bread
2 tablespoons butter, softened
1 cup (4 ounces) shredded Cheddar cheese
½ cup (2 ounces) shredded Monterey Jack cheese
1 package (10 ounces) frozen spinach, thawed and well drained
1¼ cups milk
6 eggs, lightly beaten
¼ teaspoon salt
⅛ teaspoon ground black pepper

Spread bread with butter; arrange in single layer in greased 13×9-inch baking dish. Sprinkle with cheeses. Blend spinach, milk, eggs, salt and pepper in large bowl. Pour over bread and cheese. Cover; refrigerate at least 6 hours or overnight. Bake, uncovered, at 350°F about 1 hour or until puffy and lightly golden.
*Makes 4 to 6 servings*

*Broccoli & Cheese Quiche*

# Cheddar and Leek Strata

8 eggs, lightly beaten
2 cups milk
½ cup ale or beer
2 cloves garlic, minced
¼ teaspoon salt
¼ teaspoon ground black pepper
1 loaf (16 ounces) sourdough bread, cubed
2 small leeks, coarsely chopped
1 red bell pepper, chopped
1½ cups (6 ounces) shredded Swiss cheese, divided
1½ cups (6 ounces) shredded sharp Cheddar cheese, divided
Fresh sage sprig for garnish

Combine eggs, milk, ale, garlic, salt and black pepper in large bowl. Beat with wire whisk until ingredients are well blended. Place half of bread cubes on bottom of greased 13×9-inch baking dish. Sprinkle half of leeks and half of bell pepper over bread cubes. Top with ¾ cup Swiss cheese and ¾ cup Cheddar cheese. Repeat layers with remaining ingredients, ending with Cheddar cheese. Pour egg mixture evenly over top. Cover tightly with plastic wrap or foil. Weight top of strata down with slightly smaller baking dish. Refrigerate strata at least 2 hours or overnight.

Preheat oven to 350°F. Bake strata uncovered 40 to 45 minutes or until center is set. Garnish, if desired. Serve immediately. *Makes 12 servings*

# Puff Pancake with Summer Berries

Summer Berries (recipe follows)
4 tablespoons butter or margarine, divided
2 eggs
½ cup all-purpose flour
½ cup milk
1 tablespoon sugar
¼ teaspoon salt

Prepare Summer Berries; set aside. Preheat oven to 425°F. Place 2 tablespoons butter in *ovenproof* skillet. Place skillet in oven 3 minutes or until butter is bubbly. Swirl pan to coat bottom and sides.

Beat eggs in medium bowl with electric mixer at high speed. Add flour, milk, remaining 2 tablespoons butter, sugar and salt; beat until smooth. Pour batter into prepared skillet. Bake 15 minutes. *Reduce oven temperature to 350°F.* Continue baking 10 to 15 minutes or until pancake is puffed and golden brown. Serve pancake in skillet with Summer Berries.

*Makes 6 servings*

## Summer Berries

2 cups blueberries
1 cup sliced strawberries
1 cup raspberries
Sugar to taste
Whipping cream (optional)

Combine blueberries, strawberries and raspberries in medium bowl. Gently toss with sugar. Let stand 5 minutes. Top with cream, if desired.

*Cheddar and Leek Strata*

# Stuffed French Toast with Apricot and Orange
## – Marmalade Sauce –

**Apricot and Orange Marmalade
    Sauce (recipe follows)
1 cup (8 ounces) cream cheese,
    softened
½ cup (4 ounces) part-skim ricotta
    cheese
¼ cup orange marmalade
2 tablespoons sugar
1 loaf (16 ounces) Vienna bread
4 eggs
1 cup milk
1 teaspoon vanilla
    Grated nutmeg**

Prepare Apricot and Orange Marmalade Sauce. Preheat oven to 475°F. Beat cream cheese in medium bowl with electric mixer at medium speed until smooth. Beat in ricotta, marmalade and sugar.

Trim ends from bread; discard. Slice bread into 8 (1½-inch-thick) slices. Cut a pocket in each bread slice, leaving sides of bread slices intact. Carefully fill each pocket with about 3 tablespoons cream cheese mixture. Beat eggs with wire whisk in large shallow dish. Add milk and vanilla and whisk until blended. Dip 1 slice bread at a time into egg mixture, allowing bread to soak up egg mixture. Place filled slices onto lightly greased baking sheet. Sprinkle with nutmeg. Bake 5 minutes or until golden on bottom. Turn slices;

sprinkle with nutmeg. Bake 3 to 5 minutes or until golden on bottom. Serve with sauce.          *Makes 6 to 8 servings*

## Apricot and Orange Marmalade Sauce

**1 tablespoon butter or margarine
1½ cups chopped peeled fresh apricots
1 cup orange marmalade
½ teaspoon ground nutmeg**

Melt butter in medium saucepan over medium-high heat. Add apricots; cook and stir 5 to 10 minutes or until fork-tender. Add marmalade and nutmeg; stir until melted. Transfer mixture to food processor; process until apricots are finely chopped.          *Makes about 2 cups*

# Savory Bread
# Pudding

**8 slices thick-cut, day-old white bread,
    crusts trimmed
2 tablespoons unsalted butter
    substitute, softened
2 cups (8 ounces) shredded ALPINE
    LACE® Reduced Fat Baby Swiss
    Cheese, divided
1 cup grated peeled apple
½ cup egg substitute *or* 2 large eggs
2 large egg whites
2 cups 2% low fat milk
½ teaspoon salt
¼ teaspoon freshly ground black
    pepper**

**1.** Preheat the oven to 400°F. Spray a 13×9×2-inch rectangular or 3-quart oval baking dish with nonstick cooking spray. Thinly spread the bread slices with the butter. Cut each bread slice into 4 triangles, making a total of 32. In a small bowl, toss 1¾ cups of the cheese with the grated apple.

**2.** In a medium-size bowl, using an electric mixer set on high, beat the egg substitute (or the whole eggs), the egg whites, milk, salt and pepper together until frothy and light yellow.

**3.** To assemble the pudding: Line the bottom of the dish with 16 of the bread triangles. Cover with the apple-cheese mixture, then pour over half the egg mixture. Arrange the remaining 16 triangles around the edge and down the center of the dish, overlapping slightly as you go.

**4.** Pour the remaining egg mixture over the top, then sprinkle with the remaining ¼ cup of cheese. Bake, uncovered, for 35 minutes or until crisp and golden brown.

*Makes 8 servings*

# Bacon and Maple Grits Puff

8 slices bacon
2 cups milk
1¼ cups water
1 cup quick-cooking grits
½ teaspoon salt
½ cup pure maple syrup
4 eggs
Fresh chives for garnish

Preheat oven to 350°F. Grease 1½-quart round casserole or soufflé dish; set aside.

Cook bacon in large skillet over medium-high heat about 7 minutes or until crisp. Remove bacon with tongs to paper towel; set aside. Reserve 2 tablespoons bacon drippings. Combine milk, water, grits and salt in medium saucepan. Bring to a boil over medium heat, stirring frequently. Simmer 2 to 3 minutes or until mixture thickens, stirring constantly. Remove from heat; stir in syrup and reserved 2 tablespoons bacon drippings.

Crumble bacon; reserve ¼ cup for garnish. Stir remaining crumbled bacon into grits mixture. Beat eggs in medium bowl. Gradually stir small amount of grits mixture into eggs, then stir eggs into remaining grits mixture. Pour into prepared casserole. Bake 1 hour and 20 minutes or until knife inserted in center comes out clean. Top with reserved ¼ cup bacon. Garnish, if desired. Serve immediately. *Makes 6 to 8 servings*

**Note:** *Puff will fall slightly after removing from oven.*

# BOUNTIFUL BREADS

*Rediscover the joys of fresh-from-the-oven breads. You'll find rich cinnamon rolls and berry-filled muffins for breakfasts on the run, fruit-filled scones and warm glazed doughnuts for afternoon snacks, and savory breadsticks and flaky biscuits to serve with evening meals.*

## Cinnamon Buns

**1 recipe Sweet Yeast Dough (page 244)**

**½ cup granulated sugar**

**2 teaspoons ground cinnamon**

**2 tablespoons butter or margarine, melted**

**½ cup raisins (optional)**

**2 cups sifted powdered sugar**

**3 tablespoons milk**

**½ teaspoon vanilla**

Prepare Sweet Yeast Dough; let rise as directed.

Combine granulated sugar and cinnamon in small bowl; set aside. Grease 2 (9-inch) round cake pans. Cut dough in half. Roll one half of dough into 12×8-inch rectangle. Brush rectangle with half of melted butter; sprinkle with half of sugar mixture and half of raisins, if desired. Starting with 1 (12-inch) side, roll up jelly-roll style. *(Do not roll dough too tightly because centers of rolls will pop up as they rise.)* Repeat with remaining dough.

Cut each roll into 12 (1-inch) slices. Place slices ½ inch apart in prepared pans. (Rolls will spread as they rise.) Cover with towel; let rise in warm place about 1 hour or until doubled in bulk.

Preheat oven to 350°F. Bake 20 to 25 minutes or until rolls are golden brown. Cool in pans on wire racks 5 minutes. Combine powdered sugar, milk and vanilla in small bowl until smooth. Spread mixture over rolls. Serve warm. *Makes 24 buns*

*Cinnamon Buns*

# Sweet Yeast Dough

    4 to 4¼ cups all-purpose flour, divided
    ½ cup sugar
    2 packages active dry yeast
    1 teaspoon salt
    ¾ cup milk
    4 tablespoons butter or margarine
    2 eggs
    1 teaspoon vanilla

Combine 1 cup flour, sugar, yeast and salt in large bowl; set aside.

Combine milk and butter in 1-quart saucepan. Heat over low heat until mixture is 120° to 130°F. Gradually beat milk mixture into flour mixture with electric mixer at low speed. Increase speed to medium; beat 2 minutes. Reduce speed to low. Beat in eggs, vanilla and 1 cup flour. Increase speed to medium; beat 2 minutes. Stir in enough additional flour, about 2 cups, to make soft dough.

Turn out dough onto lightly floured surface; flatten slightly. Knead about 5 minutes or until smooth and elastic, adding remaining ¼ cup flour to prevent sticking if necessary. Shape dough into a ball; place in large greased bowl. Turn to coat with grease. Cover with towel; let rise in warm place 1½ to 2 hours or until doubled in bulk. Punch down dough, knead on lightly floured surface 1 minute. Cover with towel; let rest 10 minutes.

**Note:** *Use this dough to make Cinnamon Buns (page 242) and Cheese-Filled Almond Braids (page 250).*

**Refrigerator Sweet Yeast Dough:** Prepare Sweet Yeast Dough as directed, except cover with greased plastic wrap; refrigerate 3 to 24 hours. Punch down dough. Knead dough on lightly floured surface 1 to 2 minutes. Cover with towel; let dough rest 20 minutes before shaping and second rising. (Second rising may take up to 1½ hours.)

# Pecan Sticky Buns

**DOUGH\***
    4 to 5 cups flour, divided
    ½ cup granulated sugar
    1½ teaspoons salt
    2 packages active dry yeast
    ¾ cup warm milk (105° to 115°F)
    ½ cup warm water (105° to 115°F)
    ¼ cup (½ stick) MAZOLA® Margarine
        or butter, softened
    2 eggs

**GLAZE**
    ½ cup KARO® Dark or Light Corn
        Syrup
    ½ cup packed light brown sugar
    ¼ cup (½ stick) MAZOLA® Margarine
        or butter
    1 cup pecans, coarsely chopped

**FILLING**
    ½ cup packed light brown sugar
    1 teaspoon cinnamon
    2 tablespoons MAZOLA® Margarine or
        butter, melted

*\*To use frozen bread dough, thaw 2 loaves (1 pound each) frozen bread dough in refrigerator overnight. Press loaves together and roll into a 20×12-inch rectangle; complete as recipe directs.*

**FOR DOUGH:** In large bowl combine 2 cups flour, granulated sugar, salt and yeast. Stir in milk, water and softened margarine until blended. Stir in eggs and enough additional flour (about 2 cups) to make a soft dough. Knead on floured surface until smooth and elastic, about 8 minutes. Cover dough and let rest on floured surface 10 minutes.

**FOR GLAZE:** Meanwhile, in small saucepan over low heat stir corn syrup, brown sugar and margarine until smooth. Pour into 13×9×2-inch baking pan. Sprinkle with pecans; set aside.

**FOR FILLING:** Combine brown sugar and cinnamon; set aside. Roll dough to a 20×12-inch rectangle. Brush dough with 2 tablespoons melted margarine; sprinkle with brown sugar mixture. Starting from a long side, roll up jelly-roll fashion. Pinch seam to seal. Cut into 15 slices; place cut-side up in prepared pan. Cover tightly. Refrigerate 2 to 24 hours.

To bake, preheat oven to 375°F. Remove pan from refrigerator; uncover and let stand at room temperature 10 minutes. Bake 28 to 30 minutes or until tops are browned. Invert onto serving tray. Serve warm or cool completely.

*Makes 15 buns*

# Quicky Sticky Buns

**3 tablespoons packed brown sugar, divided**
**¼ cup KARO® Light or Dark Corn Syrup**
**¼ cup coarsely chopped pecans**
**2 tablespoons softened MAZOLA® margarine, divided**
**1 can (8 ounces) refrigerated crescent dinner rolls**
**1 teaspoon cinnamon**

Preheat oven to 350°F. In small bowl combine 2 tablespoons of the brown sugar, the corn syrup, pecans and 1 tablespoon of the margarine. Spoon about 2 teaspoons mixture into each of 9 (2½-inch) muffin pan cups. Unroll entire crescent roll dough; pinch seams together to form 1 rectangle. Combine remaining 1 tablespoon brown sugar and the cinnamon. Spread dough with remaining 1 tablespoon margarine; sprinkle with cinnamon mixture. Roll up from short end. Cut into 9 slices. Place one slice in each prepared muffin pan cup. Bake 25 minutes or until golden brown. Immediately invert pan onto cookie sheet or tray; cool 10 minutes.        *Makes 9 buns*

**Prep Time:** 15 minutes
**Bake Time:** 25 minutes, plus cooling

## Thyme-Cheese Bubble Loaf

1 package active dry yeast
1 teaspoon sugar
1 cup warm water (105° to 115°F)
3 cups all-purpose flour
1 teaspoon salt
2 tablespoons vegetable oil
1 cup shredded Monterey Jack cheese (4 ounces)
4 tablespoons butter or margarine, melted
¼ cup chopped parsley
3 teaspoons finely chopped fresh thyme *or* ¾ teaspoon dried thyme leaves

Sprinkle yeast and sugar over warm water in small bowl; stir until dissolved. Let stand 5 minutes or until mixture is bubbly.

Combine flour and salt in food processor. With food processor running, add yeast mixture and oil. Process until soft dough forms. If too dry, add 1 to 2 tablespoons water. If too wet, add 1 to 2 tablespoons additional flour until dough leaves side of bowl. (Dough will be sticky.) Place in large greased bowl; turn to coat with grease. Cover with towel; let rise in warm place about 1 hour or until doubled in bulk.

Punch down dough; knead in cheese on lightly floured surface until evenly distributed. Cover with towel; let rest 10 minutes. Grease 1½-quart casserole dish or 8½×4½-inch loaf pan; set aside. Combine butter, parsley and thyme in small bowl. Roll out dough into 8×6-inch rectangle. Cut into 48 squares. Shape each square into a ball. Dip into parsley mixture. Place in prepared pan. Cover with towel; let rise in warm place about 45 minutes or until doubled in bulk. Preheat oven to 375°F. Bake 35 to 40 minutes or until top is golden and loaf sounds hollow when tapped. Immediately remove from casserole dish; cool on wire rack 30 minutes. Serve warm. Store in refrigerator.

*Makes 1 loaf*

## Bacon Brunch Buns

1 loaf (1 pound) frozen bread dough
¼ cup unsalted butter or margarine, melted
2 tablespoons (½ package) HIDDEN VALLEY RANCH® Original Ranch® with Bacon Salad Dressing Mix
1 cup shredded Cheddar cheese
2 egg yolks
1½ tablespoons cold water
3 tablespoons sesame seeds

Thaw bread dough following package directions. Preheat oven to 375°F. On floured board, roll dough into rectangle about 18×7 inches. In small bowl, whisk together butter and salad dressing mix. Spread mixture on dough; sprinkle with cheese. Roll up tightly, jelly-roll style, pinching seam to seal. Cut into 16 slices. Place slices cut-side down on greased jelly-roll pan. Cover with plastic wrap and let rise until doubled in bulk, about 1 hour. In small bowl, beat egg yolks and water; brush mixture over buns. Sprinkle with sesame seeds. Bake until golden brown, 25 to 30 minutes. Serve warm.

*Makes 16 buns*

*Thyme-Cheese Bubble Loaf*

## Petit Pain au Chocolat

3 to 3½ cups all-purpose flour
3 tablespoons granulated sugar
1 package (¼ ounce) active dry yeast
1 teaspoon salt
1 cup plus 1 tablespoon milk, divided
3 tablespoons butter or margarine
1 egg, lightly beaten
1 milk chocolate candy bar
   (7 ounces), cut into 16 pieces
2 teaspoons colored sugar

Combine 3 cups flour, granulated sugar, yeast and salt in large bowl; set aside. Combine 1 cup milk and butter in small saucepan. Heat over low heat until mixture is 120° to 130°F. (Butter does not need to completely melt.) Gradually stir milk mixture and egg into flour mixture to make soft dough that forms a ball.

Turn out dough onto lightly floured surface; flatten slightly. Knead 8 to 10 minutes or until smooth and elastic, adding remaining ½ cup flour to prevent sticking if necessary. Shape dough into a ball. Place in large greased bowl; turn to coat with grease. Cover with towel; let rise in warm place about 1 hour or until doubled in bulk.

Punch down dough. Knead on lightly floured surface 1 minute. Roll back and forth to form a loaf. Cut loaf into 8 pieces. Roll 1 dough piece into a 6-inch round. Place 2 pieces chocolate in center. Fold edge into center around chocolate. Place seam side down on lightly greased baking sheet. Repeat with remaining dough pieces, placing rolls 3 inches apart on baking sheet. Cover rolls lightly with towel and let rise in warm place 20 to 30 minutes or until slightly puffed. Brush tops with remaining 1 tablespoon milk. Sprinkle with colored sugar.

Preheat oven to 400°F. Bake 12 to 15 minutes or until rolls are golden brown. Serve immediately. *Makes 8 rolls*

## — Country Biscuits —

2 cups all-purpose flour
1 tablespoon baking powder
1 teaspoon salt
⅓ CRISCO® Stick or ⅓ cup CRISCO all-
   vegetable shortening
¾ cup milk

**1. Preheat** oven to 425°F. **Combine** flour, baking powder and salt in medium bowl. **Cut** in shortening using pastry blender (or two knives) to form coarse crumbs. **Add** milk. **Mix** with fork until dry mixture is moistened. **Form** dough into a ball.

**2. Transfer** dough to lightly floured surface. **Knead** gently 8 to 10 times. **Roll** out dough to ½-inch thickness. **Cut** with floured 2-inch round cutter. **Place** on ungreased baking sheet.

**3. Bake** at 425°F 12 to 14 minutes or until golden. *Makes 12 to 16 biscuits*

*Petit Pain au Chocolat*

# Cheese-Filled — Almond Braids —

**1 recipe Sweet Yeast Dough (page 244)**
**2 packages (8 ounces each) cream cheese, softened**
**⅔ cup granulated sugar**
**2 eggs, separated**
**2 tablespoons all-purpose flour**
**1½ teaspoons almond extract**
**1 tablespoon water**
**¼ cup sliced almonds**
**Additional granulated sugar (optional)**
**Powdered sugar (optional)**

Prepare Sweet Yeast Dough; let rise as directed. Combine cream cheese, ⅔ cup granulated sugar, egg yolks, flour and almond extract in large bowl. Beat with electric mixer at low speed until combined. Increase speed to medium; beat until smooth, scraping down side of bowl once. Cover with plastic wrap; refrigerate until needed.

Grease 2 large baking sheets. Cut dough into halves. Roll out one half of dough into 12×9-inch rectangle on lightly floured surface with lightly floured rolling pin. Place rolling pin on 1 side of dough. Gently roll dough over rolling pin once. Carefully lift rolling pin and dough, unrolling dough onto prepared baking sheet. Score dough lengthwise into 3 (3-inch-wide) sections with tip of sharp knife, taking care not to cut completely through dough. Spread half of cream cheese mixture lengthwise down middle section of dough.

Score 2 outer sections of dough with tip of sharp knife to mark 1-inch-wide diagonal strips. Cut diagonal strips with scissors or sharp knife to within ½ inch of filling.

Starting at 1 end, fold strips over filling. Alternate folding strips from left and right, overlapping strips in center to create a braided pattern. Repeat with remaining dough and cream cheese mixture. Cover braids with towels; let rise in warm place about 45 minutes or until doubled in bulk.

Preheat oven to 350°F. Combine egg whites with 1 tablespoon water in small bowl. Brush braids with egg white mixture and sprinkle with almonds. Sprinkle additional granulated sugar over almonds, if desired. Bake on 2 racks in oven 25 to 30 minutes or until braids are golden brown and sound hollow when tapped. (Rotate baking sheets top to bottom halfway through baking.) Immediately remove from baking sheets; cool completely on wire racks. Dust with powdered sugar, if desired.

*Makes 2 coffee cakes or about 24 servings*

*Cheese-Filled Almond Braid*

## Streusel-Topped Blueberry Muffins

1½ cups plus ⅓ cup all-purpose flour, divided
½ cup plus ⅓ cup sugar, divided
1 teaspoon ground cinnamon
3 tablespoons butter or margarine, cut into small pieces
2 teaspoons baking powder
½ teaspoon salt
1 cup milk
¼ cup butter or margarine, melted and slightly cooled
1 egg, beaten
1 teaspoon vanilla
1 cup fresh blueberries

Preheat oven to 375°F. Grease or paper-line 12 (2½-inch) muffin cups; set aside.

Combine ⅓ cup flour, ⅓ cup sugar and cinnamon in small bowl. Cut in 3 tablespoons butter with pastry blender until mixture resembles coarse crumbs; set aside. Combine remaining 1½ cups flour, ½ cup sugar, baking powder and salt in large bowl. Combine milk, ¼ cup melted butter, egg and vanilla in small bowl. Stir into flour mixture just until moistened. Fold in blueberries. Spoon evenly into prepared muffin cups. Sprinkle reserved topping over top of each muffin.

Bake 20 to 25 minutes or until wooden pick inserted in center comes out clean. Remove from pan; cool completely.

*Makes 12 muffins*

## Apple Cheddar Muffins

2 cups sifted all-purpose flour
⅓ cup sugar
1 tablespoon baking powder
½ teaspoon salt
¼ teaspoon ground nutmeg
½ cup egg substitute *or* 2 large eggs
¾ cup 2% low fat milk
¼ cup unsalted butter, melted
1 cup grated, cored, peeled baking apples, such as Granny Smith, Rome Beauty or Winesap
¾ cup (3 ounces) shredded ALPINE LACE® Fat Free Pasteurized Process Skim Milk Cheese Product—For Cheddar Lovers

**1.** Preheat the oven to 400°F. Spray 12 regular-size muffin cups with nonstick cooking spray.

**2.** In a large bowl, sift together the flour, sugar, baking powder, salt and nutmeg. In a small bowl, whisk the egg substitute (or the whole eggs) with the milk and butter until blended.

**3.** Using a wooden spoon, make a hole in the center of the flour mixture, then pour in the egg mixture all at once. Stir just until the flour disappears. *(Avoid overmixing!)* Fold in the apples and cheese. Spoon the batter into the muffin cups until three-fourths full.

**4.** Bake the muffins for 20 to 25 minutes or until golden brown. Cool the muffins in the pan on a wire rack for 5 minutes, then lift them out with a spatula. They're delicious when served hot with honey!

*Makes 12 muffins*

*Apple Cheddar Muffins*

## Oreo® Muffins

1¾ cups all-purpose flour
½ cup sugar
1 tablespoon DAVIS® Baking Powder
½ teaspoon salt
¾ cup milk
⅓ cup sour cream
1 egg
¼ cup FLEISCHMANN'S® Margarine,
   melted
20 OREO® Chocolate Sandwich Cookies,
   coarsely chopped

In medium bowl, combine flour, sugar,
baking powder and salt; set aside.

In small bowl, combine milk, sour cream
and egg; stir into flour mixture with
margarine until just blended. Gently stir in
cookies. Spoon batter into 12 greased
2½-inch muffin-pan cups.

Bake at 400°F for 20 to 25 minutes or
until toothpick inserted in center comes
out clean. Remove from pan; cool on wire
rack. Serve warm or cold.

*Makes 12 muffins*

## Berry Filled Muffins

1 package DUNCAN HINES® Blueberry
   Muffin Mix
1 egg
½ cup water
¼ cup strawberry jam
2 tablespoons sliced natural almonds

**1.** Preheat oven to 400°F. Place 8
(2½-inch) paper or foil liners in muffin
cups; set aside.

**2.** Rinse blueberries from Mix with cold
water and drain.

**3.** Empty muffin mix into bowl. Break up
any lumps. Add egg and water. Stir until
moistened, about 50 strokes. Fill cups half
full with batter.

**4.** Fold blueberries into jam. Spoon on
top of batter in each cup. Spread gently.
Cover with remaining batter. Sprinkle
with almonds. Bake at 400°F for 17 to
20 minutes or until set and golden brown.
Cool in pan 5 to 10 minutes. Loosen
carefully before removing from pan.

*Makes 8 muffins*

**Tip:** For a delicious flavor variation, try using
blackberry or red raspberry jam for the
strawberry jam.

# Chocolate Pumpkin Muffins

1½ cups all-purpose flour
½ cup granulated sugar
2 teaspoons baking powder
½ teaspoon ground cinnamon
½ teaspoon salt
1 cup milk
½ cup LIBBY'S® Solid Pack Pumpkin
¼ cup margarine or butter, melted
1 egg
1 cup (6-ounce package) NESTLÉ®
   TOLL HOUSE® Semi-Sweet
   Chocolate Morsels
⅓ cup finely chopped nuts

**PREHEAT** oven to 400°F. Grease 12 (2½-inch) muffin cups.

**COMBINE** flour, sugar, baking powder, cinnamon and salt in large bowl; make well in center. In small bowl, combine milk, pumpkin, margarine and egg; add to well in flour mixture. Add morsels; stir just until dry ingredients are moistened. Spoon into prepared muffin cups, filling each ¾ full. Sprinkle 1 teaspoon nuts over each muffin.

**BAKE** 18 to 20 minutes or until wooden pick inserted into center comes out clean. Cool 5 minutes; remove from pans. Cool completely on wire racks.

*Makes 12 muffins*

# White Chocolate Chunk Muffins

2½ cups all-purpose flour
1 cup packed brown sugar
⅓ cup unsweetened cocoa powder
2 teaspoons baking soda
½ teaspoon salt
1⅓ cups buttermilk
6 tablespoons butter or margarine, melted
2 eggs, beaten
1½ teaspoons vanilla
1½ cups chopped white chocolate

Preheat oven to 400°F. Grease 12 (3½-inch) large muffin cups; set aside.

Combine flour, sugar, cocoa, baking soda and salt in large bowl. Combine buttermilk, butter, eggs and vanilla in small bowl until blended. Stir into flour mixture just until moistened. Fold in white chocolate. Spoon into prepared muffin cups, filling half full.

Bake 25 to 30 minutes or until wooden pick inserted in center comes out clean. Cool in pan on wire rack 5 minutes. Remove from pan. Cool on wire rack 10 minutes. Serve warm or cool completely.

*Makes 12 jumbo muffins*

## Honey Currant Scones

2½ cups all-purpose flour
2 teaspoons grated orange peel
1 teaspoon baking powder
½ teaspoon baking soda
½ teaspoon salt
½ cup butter or margarine
½ cup currants
½ cup sour cream
⅓ cup honey
1 egg, slightly beaten

Preheat oven to 375°F. Grease baking sheet; set aside. Combine flour, orange peel, baking powder, baking soda and salt in large bowl. Cut in butter with pastry blender or 2 knives until mixture resembles coarse crumbs. Add currants. Combine sour cream, honey and egg in medium bowl until well blended. Stir into flour mixture until soft dough forms. Turn out dough onto lightly floured surface. Knead dough 10 times. Shape dough into 8-inch square. Cut into 4 squares; cut each square diagonally in half, making 8 triangles. Place triangles 1 inch apart on prepared baking sheet.

Bake 15 to 20 minutes or until golden brown and wooden pick inserted in center comes out clean. Remove from baking sheet. Cool on wire rack 10 minutes. Serve warm or cool completely.

*Makes 8 scones*

Favorite recipe from **National Honey Board**

## Buttermilk Oatmeal Scones

2 cups all-purpose flour, sifted
1 cup uncooked rolled oats
⅓ cup granulated sugar
1 tablespoon baking powder
½ teaspoon baking soda
⅛ teaspoon salt
6 tablespoons cold unsalted margarine, cut into small pieces
1 cup buttermilk
Additional buttermilk and granulated sugar for scone tops

Preheat oven to 375°F. Grease baking sheets; set aside.

Combine flour, oats, sugar, baking powder, baking soda and salt in large bowl. Cut in margarine with pastry blender or process in food processor until mixture resembles coarse crumbs. Add buttermilk; stir with fork until soft dough forms. Turn out dough onto lightly floured surface; knead 10 to 12 times. Roll out dough to ½-inch-thick rectangle with lightly floured rolling pin. Cut dough into circles with lightly floured 1½-inch biscuit cutter. Place biscuits on prepared baking sheets. Brush tops with buttermilk and sprinkle with sugar. Bake 18 to 20 minutes or until golden brown and wooden pick inserted in center comes out clean. Remove from baking sheets. Cool on wire racks 10 minutes. Serve warm or cool completely.

*Makes about 30 scones*

Favorite recipe from **The Sugar Association, Inc.**

*Honey Currant Scones*

## — Cake Doughnuts —

3¾ cups all-purpose flour
1 tablespoon baking powder
¾ teaspoon salt
1 teaspoon ground cinnamon
½ teaspoon ground nutmeg
3 eggs
¾ cup granulated sugar
1 cup applesauce
2 tablespoons butter or margarine, melted and cooled slightly
2 cups sifted powdered sugar
3 tablespoons milk
½ teaspoon vanilla
1 quart vegetable oil for frying
Colored sprinkles

Combine flour, baking powder, salt, cinnamon and nutmeg in medium bowl; set aside. Beat eggs in large bowl with electric mixer at high speed until frothy. Gradually beat in granulated sugar. Beat at high speed 4 minutes until thick. Reduce speed to low; beat in applesauce and butter. Beat in flour mixture until well blended. Place half of dough onto sheet of plastic wrap. Pat dough into 5-inch square; wrap in another sheet of plastic wrap. Repeat with remaining dough. Refrigerate 3 hours.

Blend powdered sugar, milk and vanilla in small bowl. Cover; set aside. Pour oil into 6-quart Dutch oven. Heat until thermometer registers 375°F; adjust heat to maintain temperature.

Meanwhile, roll out 1 piece dough to ⅜-inch thickness on well-floured pastry cloth. Cut with floured 3-inch doughnut cutter; repeat with remaining dough.

Reroll scraps, reserving doughnut holes. Cook, 1 at a time, 2 minutes or until golden brown on both sides, turning often. Remove with slotted spoon; drain on paper-towel-lined plate. Spread glaze over warm doughnuts; top with colored sprinkles.

*Makes 1 dozen doughnuts and holes*

## — Cheesy Focaccia —

3 cups buttermilk baking mix
2 cups (8 ounces) VELVEETA® Shredded Pasteurized Process Cheese Food
1 teaspoon dried basil leaves, crushed
¼ teaspoon dried oregano leaves, crushed
1 cup milk
6 tablespoons olive oil

**PREHEAT** oven to 375°F.

**STIR** together baking mix, process cheese food and seasonings. Add milk; mix well.

**COAT** bottom of 15×10×1-inch jelly roll pan with 2 tablespoons olive oil. Pat dough evenly into pan with floured hands. Make indentations with fingertips at 1-inch intervals over entire surface of dough. Brush remaining olive oil evenly over dough.

**BAKE** 20 minutes or until golden brown. Cut into rectangles; serve warm.

*Makes approximately 3 dozen servings*

**Prep Time:** 10 minutes
**Cooking Time:** 20 minutes

*Cake Doughnuts and Doughnut Holes*

## Jalapeño-Bacon Corn Bread

4 slices bacon
¼ cup minced green onions with tops
2 jalapeño peppers, stemmed, seeded and minced
1 cup yellow cornmeal
1 cup all-purpose flour
2½ teaspoons baking powder
½ teaspoon baking soda
½ teaspoon salt
1 egg
¾ cup plain yogurt
¾ cup milk
¼ cup butter or margarine, melted
½ cup (2 ounces) shredded Cheddar cheese

Preheat oven to 400°F. Cook bacon in skillet until crisp; drain on paper towels. Pour 2 tablespoons of the bacon drippings into 9-inch cast-iron skillet or 9-inch square baking pan. Crumble bacon into small bowl; add green onions and peppers.

Combine cornmeal, flour, baking powder, baking soda and salt in large bowl. Beat egg slightly in medium bowl; add yogurt and whisk until smooth. Whisk in milk and butter. Pour liquid mixture into dry ingredients; stir just until moistened. Stir in bacon mixture. Pour into skillet; sprinkle with cheese. Bake 20 to 25 minutes or until a wooden pick inserted in center comes out clean. Cut into wedges or squares; serve hot.

*Makes 9 to 12 servings*

## Cornmeal Sticks

2 cups cold water
1½ cups yellow cornmeal
¾ teaspoon salt
6 ounces sharp Cheddar cheese, finely shredded (1½ cups)
CRISCO® all-vegetable shortening for deep frying

**1. Combine** water, cornmeal and salt in a heavy saucepan. **Mix** until smooth. **Cook** over medium heat, stirring constantly, until mixture is very stiff, thick and pulls away from side of pan. (This takes 6 to 9 minutes.)

**2. Remove** from heat. **Add** cheese. **Stir** until melted.

**3. Pat** mixture evenly into ungreased 13×9×2-inch baking dish. **Let** stand uncovered 30 minutes at room temperature. *Do not chill dough.*

**4. Cut** dough into 3 lengthwise sections and 18 crosswise strips.

**5. Heat** shortening to 365°F in a large saucepan or deep fryer.

**6. Add** sticks to hot shortening, one at a time, frying 3 sticks at a time for 3 minutes or until golden brown. (If sticks run together, cut apart after frying.) **Remove** with slotted spatula. **Drain** on paper towels. **Serve** warm.

*Makes 4½ dozen cornmeal sticks*

**Prep Time:** 30 minutes, plus chilling
**Bake Time:** 28 minutes

*Jalapeño-Bacon Corn Bread*

## Cheddar and Onion Whole Wheat Loaf

½ cup egg substitute *or* 2 large eggs
⅔ cup 2% low fat milk
1⅓ cups whole wheat flour
1 cup all-purpose flour
1½ tablespoons baking powder
¾ teaspoon salt
½ teaspoon coarsely ground black pepper
3 tablespoons unsalted butter, at room temperature
1 cup (4 ounces) shredded ALPINE LACE® Reduced Fat Cheddar Cheese
1 cup minced yellow onion

**1.** Preheat the oven to 350°F. Spray a 9×5×3-inch loaf pan with nonstick cooking spray. In a cup, whisk the egg substitute (or the whole eggs) with the milk. In a large bowl, stir together both of the flours, the baking powder, salt and pepper. Using a pastry blender or 2 knives, cut in the butter until coarse crumbs form.

**2.** Using a wooden spoon, make a hole in the center of the flour mixture, then pour in the egg mixture all at once. Stir just until the flour disappears. *(Avoid overmixing!)* Fold in the cheese and onion, then spoon the batter into the pan.

**3.** Bake the bread for 1 hour and 10 minutes or until a toothpick inserted in the center comes out with moist crumbs. Cool the bread in the pan on a wire rack for 5 minutes, then remove from the pan to the rack to cool completely.

*Makes one 9-inch loaf*

## Blueberry Oat Bread

2 cups flour
1 cup uncooked quick or old-fashioned oats
1 tablespoon baking powder
1 teaspoon salt
½ teaspoon baking soda
½ teaspoon cinnamon
2 eggs
1 cup milk
½ cup sugar
⅓ cup KARO® Light Corn Syrup
¼ cup MAZOLA® Corn Oil
1½ cups fresh or frozen blueberries

Preheat oven to 350°F. Grease and flour 9×5×3-inch loaf pan. In large bowl combine flour, oats, baking powder, salt, baking soda and cinnamon. In small bowl combine eggs, milk, sugar, corn syrup and corn oil until blended; set aside. Toss blueberries in flour mixture. Stir in egg mixture until well blended. Pour batter into prepared pan. Bake 60 to 70 minutes or until toothpick inserted into center comes out clean. Cool in pan 10 minutes. Remove from pan; cool on wire rack.

*Makes 1 loaf or 12 servings*

**Prep Time:** 15 minutes
**Bake Time:** 70 minutes, plus cooling

## Cherry Walnut Breads

2 cups all-purpose flour
½ cup packed light brown sugar
1 teaspoon baking powder
½ teaspoon baking soda
½ teaspoon ground cinnamon
¼ teaspoon ground allspice
⅛ teaspoon salt
4 tablespoons butter or margarine, softened
¾ cup milk
1 egg
1 can (16 ounces) light sweet cherries, well drained*
½ cup chopped walnuts

*One can (16 ounces) dark sweet cherries can be substituted for the light sweet cherries.

Preheat oven to 400°F. Grease 3 clean, empty (16-ounce) cans; set aside. Combine flour, brown sugar, baking powder, baking soda, cinnamon, allspice and salt in medium bowl. Stir in butter. (Mixture will be crumbly.) Stir in milk and egg. Stir in cherries and walnuts. Spoon batter into prepared cans. Bake 50 to 55 minutes or until wooden skewer inserted in center comes out clean. Remove breads from cans. Cool on wire racks 10 minutes. Serve warm or cool completely.

*Makes 3 loaves (10 slices each)*

**Tip:** To make 1 loaf, bake batter in greased 8½×4½×2½-inch loaf pan 55 to 60 minutes.

Favorite recipe from **Canned Food Information Council**

## Pick-of-the-Garden Bread

3 cups all-purpose flour
1½ tablespoons baking powder
1 teaspoon salt
⅛ teaspoon cayenne pepper
6 tablespoons unsalted butter, at room temperature
6 ounces (1 carton) ALPINE LACE® Fat Free Cream Cheese with Garden Vegetables
¾ cup 2% low fat milk
½ cup egg substitute *or* 2 large eggs
¾ cup grated zucchini
½ cup grated peeled carrot
½ cup finely chopped green onions

**1.** Preheat the oven to 350°F. Spray a 9×5×3-inch loaf pan with nonstick cooking spray. In a large bowl, stir together the flour, baking powder, salt and pepper. Using a pastry blender, cut in the butter until coarse crumbs form.

**2.** In a small bowl, using an electric mixer set on medium, beat the cream cheese, milk and egg substitute until almost blended.

**3.** Using a wooden spoon, make a hole in the center of the flour mixture and pour in the cheese mixture all at once. Stir just until the flour disappears. *(Avoid overmixing!)* Fold in the zucchini, carrot and green onions. Spoon batter into pan.

**4.** Bake for 1 hour and 20 minutes or until a toothpick inserted in the center comes out with moist crumbs. Cool the bread in the pan on a wire rack for 5 minutes, then remove from the pan to the rack to cool completely. *Makes 1 loaf*

# COOKIES & CANDIES

*Tickle your taste buds with cookies that are chock-full of tasty chips, fudgy brownies that ooze with chocolatey goodness or velvety fudges and silky truffles that melt in your mouth. There's more in this chapter than the usual baker's dozen to satisfy even the sweetest tooth.*

## HERSHEY'S Great American Chocolate Chip Cookies

1 cup (2 sticks) butter, softened
¾ cup granulated sugar
¾ cup packed light brown sugar
1 teaspoon vanilla extract
2 eggs
2¼ cups all-purpose flour
1 teaspoon baking soda
½ teaspoon salt
2 cups (12-ounce package) HERSHEY'S Semi-Sweet Chocolate Chips
1 cup chopped nuts (optional)

Heat oven to 375°F. In large mixer bowl, beat butter, granulated sugar, brown sugar and vanilla until creamy. Add eggs; beat well. Stir together flour, baking soda and salt; gradually add to butter mixture, beating well. Stir in chocolate chips and nuts, if desired. Drop dough by rounded teaspoonfuls onto ungreased cookie sheet. Bake 8 to 10 minutes or until lightly browned. Cool slightly; remove from cookie sheet to wire rack. Cool completely. *Makes about 6 dozen cookies*

**HERSHEY'S Great American Chocolate Chip Pan Cookies:** Spread dough into greased 15½×10½×1-inch jelly-roll pan. Bake at 375°F for 20 minutes or until lightly browned. Cool completely in pan on wire rack. Cut into bars. *Makes about 4 dozen bars*

**SKOR® & Chocolate Chip Cookies:** Omit 1 cup HERSHEY'S Semi-Sweet Chocolate Chips and nuts; replace with 1 cup finely chopped SKOR® bars. Drop onto cookie sheets and bake as directed.

*Top to bottom: Cocoa Kiss Cookies (page 278), HERSHEY'S Great American Chocolate Chip Cookies*

# White Chocolate Biggies

1½ cups butter or margarine, softened
1 cup granulated sugar
¾ cup packed light brown sugar
2 eggs
2 teaspoons vanilla
2½ cups all-purpose flour
⅔ cup unsweetened cocoa
1 teaspoon baking soda
½ teaspoon salt
1 package (10 ounces) large white chocolate chips
¾ cup pecan halves, coarsely chopped
½ cup golden raisins

Preheat oven to 350°F. Lightly grease cookie sheets or line with parchment paper. Cream butter, sugars, eggs and vanilla in large bowl. Combine flour, cocoa, baking soda and salt in medium bowl; blend into creamed mixture until smooth. Stir in white chocolate chips, pecans and raisins.

Scoop out about ⅓ cupful of dough for each cookie. Place on prepared cookie sheets, spacing about 4 inches apart. Press each cookie to flatten slightly.

Bake 12 to 14 minutes or until firm in center. Cool 5 minutes on cookie sheets, then remove to wire racks to cool completely.

*Makes about 2 dozen cookies*

# Sour Cream Chocolate Chip Cookies

1 BUTTER FLAVOR* CRISCO® Stick or 1 cup BUTTER FLAVOR CRISCO all-vegetable shortening
1 cup firmly packed brown sugar
½ cup granulated sugar
1 egg
½ cup dairy sour cream
¼ cup warm honey
2 teaspoons vanilla
2½ cups all-purpose flour
1½ teaspoons baking powder
½ teaspoon salt
2 cups semi-sweet or milk chocolate chips
1 cup coarsely chopped walnuts

*Butter Flavor Crisco is artificially flavored.*

**1. Preheat** oven to 375°F. **Grease** cookie sheets with shortening.

**2. Combine** shortening, brown sugar and granulated sugar in large bowl. **Beat** at medium speed of electric mixer until well blended. **Beat** in egg, sour cream, honey and vanilla. **Beat** until just blended.

**3. Combine** flour, baking powder and salt. **Mix** into creamed mixture at low speed until just blended. **Stir** in chocolate chips and nuts.

**4. Drop** slightly rounded measuring tablespoonfuls of dough 2 inches apart onto cookie sheet.

**5. Bake** 10 to 12 minutes or until set. **Cool** 2 minutes on cookie sheet. **Remove** to cooling rack.

*Makes about 5 dozen cookies*

## Oatmeal Chocolate Chip Cookies

1 can (20 ounces) DOLE® Crushed Pineapple
1½ cups brown sugar, packed
1 cup margarine, softened
1 egg
¼ teaspoon almond extract
4 cups rolled oats
2 cups all-purpose flour
1 teaspoon baking powder
1 teaspoon salt
1 teaspoon ground cinnamon
½ teaspoon ground nutmeg
1 package (12 ounces) semisweet chocolate chips
¾ cup DOLE® Slivered Almonds, toasted
2 cups flaked coconut

•DRAIN pineapple well, reserving ½ cup juice.

•CREAM brown sugar and margarine until light and fluffy in large bowl. Beat in egg. Beat in pineapple, reserved juice and almond extract. Combine oats, flour, baking powder, salt, cinnamon and nutmeg in small bowl. Add to creamed mixture; beat until blended. Stir in chocolate chips, almonds and coconut. Drop by heaping tablespoonfuls onto greased cookie sheets. Flatten cookies slightly with back of spoon. Bake at 350°F 20 to 25 minutes or until golden. Cool on wire racks. *Makes about 5 dozen cookies*

## Pudding Chip Cookies

1 cup margarine, softened
¾ cup firmly packed light brown sugar
¼ cup granulated sugar
1 package (4-serving size) JELL-O® Instant Pudding and Pie Filling, Butter Pecan, Butterscotch, Chocolate, Milk Chocolate, Chocolate Fudge, French Vanilla or Vanilla Flavor
1 teaspoon vanilla
2 eggs
2¼ cups all-purpose flour
1 teaspoon baking soda
1 package (12 ounces) BAKER'S® Semi-Sweet Real Chocolate Chips
1 cup chopped nuts (optional)

PREHEAT oven to 375°F. Beat margarine, sugars, pudding mix and vanilla in large bowl until smooth and creamy. Beat in eggs. Gradually add flour and baking soda. Stir in chips and nuts. (Dough will be stiff.) Drop by teaspoonfuls 2 inches apart onto ungreased cookie sheets.

BAKE 8 to 10 minutes or until lightly browned. Remove from cookie sheets; cool on racks.

*Makes about 7 dozen cookies*

**Prep Time:** 30 minutes
**Baking Time:** 30 minutes

# Anna's Icing Oatmeal Sandwich Cookies

## COOKIES

¾ BUTTER FLAVOR* CRISCO® Stick or
   ¾ cup BUTTER FLAVOR CRISCO
   all-vegetable shortening
1¼ cups firmly packed light brown
   sugar
1 egg
⅓ cup milk
1½ teaspoons vanilla
3 cups quick oats, uncooked
1 cup all-purpose flour
½ teaspoon baking soda
½ teaspoon salt

## FROSTING

2 cups confectioners' sugar
¼ BUTTER FLAVOR* CRISCO Stick or
   ¼ cup BUTTER FLAVOR CRISCO
   all-vegetable shortening
½ teaspoon vanilla
Milk

*Butter Flavor Crisco is artificially flavored.*

**1. Heat** oven to 350°F. **Grease** baking sheets with shortening. **Place** sheets of foil on countertop for cooling cookies.

**2. *For Cookies,* combine** shortening, brown sugar, egg, milk and vanilla in large bowl. **Beat** at medium speed of electric mixer until well blended.

**3. Combine** oats, flour, baking soda and salt. **Mix** into creamed mixture at low speed just until blended. **Drop** tablespoonfuls of dough 2 inches apart onto prepared sheets. **Bake** one sheet at a time at 375°F for 10 to 12 minutes, or until lightly browned. *Do not overbake.* **Cool** 2 minutes on baking sheets.

**Remove** cookies to foil to cool completely.

**4. *For Frosting,* combine** confectioners' sugar, shortening and vanilla in medium bowl. **Beat** at low speed, adding enough milk for good spreading consistency. **Spread** on bottoms of half the cookies. **Top** with remaining cookies.      *Makes 16 cookies*

# Peanut Butter Chip Oatmeal Cookies

1 cup (2 sticks) butter or margarine, softened
¼ cup shortening
2 cups packed light brown sugar
1 tablespoon milk
2 teaspoons vanilla extract
1 egg
2 cups all-purpose flour
1⅔ cups (10-ounce package) REESE'S® Peanut Butter Chips
1½ cups quick-cooking or regular rolled oats
½ cup chopped walnuts
½ teaspoon baking soda
½ teaspoon salt

Heat oven to 375°F. In large mixer bowl, beat butter, shortening, brown sugar, milk, vanilla and egg until light and fluffy. Add remaining ingredients; mix until well blended. Drop dough by rounded teaspoonfuls about 2 inches apart onto ungreased cookie sheet. Bake until light brown, 10 to 12 minutes for soft cookies or 12 to 14 minutes for crisp cookies. Remove from cookie sheet to wire rack. Cool completely.      *Makes 6 dozen cookies*

*Anna's Icing Oatmeal
Sandwich Cookies*

## Oatmeal Scotch Chippers

1¼ BUTTER FLAVOR* CRISCO® Stick or
   1¼ cups BUTTER FLAVOR CRISCO
   all-vegetable shortening
1½ cups firmly packed brown sugar
 1 cup granulated sugar
 3 eggs
1¼ cups JIF® Extra Crunchy Peanut
   Butter
4½ cups old-fashioned oats (not instant
   or quick), uncooked
 2 teaspoons baking soda
 1 cup semi-sweet chocolate chips
 1 cup butterscotch-flavored chips
 1 cup chopped walnuts

*Butter Flavor Crisco is artificially flavored.*

**1. Preheat** oven to 350°F. **Combine** shortening, brown sugar and granulated sugar in large bowl. **Beat** at medium speed of electric mixer until well blended. **Beat** in eggs. **Add** peanut butter. **Beat** until blended.

**2. Combine** oats and baking soda. **Stir** into creamed mixture with spoon. **Stir** in chocolate chips, butterscotch chips and nuts until blended.

**3. Drop** rounded teaspoonfuls of dough 2 inches apart onto ungreased cookie sheet.

**4. Bake** 10 to 11 minutes or until lightly browned. **Cool** 2 minutes on cookie sheet. **Remove** to cooling rack.

*Makes about 6 dozen cookies*

## Chocolate-Dipped Oat Cookies

 2 cups uncooked rolled oats
 ¾ cup packed brown sugar
 ½ cup vegetable oil
 ½ cup finely chopped walnuts
 1 egg
 2 teaspoons grated orange peel
 ¼ teaspoon salt
 1 package (12 ounces) milk chocolate
   chips

Combine oats, sugar, oil, walnuts, egg, orange peel and salt in large bowl until blended. Cover; refrigerate overnight.

Preheat oven to 350°F. Lightly grease cookie sheets or line with parchment paper. Melt chocolate chips in top of double boiler over hot, not boiling, water; keep warm. Shape oat mixture into large marble-sized balls. Place 2 inches apart on prepared cookie sheets.

Bake 10 to 12 minutes or until golden and crisp. Cool 10 minutes on wire racks. Dip tops of cookies, one at a time, into melted chocolate. Place on waxed paper; cool until chocolate is set.

*Makes about 6 dozen cookies*

*Oatmeal Scotch Chippers*

# Elvis Would Have Loved These Peanut Butter Cookies

## COOKIES

1¼ cups firmly packed light brown
    sugar
¾ cup creamy peanut butter
½ CRISCO® Stick or ½ cup CRISCO
    all-vegetable shortening
1 cup mashed banana
3 tablespoons milk
1½ teaspoons vanilla
1 egg
2 cups all-purpose flour
¾ teaspoon baking soda
¾ teaspoon salt
1½ cups milk chocolate chunks or semi-
    sweet chocolate chips
1 cup coarsely chopped pecans

## FROSTING

2 tablespoons BUTTER FLAVOR*
    CRISCO all-vegetable shortening
1½ cups miniature marshmallows
¼ cup creamy peanut butter
½ teaspoon vanilla
1¼ cups confectioners' sugar
    Hot water
1 cup peanut butter chips

*Butter Flavor Crisco is artificially flavored.*

1. **Heat** oven to 350°F. **Place** sheets of foil on countertop for cooling cookies.

2. *For Cookies,* **place** brown sugar, peanut butter, ½ cup shortening, banana, milk and vanilla in large bowl. **Beat** at medium speed of electric mixer until well blended. **Add** egg. **Beat** just until blended.

3. **Combine** flour, baking soda and salt. **Add** to shortening mixture. **Beat** at low speed just until blended. **Stir** in chocolate chips and pecans.

4. **Drop** dough by rounded measuring tablespoonfuls 2 inches apart onto ungreased baking sheets.

5. **Bake** one baking sheet at a time at 350°F for 11 to 13 minutes or until cookies are light brown around edges. *Do not overbake.* **Cool** 2 minutes on baking sheet. **Remove** cookies to foil to cool completely.

6. *For Frosting,* **melt** 2 tablespoons shortening in medium saucepan on low heat. **Add** marshmallows and peanut butter. **Heat** until melted, stirring constantly until well blended. **Remove** from heat. **Stir** in vanilla.

7. **Place** confectioners' sugar in medium bowl. **Add** marshmallow mixture and 1 tablespoon of hot water at a time, beating until desired consistency. **Frost** cookies. **Sprinkle** with peanut butter chips.

*Makes about 4 dozen cookies*

*Elvis Would Have Loved These Peanut Butter Cookies*

# Double-Dipped Chocolate Peanut — Butter Cookies —

1¼ cups all-purpose flour
½ teaspoon baking powder
½ teaspoon baking soda
½ teaspoon salt
½ cup butter or margarine, softened
½ cup granulated sugar plus additional for tops of cookies, divided
½ cup packed light brown sugar
½ cup creamy or chunky peanut butter
1 large egg
1 teaspoon vanilla
1½ cups semisweet chocolate chips
3 teaspoons shortening, divided
1½ cups milk chocolate chips

Preheat oven to 350°F. Place flour, baking powder, baking soda and salt in small bowl; stir to combine. Beat butter, ½ cup granulated sugar and brown sugar in large bowl with electric mixer at medium speed until light and fluffy. Beat in peanut butter, egg and vanilla. Gradually stir in flour mixture until well blended.

Roll heaping tablespoonfuls of dough into 1½-inch balls. Place balls 2 inches apart on ungreased cookie sheets. (If dough is too soft to roll into balls, refrigerate 30 minutes.) Dip fork into granulated sugar; press criss-cross fashion onto each ball, flattening to ½-inch thickness. Bake 12 minutes or until set. Let cookies stand on cookie sheets 2 minutes. Remove cookies with spatula to wire racks; cool completely. Melt semisweet chocolate chips and 1½ teaspoons shortening in top of double boiler over hot, not boiling, water. Dip one side of each cookie into chocolate, coating one third the way up; place on waxed paper. Let stand until chocolate is set, about 30 minutes. Melt milk chocolate chips with 1½ teaspoons shortening in top of double boiler over hot, not boiling, water. Dip opposite side of each cookie into chocolate, coating one third the way up; place on waxed paper. Let stand until set. Store cookies between sheets of waxed paper at room temperature.

*Makes about 2 dozen cookies*

# Easy Peanutty — Snickerdoodles —

2 tablespoons sugar
2 teaspoons ground cinnamon
1 package (15 ounces) golden sugar cookie mix
1 egg
1 tablespoon water
1 cup REESE'S® Peanut Butter Chips

Preheat oven to 375°F. In small bowl combine sugar and cinnamon. In medium bowl combine cookie mix (and enclosed flavor packet), egg and water; mix with spoon or fork until thoroughly blended. Stir in peanut butter chips. Shape dough into 1-inch balls. (If dough is too soft, cover and chill about 1 hour.) Roll balls in cinnamon-sugar. Place on ungreased cookie sheet.

Bake 8 to 10 minutes or until very lightly browned. Cool slightly; remove from cookie sheet to wire rack. Cool completely.

*Makes about 2 dozen cookies*

*Double-Dipped Chocolate Peanut Butter Cookies*

## Peanut Butter Secrets

### COOKIES

1¼ cups firmly packed light brown sugar
¾ cup creamy peanut butter
½ CRISCO® Stick or ½ cup CRISCO all-vegetable shortening
3 tablespoons milk
1 tablespoon vanilla
1 egg
1¾ cups all-purpose flour
¾ teaspoon salt
¾ teaspoon baking soda
40 to 45 chocolate-covered miniature peanut butter cups, unwrapped

### GLAZE

1 teaspoon BUTTER FLAVOR* CRISCO all-vegetable shortening
1 cup semi-sweet chocolate chips
2 tablespoons creamy peanut butter

*Butter Flavor Crisco is artificially flavored.*

**1. Heat** oven to 375°F. **Place** sheets of foil on countertop for cooling cookies.

**2. For Cookies, combine** brown sugar, peanut butter, shortening, milk and vanilla in large bowl. **Beat** at medium speed of electric mixer until well blended. **Add** egg. **Beat** just until blended.

**3. Combine** flour, salt and baking soda. **Add** to creamed mixture at low speed. **Mix** just until blended.

**4. Form** rounded teaspoonfuls of dough around each peanut butter cup. **Enclose** entirely. **Place** 2 inches apart on ungreased cookie sheets.

**5. Bake** one cookie sheet at a time at 375°F for 7 to 8 minutes or until set and just beginning to brown. *Do not overbake.* **Cool** 2 minutes on cookie sheets. **Remove** cookies to foil to cool completely.

**6. For Glaze, combine** shortening, chocolate chips and peanut butter in microwave-safe bowl. **Microwave** at MEDIUM (50% power). **Stir** after 1 minute. **Repeat** until smooth. **Dip** cookie tops in glaze.

*Makes about 3½ dozen cookies*

## Ice Cream Cookie Sandwich

2 pints chocolate chip ice cream, softened
1 package DUNCAN HINES® Moist Deluxe Dark Dutch Fudge Cake Mix
½ cup butter or margarine, softened

**1.** Line bottom of 9-inch round cake pan with aluminum foil. Spread ice cream in pan; freeze until firm. Run knife around edge of pan to loosen ice cream. Remove from pan; wrap in foil and return to freezer.

**2.** Preheat oven to 350°F. Line bottoms of two 9-inch round cake pans with aluminum foil. Place cake mix in large bowl. Add butter; mix thoroughly until crumbs form. Place half the cake mix in each pan; press lightly. Bake 15 minutes or until browned around edges; do not overbake. Cool 10 minutes; remove from pans. Remove foil from cookie layers; cool completely.

**3.** To assemble, place one cookie layer on serving plate. Top with ice cream. Peel off foil. Place second cookie layer on top. Wrap in foil and freeze 2 hours. Let stand at room temperature for 5 to 10 minutes before cutting.          *Makes 10 to 12 servings*

## Chocolate Chip Rugalach

1 cup (2 sticks) butter or margarine, slightly softened
2 cups all-purpose flour
1 cup vanilla ice cream, softened
½ cup strawberry jam
1 cup BAKER'S® Semi-Sweet Real Chocolate Chips
1 cup finely chopped nuts
    Powdered sugar

**BEAT** butter and flour. Beat in ice cream until well blended. Divide dough into 4 balls; wrap each in waxed paper. Refrigerate until firm, about 1 hour.

**PREHEAT** oven to 350°F. Roll dough, one ball at a time, on floured surface into 11×6-inch rectangle, about ⅛ inch thick. Spread with 2 tablespoons of the jam; sprinkle with ¼ cup of the chips and ¼ cup of the nuts. Roll up lengthwise as for jelly roll. Place on ungreased cookie sheet. Cut 12 diagonal slits in roll, being careful not to cut all the way through. Repeat with the remaining dough.

**BAKE** for 35 minutes or until golden brown. Cool 5 minutes on cookie sheet. Cut through each roll; separate pieces. Finish cooling on wire racks. Sprinkle with powdered sugar, if desired.

*Makes 4 dozen pieces*

## Nestlé® Crunch Pizza Cookie

1 cup plus 2 tablespoons all-purpose flour
¼ teaspoon baking soda
¼ teaspoon salt
½ cup (1 stick) butter or margarine, softened
6 tablespoons granulated sugar
6 tablespoons packed brown sugar
1 egg
½ teaspoon vanilla extract
1¾ cups (8-ounce package) NESTLÉ® CRUNCH Baking Pieces, *divided*
½ cup peanut butter

**COMBINE** flour, baking soda and salt in small bowl.

**BEAT** butter, granulated sugar and brown sugar in large mixer bowl. Beat in egg and vanilla. Gradually beat in flour mixture. Stir in ½ *cup* Crunch Baking Pieces. Spread or pat dough onto bottom of greased 13×9-inch baking pan or 12-inch pizza pan.

**BAKE** in preheated 350°F oven for 14 to 18 minutes or until set and deep golden brown. Remove from oven. Drop peanut butter by spoonfuls onto hot crust; let stand for 5 minutes to soften. Gently spread over crust. Sprinkle *remaining* Crunch Baking Pieces in single layer over peanut butter. Serve warm or at room temperature.          *Makes about 12 servings*

# Espresso Chocolate Chip Kisses

1¼ cups firmly packed light brown sugar
¾ BUTTER FLAVOR* CRISCO® Stick or ¾ cup BUTTER FLAVOR CRISCO all-vegetable shortening
2 tablespoons milk
1 teaspoon vanilla
½ teaspoon brandy extract
1 egg
1¾ cups all-purpose flour
1 teaspoon instant coffee
1 teaspoon salt
¾ teaspoon baking soda
⅓ cup milk chocolate chips
⅓ cup semi-sweet chocolate chips
½ cup coarsely chopped walnuts (optional)**
32 chocolate kisses, unwrapped

*Butter Flavor Crisco is artifically flavored.

**If nuts are omitted, add an additional ½ cup semi-sweet chocolate chips.

**1. Heat** oven to 375°F. **Place** sheets of foil on countertop for cooling cookies.

**2. Combine** brown sugar, shortening, milk, vanilla and brandy extract in large bowl. **Beat** at medium speed of electric mixer until well blended. **Beat** egg into creamed mixture.

**3. Combine** flour, instant coffee, salt and baking soda. **Mix** into creamed mixture just until blended. **Stir** in milk and semi-sweet chocolate chips and walnut pieces, if desired.

**4. Drop** rounded measuring tablespoonfuls of dough 3 inches apart onto ungreased baking sheets.

**5. Bake** one baking sheet at a time at 375°F for 8 to 10 minutes for chewy cookies or 11 to 13 minutes for crisp cookies. *Do not overbake.* **Place** 1 chocolate kiss in center of each cookie. **Cool** 2 minutes on baking sheets. **Remove** to foil to cool completely.

*Makes about 3 dozen cookies*

# Cocoa Kiss Cookies

1 cup (2 sticks) butter or margarine, softened
⅔ cup sugar
1 teaspoon vanilla extract
1⅔ cups all-purpose flour
¼ cup HERSHEY®'S Cocoa
1 cup finely chopped pecans
1 bag (9 ounces) HERSHEY®'S KISSES Milk Chocolates
Powdered sugar

In large bowl, beat butter, sugar and vanilla until creamy. Stir together flour and cocoa; gradually add to butter mixture, beating until blended. Add pecans; beat until well blended. Refrigerate dough about 1 hour or until firm enough to handle. Heat oven to 375°F. Remove wrappers from chocolate pieces. Mold scant tablespoon of dough around each chocolate piece, covering completely. Shape into balls. Place on ungreased cookie sheet. Bake 10 to 12 minutes or until set. Cool slightly, about 1 minute; remove from cookie sheet to wire rack. Cool completely. Roll in powdered sugar. Roll in sugar again just before serving, if desired.

*Makes about 4½ dozen cookies*

*Espresso Chocolate Chip Kisses*

# Danish Raspberry Ribbons

1 cup butter, softened
½ cup granulated sugar
1 large egg
2 tablespoons milk
2 tablespoons vanilla
¼ teaspoon almond extract
2⅔ cups all-purpose flour
6 tablespoons seedless raspberry jam
   Glaze (recipe follows)

Beat butter and sugar in large bowl with electric mixer at medium speed until light and fluffy, scraping down side of bowl once. Beat in egg, milk, vanilla and almond extract until well blended, scraping down side of bowl once. Gradually add 1½ cups flour. Beat at low speed until well blended, scraping down side of bowl occasionally. Stir in enough remaining flour with spoon to form stiff dough. Form dough into a disc; wrap in plastic wrap and refrigerate until firm, at least 30 minutes or overnight.

Preheat oven to 375°F. Cut dough into 6 equal pieces. Rewrap 3 dough pieces and return to refrigerator. Shape remaining 3 pieces of dough into 12-inch-long, ¾-inch-thick ropes. Place ropes 2 inches apart on ungreased cookie sheets. Make a lengthwise ¼-inch-deep groove down center of each rope. Bake 12 minutes. Take strips out of oven; spoon 1 tablespoon jam along each groove. Return to oven; bake 5 to 7 minutes longer or until strips are light golden brown. Cool strips 15 minutes on cookie sheets.

Prepare Glaze. Drizzle strips with Glaze; let stand 5 minutes. Cut cookie strips at 45° angle into 1-inch slices. Remove cookies with spatula to wire racks; cool completely. Repeat with remaining dough.

Store tightly covered between sheets of waxed paper at room temperature.

*Makes about 5½ dozen cookies*

## Glaze

½ cup powdered sugar
1 tablespoon milk
1 teaspoon vanilla

Blend ingredients in small bowl until smooth. *Makes scant ¼ cup glaze*

*Danish Raspberry Ribbons*

# — Almond Biscotti —

¼ cup finely chopped slivered
  almonds
½ cup sugar
2 tablespoons margarine
4 large egg whites, lightly beaten
2 teaspoons almond extract
2 cups all-purpose flour
2 teaspoons baking powder
¼ teaspoon salt

Preheat oven to 375°F. Place almonds in small baking pan. Bake 7 to 8 minutes or until golden brown. (Watch almonds carefully; they burn easily.) Set aside.

Beat sugar and margarine in medium bowl with electric mixer until smooth. Add egg whites and almond extract; mix well. Combine flour, baking powder and salt in large bowl; mix well. Stir egg white mixture and almonds into flour mixture until well blended.

Spray two 9×5-inch loaf pans with nonstick cooking spray. Evenly divide dough between prepared pans; spread dough evenly onto bottoms of pans with wet fingertips. Bake 15 minutes or until knife inserted in centers comes out clean. Remove from oven; turn out onto cutting board.

As soon as loaves are cool enough to handle, cut each loaf into 16 (½-inch-thick) slices. Place slices on baking sheets covered with parchment paper or sprayed with cooking spray. Bake 5 minutes; turn over. Bake 5 minutes more or until golden brown. Serve warm or cool completely and store in airtight container.

*Makes 32 biscotti*

# Gooey Caramel — Chocolate Bars —

2 cups all-purpose flour
1 cup granulated sugar
¼ teaspoon salt
4 sticks butter or margarine, divided
1 cup packed light brown sugar
⅓ cup light corn syrup
1 cup (6 ounces) semisweet chocolate
  chips

Preheat oven to 350°F. Line 13×9-inch baking pan with foil. Combine flour, granulated sugar and salt in medium bowl; stir until blended. Cut in 1¾ sticks (14 tablespoons) butter until mixture resembles coarse crumbs. Press onto bottom of prepared pan.

Bake 18 to 20 minutes until lightly browned around edges. Remove pan to wire rack; cool completely.

Combine 2 sticks butter, brown sugar and corn syrup in heavy, medium saucepan. Cook over medium heat 5 to 8 minutes or until mixture boils, stirring frequently. Boil gently 2 minutes, without stirring. Immediately pour over cooled base; spread evenly to edges of pan with metal spatula. Cool completely.

Melt chocolate in double boiler over hot (not boiling) water. Stir in remaining 2 tablespoons butter. Pour over cooled caramel layer and spread evenly to edges of pan with metal spatula. Refrigerate 10 to 15 minutes until chocolate begins to set. Remove; cool completely. Cut into bars.

*Makes 3 dozen bars*

*Almond Biscotti*

# Oatmeal Carmelita Bars

¾ BUTTER FLAVOR* CRISCO® Stick or ¾ cup BUTTER FLAVOR CRISCO all-vegetable shortening, melted
1½ cups quick oats (not instant or old fashioned), uncooked
¾ cup firmly packed brown sugar
½ cup all-purpose flour
½ cup whole wheat flour
½ teaspoon baking soda
¼ teaspoon cinnamon
1⅓ cups milk chocolate chips
½ cup chopped walnuts
1 jar (12.5 ounces) *or* ¾ cup caramel ice cream topping
3 tablespoons all-purpose flour

*Butter Flavor Crisco is artificially flavored.*

**1. Preheat** oven to 350°F. **Grease** bottom and sides of 9×9×2-inch pan with shortening.

**2. Combine** ¾ cup shortening, oats, sugar, ½ cup all-purpose flour, whole wheat flour, baking soda and cinnamon in large bowl. **Mix** at low speed of electric mixer until crumbs form. **Reserve** ½ cup for topping. **Press** remaining crumbs into pan.

**3. Bake** for 10 minutes. **Sprinkle** chocolate chips and nuts over crust.

**4. Combine** caramel topping and 3 tablespoons all-purpose flour. **Stir** until well blended. **Drizzle** over chocolate chips and nuts. **Sprinkle** reserved crumbs over caramel topping.

**5. Return** to oven. **Bake** for 20 to 25 minutes or until golden brown. **Run** spatula around edge of pan before cooling. **Cool** completely in pan on wire rack. **Cut** into bars.　　*Makes 3 dozen bars*

# Luscious Lemon Bars

4 teaspoons lemon peel
2 cups all-purpose flour
1 cup butter
½ cup powdered sugar
¼ teaspoon salt
1 cup granulated sugar
3 large eggs
⅓ cup fresh lemon juice
Sifted powdered sugar

Preheat oven to 350°F. Grease 13×9-inch baking pan. Place 1 teaspoon lemon peel, flour, butter, powdered sugar and salt in food processor. Process until mixture forms coarse crumbs. Press mixture evenly into prepared pan. Bake 18 to 20 minutes or until golden brown. Beat remaining 3 teaspoons lemon peel, granulated sugar, eggs and lemon juice in medium bowl with electric mixer at medium speed until well blended. Pour over warm crust. Return to oven; bake 18 to 20 minutes or until center is set and edges are golden brown. Remove pan to wire rack; cool completely. Dust with sifted powdered sugar; cut into 2×1½-inch bars. Store tightly covered at room temperature. Do not freeze.

*Makes 3 dozen bars*

*Luscious Lemon Bars*

## Fudgy Chocolate Mint Oatmeal Squares

1¼ cups all-purpose flour
½ teaspoon baking soda
1 cup packed brown sugar
½ cup (1 stick) butter or margarine, softened
1 egg
1½ cups oats
1 cup chopped nuts
1½ cups (10-ounce package) NESTLÉ® TOLL HOUSE® Mint-Chocolate Morsels
1¼ cups (14-ounce can) CARNATION® Sweetened Condensed Milk
2 tablespoons butter or margarine

**COMBINE** flour and baking soda in small bowl. Beat sugar and ½ cup butter in large mixer bowl until creamy. Beat in egg. Gradually beat in flour mixture. Stir in oats and nuts. Press 2 cups oat mixture onto bottom of greased 13×9-inch baking pan with dampened fingers.

**MELT** morsels, sweetened condensed milk and 2 tablespoons butter in heavy saucepan over low heat, stirring constantly until smooth; pour over crust. Crumble remaining oat mixture over filling.

**BAKE** in preheated 350°F oven for 25 to 30 minutes or until filling is set and topping begins to brown. Cool in pan on wire rack.

*Makes about 2½ dozen squares*

## Mississippi Mud Brownies

1 package DUNCAN HINES® Fudge Brownie Mix, Family Size
2 eggs
⅓ cup water
⅓ cup CRISCO® Oil or CRISCO® PURITAN® Canola Oil
1 jar (7 ounces) marshmallow creme
1 container (16 ounces) DUNCAN HINES® Creamy Homestyle Milk Chocolate Layer Cake Frosting, melted

**1.** Preheat oven to 350°F. Grease bottom of 13×9-inch pan.

**2.** Combine brownie mix, eggs, water and oil in large bowl. Stir with spoon until well blended, about 50 strokes. Spread in pan. Bake at 350°F for 25 to 28 minutes or until set.

**3.** Spread marshmallow creme gently over hot brownies. Pour 1¼ cups melted milk chocolate frosting over marshmallow cream. Swirl with knife to marbleize. Cool completely. Cut into bars.

*Makes 20 to 24 brownies*

**Note:** *Store leftover melted frosting in original container. Refrigerate.*

# Rich Chocolate Caramel Brownies

1 package (18.25 to 18.5 ounces) devil's food or chocolate cake mix
1 cup chopped nuts
½ cup (1 stick) butter or margarine, melted
1 cup *undiluted* CARNATION® Evaporated Milk, *divided*
35 (10 ounces) light caramels, unwrapped
1 cup (6 ounces) NESTLÉ® TOLL HOUSE® Semi-Sweet Chocolate Morsels

**COMBINE** cake mix and nuts in large bowl; stir in butter. Stir in ⅔ *cup* evaporated milk (batter will be thick). Spread half of batter into greased 13×9-inch baking pan.

**BAKE** in preheated 350°F oven for 15 minutes.

**COMBINE** caramels and *remaining* evaporated milk in small saucepan; stir over low heat until caramels are melted. Sprinkle chocolate morsels over baked layer; drizzle caramel mixture over top. Drop remaining batter by heaping teaspoons over caramel mixture. Return to 350°F oven for 20 to 25 minutes (top layer will be soft). Cool completely on wire rack.          *Makes about 48 brownies*

# Outrageous Brownies

½ cup MIRACLE WHIP® Salad Dressing
2 eggs, beaten
¼ cup cold water
1 (21.5-ounce) package fudge brownie mix
3 (7-ounce) milk chocolate bars, divided
Walnut halves (optional)

**PREHEAT** oven to 350°F.

**MIX** together salad dressing, eggs and water until well blended. Stir in brownie mix, mixing just until moistened.

**COARSELY** chop 2 chocolate bars; stir into brownie mixture. Pour into greased 13×9-inch baking pan.

**BAKE** 30 to 35 minutes or until edges begin to pull away from sides of pan. Immediately top with 1 chopped chocolate bar. Let stand about 5 minutes or until melted; spread evenly over brownies. Garnish with walnut halves, if desired. Cool. Cut into squares.

*Makes about 24 brownies*

# Decadent Blonde Brownies

1½ cups all-purpose flour

1 teaspoon baking powder

½ teaspoon salt

½ cup butter or margarine, softened

¾ cup granulated sugar

¾ cup packed light brown sugar

2 large eggs

2 teaspoons vanilla

1 package (10 ounces) semisweet chocolate chunks*

1 jar (3½ ounces) macadamia nuts, coarsely chopped to measure ¾ cup

*If chocolate chunks are not available, cut 10-ounce-thick chocolate candy bar into ½-inch pieces to equal 1½ cups.

Preheat oven to 350°F. Grease 13×9-inch baking pan. Combine flour, baking powder and salt in small bowl.

Beat butter, granulated sugar and brown sugar in large bowl with electric mixer at medium speed until light and fluffy. Beat in eggs and vanilla. Add flour mixture. Beat at low speed until well blended. Stir in chocolate chunks and macadamia nuts. Spread batter evenly into prepared baking pan. Bake 25 to 30 minutes or until golden brown. Remove pan to wire rack; cool completely. Cut into 3¼×1½-inch bars.

*Makes 2 dozen brownies*

# Marshmallow Krispie Bars

1 package DUNCAN HINES® Fudge Brownie Mix, Family Size

1 package (10½ ounces) miniature marshmallows

1½ cups semi-sweet chocolate chips

1 cup JIF® Creamy Peanut Butter

1 tablespoon butter or margarine

1½ cups crisp rice cereal

**1.** Preheat oven to 350°F. Grease bottom of 13×9-inch pan.

**2.** Prepare and bake brownies following package directions for basic recipe. Remove from oven. Sprinkle marshmallows on hot brownies. Return to oven. Bake for 3 minutes longer.

**3.** Place chocolate chips, Jif® Creamy Peanut Butter and butter in medium saucepan. Cook over low heat, stirring constantly, until chips are melted. Add rice cereal; mix well. Spread mixture over marshmallow layer. Refrigerate until chilled. Cut into bars.

*Makes about 2 dozen bars*

**Tip:** For a special presentation, cut cookies into diamond shapes.

*Decadent Blonde Brownies*

## —— Mint Truffles ——

**1 package (10 ounces) mint chocolate chips**
**⅓ cup whipping cream**
**¼ cup butter or margarine**
**1 container (3½ ounces) chocolate sprinkles**

Melt chips with whipping cream and butter in heavy, medium saucepan over low heat, stirring occasionally. Pour into pie pan. Refrigerate until mixture is fudgy, but soft, about 2 hours.

Shape tablespoonfuls of the mixture into 1¼-inch balls. Place balls on waxed paper. Place sprinkles in shallow bowl. Roll balls in sprinkles; place in petit four or candy cases. (If coating mixture won't stick because truffle has set, roll between your palms until outside is soft.) Truffles can be refrigerated 2 to 3 days or frozen several weeks. *Makes about 24 truffles*

## White Chocolate —— Truffles ——

**12 ounces white chocolate, coarsely chopped**
**⅓ cup whipping cream**
**2 tablespoons orange liqueur**
**1 teaspoon grated orange zest**
**1 to 1¼ cups powdered sugar**

Melt white chocolate with whipping cream in heavy, medium saucepan over low heat, stirring constantly. Whisk in liqueur and zest until blended. Pour into pie pan. Refrigerate until mixture is fudgy, but soft, about 2 hours.

Shape tablespoonfuls of the mixture into 1¼-inch balls. Place balls on waxed paper. Sift sugar into shallow bowl. Roll balls in sugar; place in petit four or candy cases. Truffles can be refrigerated 2 to 3 days or frozen several weeks.

*Makes about 36 truffles*

## – Coconut Bonbons –

**2 cups powdered sugar**
**1 cup flaked coconut**
**3 tablespoons evaporated milk**
**2 tablespoons butter or margarine, softened**
**1 teaspoon vanilla**
**1 cup (6 ounces) semisweet chocolate chips**
**1 tablespoon shortening**

Line baking sheet with waxed paper; set aside. Combine sugar, coconut, evaporated milk, butter and vanilla in medium bowl. Shape into ½-inch balls, using about ½ teaspoonfuls of mixture; place on prepared baking sheet. Refrigerate until firm. Melt chips with shortening in heavy, small saucepan over very low heat, stirring constantly. Dip bonbons in melted chocolate. Remove excess chocolate by scraping bottoms of bonbons across rim of saucepan; return to prepared baking sheet. Refrigerate until firm; store in refrigerator. *Makes about 24 bonbons*

*Mint Truffles*

## Double Chocolate Truffles

½ cup whipping cream
1 tablespoon butter or margarine
4 bars (1 ounce each) HERSHEY'S
    Semi-Sweet Baking Chocolate,
    broken into pieces
1 HERSHEY'S Milk Chocolate Bar
    (7 ounces), broken into pieces
1 tablespoon amaretto (almond-
    flavored liqueur) *or* ¼ to
    ½ teaspoon almond extract
Ground almonds

In small saucepan, combine whipping cream and butter. Cook over medium heat, stirring constantly, just until mixture is very hot. *Do not boil.* Remove from heat; add chocolate, chocolate bar pieces and liqueur. Stir with whisk until smooth. Press plastic wrap directly onto surface; cool several hours or until mixture is firm enough to handle. Shape into 1-inch balls; roll in almonds to coat. Refrigerate until firm, about 2 hours. Store in tightly covered container in refrigerator.

*Makes about 2 dozen candies*

## Peanut Butter Fudge

1 (16-ounce) box DOMINO® Light
    Brown Sugar (approximately
    2¼ cups)
½ cup milk
2 tablespoons butter
¾ cup peanut butter
1 teaspoon vanilla
½ cup chopped peanuts

Butter a 9×5-inch loaf pan; set aside. Heat sugar, milk and butter in a heavy, 2-quart saucepan. Bring to a boil, stirring constantly until the sugar is dissolved. Continue boiling 5 minutes longer, stirring constantly. Cool 10 minutes. Add peanut butter, vanilla and peanuts. Stir until well blended. Pour into prepared pan. Refrigerate at least 3 hours.

*Makes about 27 candies*

## Rum Truffles

2 cups (12 ounces) semisweet
    chocolate chips
½ cup whipping cream
1½ teaspoons rum extract
1 teaspoon vanilla
½ cup powdered sugar
¼ cup unsweetened cocoa powder

Melt chips with whipping cream in heavy, medium saucepan over low heat, stirring occasionally. Whisk in rum extract and vanilla until blended. Pour into pie pan. Refrigerate until mixture is fudgy, but soft, about 1 hour 15 minutes.

Shape tablespoonfuls of the mixture into 1¼-inch balls. Place balls on waxed paper. Sift powdered sugar and cocoa into shallow bowl. Roll balls in sugar-cocoa mixture; place in petit four or candy cases. (If coating mixture won't stick because truffle has set, roll between your palms until outside is soft.) Truffles can be refrigerated 2 to 3 days or frozen several weeks. *Makes about 30 truffles*

*Double Chocolate Truffles*

# Double Chocolate-Creme Fudge

4 cups sugar
1 can (12 ounces) evaporated milk
2 cups (11½ ounces) milk chocolate chips
1 cup (6 ounces) semisweet chocolate chips
1 jar (7 ounces) marshmallow creme
¼ cup butter or margarine
   Dash salt
1 teaspoon vanilla
2½ to 3 cups chopped pecans, divided

Butter 13×9-inch baking pan; set aside. Lightly butter side of heavy, large saucepan. Combine sugar, evaporated milk, both chips, marshmallow creme, butter and salt in prepared saucepan. Cook over medium heat, stirring constantly, until sugar dissolves and mixture comes to a boil. Wash down side of pan with pastry brush frequently dipped in hot water to remove sugar crystals.

Add candy thermometer. Stir mixture occasionally. Continue to cook until mixture reaches the soft-ball stage (238°F). Pour into large heat-proof mixer bowl. Cool to lukewarm (about 110°F).

Add vanilla and beat with heavy-duty electric mixer until thick. Beat in 1 cup of chopped pecans when candy starts to lose its gloss. Immediately spread into prepared pan. Sprinkle remaining chopped pecans over fudge; gently press into fudge. Score fudge into squares with knife. Refrigerate until firm. Cut into squares. Store in refrigerator.

*Makes about 4 pounds*

# Peanut Butter Cups

2 cups (12 ounces) semisweet chocolate chips
1 cup (6 ounces) milk chocolate chips
1½ cups confectioners' sugar
1 cup crunchy or smooth peanut butter
½ cup vanilla wafer crumbs (about 11 wafers)
6 tablespoons butter or margarine, softened

Line 12 (2½-inch) muffin cups with double-thickness paper cups or foil cups; set aside. Melt both chips in heavy, small saucepan over very low heat, stirring constantly. Spoon about 1 tablespoonful of the chocolate into each cup. With back of spoon, bring chocolate up side of each cup. Refrigerate until firm, about 20 minutes. Combine sugar, peanut butter, crumbs and butter in medium bowl. Spoon 2 tablespoons of the peanut butter mixture into each chocolate cup. Spread with small spatula. Spoon about 1 tablespoon remaining chocolate over each peanut butter cup. Refrigerate until firm.

*Makes 12 cups*

**Note:** *To remove paper cups, cut slit in bottom of paper and peel paper up from bottom. Do not peel paper down from top edge.*

## English Toffee

1 cup butter or margarine
1 cup granulated sugar
1 cup BLUE DIAMOND® Chopped
   Natural Almonds
⅓ cup semi-sweet real chocolate pieces

Combine butter and sugar in heavy skillet; cook, stirring, until boiling point is reached. Boil mixture over medium heat, stirring constantly, to soft-crack stage, 270° to 280°F or until a little mixture dropped in cold water stretches into threads that are hard but not brittle. Remove from heat and stir in ½ cup of the almonds. Pour into buttered 11×7-inch pan; let stand 10 minutes or until top is set. Sprinkle chocolate over top of candy. When chocolate has melted, smooth with spatula; sprinkle remaining almonds over chocolate. Let stand until set; break into bite-size pieces.

*Makes about 1½ pounds*

## Almond Butterscotch Brittle

2 cups packed light brown sugar
⅔ cup light corn syrup
¼ cup water
¼ cup half and half
¼ cup butter
1 cup BLUE DIAMOND® Chopped
   Natural Almonds

Butter 13×9×2-inch baking pan. In large saucepan combine brown sugar, corn syrup, water and half and half; bring to a boil, stirring constantly until sugar dissolves. Cook, stirring often, until candy thermometer reaches 260°F or until small amount of mixture dropped into very cold water forms a hard ball. Add butter and cook, stirring, until 280°F is reached or until small amount of mixture dropped into very cold water separates into threads which are hard but not brittle (the soft-crack stage). Remove from heat; quickly stir in almonds. Pour into prepared pan. When set, turn out of pan and break into bite-size pieces.

*Makes about 1¼ pounds*

## Family Friendship Praline

1 cup pecan halves
½ cup butter (do not use margarine)
⅓ cup granulated sugar
⅓ cup packed light brown sugar
1 tablespoon light corn syrup
1 teaspoon vanilla

Line 8-inch round pan with foil, extending foil beyond edge of pan; butter foil lightly. Combine pecans, butter, sugars and corn syrup in medium saucepan. Bring to a boil over medium heat. Boil, stirring constantly, about 5 minutes or until mixture turns golden brown. Remove from heat; stir in vanilla. Pour mixture into prepared pan and spread evenly. Cool completely on wire rack. Remove praline from pan using foil as handles; peel off foil.

*Makes 6 to 8 servings*

# BLUE RIBBON PIES & PASTRIES

*Whether they're filled with plump and juicy fruit, nutty pecans or creamy fillings, these first-class treats are sure to satisfy every dessert craving.*

## Luscious Cranberry and Blueberry Pie

**CRUST**

    1 unbaked 9-inch Classic CRISCO® Double Crust (page 298)

    ½ teaspoon ground mace

**FILLING**

    1 can (16 ounces) whole berry cranberry sauce

    ⅓ cup packed brown sugar

    ¼ cup granulated sugar

    2 tablespoons all-purpose flour

    2 tablespoons cornstarch

    2 tablespoons orange juice

    ½ teaspoon dried grated orange peel

    ⅛ teaspoon salt

    2 cups fresh or frozen blueberries

    2 tablespoons butter or margarine

**GLAZE**

    1 egg, beaten

**1.** *For Crust,* **prepare** 9-inch Classic CRISCO® Double Crust, adding mace to flour mixture. **Roll** and press bottom crust into 9-inch pie plate. *Do not bake.* Reserve dough scraps for decorations, if desired. **Heat** oven to 425°F.

**2.** *For Filling,* **combine** cranberry sauce, brown sugar, granulated sugar, flour, cornstarch, orange juice, orange peel and salt in large bowl. **Stir** in blueberries. **Spoon** into unbaked pie crust; dot with butter. **Moisten** pastry edge with water.

**3. Roll** out top crust; lift crust onto filled pie. **Trim** ½ inch beyond edge of pie plate. **Fold** top edge under bottom crust; flute. **Cut** blossom-shaped holes in top crust to allow steam to escape.

**4. Cut** flowers or other shapes from reserved dough. **Place** on top of pie. *For Glaze,* **brush** with egg. **Bake** at 425°F for 40 minutes or until filling in center is bubbly and crust is golden brown. **Cover** edge with foil during last 10 minutes to prevent overbrowning. **Cool** to room temperature before serving.

*Makes 1 (9-inch) pie*

*Luscious Cranberry and Blueberry Pie*

## Classic CRISCO® — Double Crust —

2 cups all-purpose flour
1 teaspoon salt
¾ CRISCO® Stick or ¾ cup CRISCO all-vegetable shortening
5 tablespoons cold water (or more as needed)

**1. Combine** flour and salt in medium bowl.

**2. Cut** in shortening using pastry blender (or 2 knives) until all flour is blended in to form pea-size chunks.

**3. Sprinkle** with water, 1 tablespoon at a time. **Toss** lightly with fork until dough forms a ball.

**4. Divide** dough in half. **Press** between hands to form two 5- to 6-inch "pancakes."

**5. Traditional rolling technique:** **Flour** dough lightly. **Roll** dough for bottom crust into circle between sheets of waxed paper on dampened countertop. **Peel** off top sheet. **Trim** one inch larger than inverted 9-inch pie plate. **Loosen** dough carefully. **Fold** into quarters. **Unfold** and press into pie plate.

**6. Easy rolling technique: Flour** dough lightly. **Roll** dough for bottom crust into circle between sheets of waxed paper on dampened countertop. **Peel** off top sheet. **Trim** one inch larger than inverted 9-inch pie plate. **Slip** into pie plate. **Remove** other sheet and press pastry to fit.

**7. To assemble, trim** edge of bottom crust even with edge of pie plate. **Add** filling to unbaked pie shell. **Moisten** pastry edge with water. **Roll** top crust same as bottom. **Lift** top crust onto filled pie. **Trim** ½ inch beyond edge of pie plate. **Fold** top edge under bottom crust. **Flute. Cut** slits in top crust or prick with fork for escape of steam. **Bake** according to filling recipes.

*Makes 1 (9-inch) double crust*

## Classic Cherry — Pie —

**CRUST**
1 unbaked 9-inch Classic CRISCO® Double Crust (page 298)

**FILLING**
3 pounds pitted red tart cherries frozen with sugar, thawed*
⅓ cup granulated sugar
⅓ cup firmly packed brown sugar
¼ cup cornstarch
½ teaspoon ground cinnamon
1½ cups reserved cherry juice*
1½ tablespoons CRISCO® Stick or BUTTER FLAVOR** CRISCO all-vegetable shortening
1 tablespoon vanilla
1 teaspoon almond extract

**GLAZE**
Milk
Additional granulated sugar

*Use 2 cans (1 pound each) red tart cherries packed in water in place of frozen. Reduce cherry liquid to 1 cup.*

**Butter Flavor Crisco is artificially flavored.*

**1. Preheat** oven to 425°F.

**2. *For Filling*, drain** cherries in large strainer over bowl, reserving 1½ cups juice. **Combine** sugars, cornstarch and cinnamon in large saucepan. **Stir** in reserved 1½ cups cherry juice. **Cook** and stir on medium heat until mixture is thick and bubbly. **Boil** and stir 1 minute. **Add** cherries and cook 1 minute or until mixture comes to a boil. **Remove** from heat. **Stir** in shortening, vanilla and almond extract. **Spoon** into unbaked pie crust. **Moisten** pastry edge with water.

**3. Cover** pie with top crust. **Fold** top edge under bottom crust; flute with fingers or fork. **Cut** slits in top crust to allow steam to escape.

**4. *For Glaze*, brush** top crust with milk. **Sprinkle** with additional granulated sugar. **Bake** at 425°F for 15 minutes. ***Reduce*** *oven temperature to 350°F.*

**5. Bake** 25 minutes or until filling in center is bubbly and crust is golden brown. **Cool** until barely warm or to room temperature before serving.

*Makes 1 (9-inch) pie*

# Butterscotch
# — Crumb Apple Pie —

**FILLING**
> 4 cups pared, cored and thinly sliced tart cooking apples (about 1½ pounds)
> 2 cups (12-ounce package) NESTLÉ® TOLL HOUSE® Butterscotch Flavored Morsels, divided
> 2 tablespoons all-purpose flour
> 1 teaspoon ground cinnamon
> 1 (9-inch) unbaked pie shell

**TOPPING**
> 1 cup (½ of 12-ounce package) NESTLÉ® TOLL HOUSE® Butterscotch Flavored Morsels, reserved from above
> ¼ cup (½ stick) butter
> ¾ cup all-purpose flour
> ⅛ teaspoon salt
> Whipped cream or ice cream (optional)

**FILLING: PREHEAT** oven to 350°F. In large bowl, stir apples, 1 cup morsels, flour and cinnamon until apples are coated. Spoon into pie shell.* Bake 20 minutes.

**TOPPING: COMBINE** over hot (not boiling) water, 1 cup morsels and butter; stir until morsels are melted and mixture is smooth. Remove from heat. Add flour and salt; blend until mixture forms large crumbs. Crumble topping over hot apple mixture.

**BAKE** an additional 30 minutes or until apples are tender. Serve warm with whipped cream or ice cream, if desired.

*Makes 1 (9-inch) pie*

*\*If using frozen pie shell, use deep-dish style, thawed. Bake pie on cookie sheet.*

# – Classic Pecan Pie –

3 eggs
1 cup sugar
1 cup KARO® Light or Dark Corn
    Syrup
2 tablespoons MAZOLA® Margarine or
    butter, melted
1 teaspoon vanilla
1½ cups pecans
    Easy-As-Pie Crust (recipe follows) *or*
    1 (9-inch) frozen deep dish pie
    crust*

*\*To use prepared frozen pie crust: Do not
thaw. Preheat oven and a cookie sheet. Pour
filling into frozen crust. Bake on cookie sheet.*

Preheat oven to 350°F. In medium bowl
with fork beat eggs slightly. Add sugar,
corn syrup, margarine and vanilla; stir
until well blended. Stir in pecans. Pour
into pie crust. Bake 50 to 55 minutes or
until knife inserted halfway between
center and edge comes out clean. Cool on
wire rack.          *Makes 8 servings*

**Prep Time:** 6 minutes
**Bake Time:** 50 minutes, plus cooling

## Easy-As-Pie Crust

1¼ cups flour
⅛ teaspoon salt
½ cup MAZOLA® Margarine
2 tablespoons cold water

In medium bowl mix flour and salt. With
pastry blender or 2 knives, cut in
margarine until mixture resembles fine
crumbs. Sprinkle water over flour mixture
while tossing with fork to blend well.
Press dough firmly into ball. On lightly
floured surface roll out to 12-inch circle.
Fit loosely into 9-inch pie plate. Trim and
flute edge.          *Makes 1 (9-inch) pie crust*

**Prep Time:** 15 minutes

# Fudgey Peanut Butter Chip —— Brownie Pie ——

2 eggs
1 teaspoon vanilla extract
1 cup sugar
½ cup (1 stick) butter or margarine,
    melted
½ cup all-purpose flour
⅓ cup HERSHEY'S Cocoa
¼ teaspoon salt
⅔ cup REESE'S® Peanut Butter Chips
1 packaged butter flavored crumb
    crust (6 ounces)
    Peanut Butter Sauce (recipe follows)
    Vanilla ice cream

Heat oven to 350°F. In small mixer bowl,
lightly beat eggs and vanilla; blend in
sugar and butter. Stir together flour, cocoa
and salt. Add to egg mixture; beat until
blended. Stir in peanut butter chips. Place
crust on baking sheet; pour chocolate
mixture into crust. Bake 45 to 50 minutes
or until set; cool completely on wire rack.
Prepare Peanut Butter Sauce; serve over
pie and ice cream.          *Makes 8 servings*

## Peanut Butter Sauce

1 cup REESE'S® Peanut Butter Chips
⅓ cup milk
¼ cup whipping cream
¼ teaspoon vanilla extract

In small saucepan over low heat, combine
peanut butter chips, milk and whipping
cream. Cook, stirring constantly, until
chips are melted and mixture is smooth.
Remove from heat; stir in vanilla. Serve
warm.

*Classic Pecan Pie*

## Decadent Pie

¾ cup packed brown sugar
¾ cup corn syrup
4 squares BAKER'S® Semi-Sweet
  Chocolate
6 tablespoons margarine or butter
3 eggs
1⅓ cups BAKER'S® ANGEL FLAKE®
  Coconut
1 cup chopped pecans
1 unbaked (9-inch) pie shell
1¾ cups (4 ounces) thawed COOL
  WHIP® Whipped Topping
1 tablespoon bourbon (optional)
  Chocolate shavings (optional)

**HEAT** oven to 350°F.

**MICROWAVE** brown sugar and corn
syrup in large microwavable bowl on
HIGH 4 minutes or until boiling. Add
chocolate and margarine. *Stir until
chocolate is completely melted.* Cool
slightly.

**ADD** eggs, one at a time, beating well
after each addition. Stir in coconut and
pecans. Pour into pie shell.

**BAKE** 1 hour or until knife inserted 1
inch from center comes out clean. Cool
on wire rack.

**COMBINE** whipped topping and
bourbon; spoon or pipe onto pie. Garnish
with chocolate shavings.

*Makes 1 (9-inch) pie*

**Prep Time:** 20 minutes
**Baking Time:** 1 hour

## Praline Pie

1 (9-inch) HONEY MAID® Honey
  Graham Pie Crust
1 egg white, slightly beaten
¼ cup FLEISCHMANN'S® Margarine,
  melted
1 cup firmly packed light brown sugar
¾ cup all-purpose flour
1 teaspoon DAVIS® Baking Powder
1 egg
1 teaspoon vanilla extract
1 cup PLANTERS® Pecans, coarsely
  chopped
  Prepared whipped topping, for
  garnish

Preheat oven to 375°F. Brush pie crust
with egg white. Bake at 375°F for 5
minutes; set aside. *Decrease oven
temperature to 350°F.*

In medium bowl, with electric mixer at
low speed, beat margarine and brown
sugar until blended. Mix in flour, baking
powder, egg and vanilla until well
combined. Stir in ¾ cup pecans. Spread
into prepared crust; sprinkle top with
remaining ¼ cup pecans. Bake at 350°F
for 25 to 30 minutes or until lightly
browned and filling is set. Cool
completely on wire rack. Garnish with
whipped topping.     *Makes 6 servings*

*Top to bottom: Decadent Pie, Chocolate
Coconut Marshmallow Pie (page 308),
Chocolate Cream Pie (page 304)*

# Chocolate Cream Pie

**Chocolate Nut Crust (recipe follows)**
**6 squares BAKER'S® Semi-Sweet Chocolate**
**½ cup corn syrup**
**1½ cups heavy cream**
**1 teaspoon vanilla extract**
**Chocolate shavings (optional)**
**Sliced strawberries (optional)**

**MICROWAVE DIRECTIONS: PREPARE** Chocolate Nut Crust. Microwave chocolate, corn syrup and ½ cup cream in large microwavable bowl on HIGH 2 minutes. *Stir until chocolate is completely melted.* Stir in vanilla. Cool to room temperature.

**BEAT** remaining 1 cup cream until soft peaks form. Gently stir in chocolate mixture. Spoon into Chocolate Nut Crust. Refrigerate until firm, about 4 hours. Garnish with additional whipped cream, chocolate shavings and strawberries.

*Makes 1 (9-inch) pie*

**Prep Time:** 30 minutes
**Chill Time:** 4 hours

## Chocolate Nut Crust

**6 squares BAKER'S® Semi-Sweet Chocolate**
**1 tablespoon margarine or butter**
**1½ cups toasted finely chopped nuts**

**MICROWAVE DIRECTIONS: LINE** 9-inch pie plate with foil.

**MICROWAVE** chocolate and margarine in large microwavable bowl on HIGH 2 minutes or until margarine is melted. *Stir until chocolate is completely melted.*

**STIR** in nuts. Press mixture onto bottom and up side of prepared pie plate. Refrigerate until firm, about 1 hour. Remove crust from pie plate; peel off foil. Return crust to pie plate or place on serving plate. Refrigerate.

*Makes 1 (9-inch) crust*

# Black Bottom Banana Cream Pie

**1 (9-inch) HONEY MAID® Honey Graham Pie Crust**
**1 egg white, slightly beaten**
**¼ cup heavy cream**
**4 (1-ounce) squares semisweet chocolate**
**¼ cup PLANTERS® Dry Roasted Peanuts, coarsely chopped**
**1 small banana, sliced**
**1 (3⅜-ounce) package ROYAL® Instant Vanilla Pudding & Pie Filling**
**2 cups cold milk**
**Whipped topping, for garnish**
**Additional coarsely chopped PLANTERS® Dry Roasted Peanuts, for garnish**

Preheat oven to 375°F. Brush pie crust with egg white. Bake at 375°F for 5 minutes; set aside. In small saucepan, over low heat, cook heavy cream and chocolate until chocolate melts. Stir in peanuts. Spread evenly into pie crust. Arrange banana slices over chocolate; set aside. Prepare pudding according to package directions for pie using cold milk; carefully pour over bananas. Chill at least 2 hours. Garnish with whipped topping and additional chopped peanuts.

*Makes 8 servings*

*Black Bottom Banana Cream Pie*

## – Boston Cream Pie –

1 cup granulated sugar
⅓ cup shortening
1 egg
1 teaspoon vanilla
1¼ cups all-purpose flour
1½ teaspoons baking powder
½ teaspoon salt
¾ cup milk
Cream Filling (recipe follows)
Chocolate Glaze (recipe follows)

Preheat oven to 350°F. Grease and flour 9-inch round cake pan. Beat together granulated sugar and shortening in large bowl until light and fluffy. Blend in egg and vanilla. Combine flour, baking powder and salt in small bowl. Add flour mixture to sugar mixture alternately with milk, beating well after each addition. Pour into prepared pan. Bake 35 minutes or until wooden toothpick inserted in center comes out clean. Cool in pan 10 minutes. Meanwhile, prepare Cream Filling. Loosen edge of cake and remove to rack to cool completely. Prepare Chocolate Glaze. When cake is cool, split in half horizontally to make 2 thin layers. To assemble, spoon Cream Filling over bottom half of cake; cover with top half. Spread top with Chocolate Glaze; cool. Serve when glaze is completely set. Refrigerate.

*Makes 1 (9-inch) pie*

**Cream Filling:** Combine ⅓ cup granulated sugar, 2 tablespoons cornstarch and ¼ teaspoon salt in 2-quart saucepan. Gradually stir in 1½ cups milk. Cook over medium heat, stirring constantly, until mixture thickens and comes to a boil. Boil 1 minute, stirring constantly. Gradually stir small amount of hot mixture into 2 slightly beaten egg yolks; mix thoroughly. Return to hot mixture in pan. Bring to a boil; boil 1 minute, stirring constantly. *Do not overcook.* Remove from heat; stir in 2 teaspoons vanilla. Cool to room temperature. Chill.

**Chocolate Glaze:** Combine 2 (1-ounce) squares unsweetened chocolate and 3 tablespoons butter in medium saucepan; stir over low heat until melted. Remove from heat; stir in 1 cup sifted powdered sugar and 1 teaspoon vanilla. Stir in 3 to 5 teaspoons water, 1 teaspoon at a time, until glaze is of desired consistency. Cool slightly.

## Chocolate Satin Pie

1½ cups (12-ounce can) *undiluted* CARNATION® Evaporated Milk
2 egg yolks
2 cups (12-ounce package) NESTLÉ® TOLL HOUSE® Semi-Sweet Chocolate Morsels
1 prepared 8-inch (6 ounces) chocolate crumb crust
Whipped cream (optional)
Chopped nuts (optional)

**WHISK** together evaporated milk and egg yolks in 2-quart saucepan. Heat over medium-low heat, stirring constantly, until mixture is very hot and thickens slightly; *do not boil.* Remove from heat; stir in morsels until chocolate is completely melted and mixture is very smooth.

**POUR** into crust; chill until firm. Top with whipped cream and sprinkle with nuts.

*Makes 10 servings*

*Boston Cream Pie*

# Chocolate Coconut Marshmallow Pie

**CRUST**
2 cups BAKER'S® ANGEL FLAKE® Coconut
½ cup chopped pecans
½ cup (1 stick) margarine or butter, melted

**FILLING**
4 squares BAKER'S® Semi-Sweet Chocolate
2 cups KRAFT® Miniature Marshmallows
½ cup milk
1 package (3 ounces) PHILADELPHIA BRAND® Cream Cheese, softened
3½ cups (8 ounces) thawed COOL WHIP® Whipped Topping
Chocolate curls (optional)

**HEAT** oven to 350°F.

**MIX** coconut, pecans and margarine in 9-inch pie plate; press onto bottom and up side of pie plate. Bake 20 minutes or until lightly browned. Cool.

**MICROWAVE** chocolate, marshmallows and milk in large microwavable bowl on HIGH 3 minutes or until marshmallows are melted. *Stir until chocolate is completely melted.*

**BEAT** in cream cheese until smooth. Refrigerate until slightly thickened. Gently stir in whipped topping. Spoon into crust. Refrigerate until firm, about 3 hours. Garnish with chocolate curls. Before cutting, dip bottom of pie plate briefly in hot water to loosen crust.

*Makes 1 (9-inch) pie*

# Chocolate Macaroon Heath® Pie

½ cup butter or margarine, melted
3 cups shredded coconut
2 tablespoons all-purpose flour
1 package (6 ounces) HEATH® Bits *or* 1 heaping cupful crushed HEATH® Bar
½ gallon chocolate ice cream, softened

Preheat oven to 375°F. Combine butter, coconut and flour. Press into 9-inch pie pan. Bake at 375°F for 10 minutes or until edge is light golden brown. Cool to room temperature. Reserve ¼ cup Heath® Bits and set aside. Combine ice cream and remaining Heath® Bits. Spread over cooled crust. Sprinkle with reserved bits. Freeze at least 3 hours. Remove from freezer; let stand 10 minutes to soften before serving.      *Makes 6 to 8 servings*

# Key Lime Pie

2 packages (4-serving size each) *or* 1 package (8-serving size) JELL-O® Brand Lime Flavor Gelatin
2 cups boiling water
2 teaspoons grated lime peel
¼ cup lime juice
1 pint vanilla ice cream, softened
1 packaged graham cracker crumb crust
COOL WHIP® Non-Dairy Whipped Topping, thawed (optional)

**COMPLETELY** dissolve gelatin in boiling water. Add lime peel and juice. Spoon in ice cream, stirring until melted and smooth. Chill until mixture will mound from spoon.

**SPOON** gelatin mixture into crust. Chill until firm, about 2 hours. Garnish with whipped topping, if desired.

*Makes 8 servings*

**Prep Time:** 15 minutes
**Chill Time:** 2 hours

# — Three-Berry Tart —

2 cups all-purpose flour
5 tablespoons unsalted butter
¼ cup ground almonds
⅓ cup plus ½ cup sifted confectioners' sugar
5 tablespoons ice water
1 tablespoon cornstarch
⅓ cup 2% low fat milk
1 cup (4 ounces) shredded ALPINE LACE® Reduced Sodium Muenster Cheese
1½ cups low fat sour cream
1 cup vanilla nonfat yogurt
1 tablespoon vanilla extract
1 teaspoon grated lemon rind
2 cups strawberries, hulled and halved
1½ cups fresh raspberries
1½ cups fresh blueberries
1 cup peeled kiwi slices
½ cup red currant jelly

**1.** To make the almond crust: Preheat the oven to 400°F. In a medium-size bowl, mix the flour, butter, almonds and the ⅓ cup of confectioners' sugar with your fingers until coarse crumbs form. Add enough ice water to form a dough. Press onto the bottom and up the side of a 12-inch tart pan with a removable bottom. Prick the dough at ½-inch intervals with the tines of a fork and bake for 15 minutes or until golden brown.

**2.** Meanwhile, to make the cheese filling: In a small saucepan, dissolve the cornstarch in the milk. Stir in the cheese and cook over medium heat until the mixture is slightly thickened and smooth. Cool for 15 minutes.

**3.** In a medium-size bowl, with an electric mixer set on medium-high, beat the sour cream, yogurt, the remaining ½ cup of confectioners' sugar, the vanilla and lemon rind for 1 minute. With the mixer running, slowly add the cheese mixture and beat until the filling is almost smooth. Pour into the tart shell and refrigerate for 30 minutes or until filling is thickened and cold.

**4.** To make the fresh fruit topping: Arrange the berries decoratively on top of the filling. In a small saucepan, melt the jelly over low heat, then carefully brush over the berries. Refrigerate for at least 1 hour before serving.

*Makes 16 servings*

## Strawberry — Devonshire Tart —

1 package (9-inch) sponge cake layer
   or dessert shell
⅓ cup tropical juice blend or orange
   juice
½ cup sour cream
1 tub (8 ounces) COOL WHIP®
   Whipped Topping, thawed
1 pint strawberries, hulled
⅓ cup strawberry jelly, melted
   Fresh mint leaves

**BRUSH** cake layer with juice.

**STIR** sour cream and 2½ cups of the whipped topping with wire whisk in medium bowl until blended. Spread over cake layer. Arrange strawberries, hulled side down, in center; brush with jelly. Garnish with remaining whipped topping and mint leaves.

**REFRIGERATE** until ready to serve.

*Makes 8 servings*

## — Oreo® Mud Pie —

26 OREO® Chocolate Sandwich Cookies
2 tablespoons FLEISCHMANN'S®
   Margarine, melted
1 pint chocolate ice cream, softened
2 pints coffee ice cream, softened
½ cup heavy cream, whipped
¼ cup PLANTERS® Walnuts, chopped
½ cup chocolate fudge topping

Finely crush 12 cookies; mix with margarine. Press crumb mixture onto bottom of 9-inch pie plate; stand

remaining 14 cookies around edge of plate. Place in freezer for 10 minutes. Evenly spread chocolate ice cream into prepared crust. Scoop coffee ice cream into balls; arrange over chocolate layer. Freeze 4 hours or until firm. To serve, top with whipped cream, walnuts and fudge topping. *Makes 8 servings*

## Cherry —— Turnovers ——

8 frozen phyllo dough sheets, thawed
¼ cup butter or margarine, melted
6 tablespoons no-sugar-added black
   cherry fruit spread
1½ tablespoons cherry-flavored liqueur
   (optional)
1 egg
1 teaspoon cold water

Preheat oven to 400°F. Lightly brush each phyllo sheet with butter; stack. Cut through all sheets to form six (5-inch) squares. Combine fruit spread and cherry liqueur, if desired. Place 1 tablespoon fruit spread mixture in center of each stack of eight phyllo squares; brush edges of phyllo with butter. Fold edges over to form triangle; gently press edges together to seal. Place on ungreased cookie sheet. Beat together egg and water; brush over phyllo triangles. Bake 10 minutes or until golden brown. Cool on wire rack. Serve warm or at room temperature.

*Makes 6 turnovers*

*Strawberry Devonshire Tart*

# Chocolate Truffle Tart

## CRUST

⅔ cup all-purpose flour
½ cup powdered sugar
½ cup ground walnuts
6 tablespoons butter or margarine, softened
⅓ cup NESTLÉ® Baking Cocoa

## FILLING

1¼ cups heavy whipping cream
¼ cup granulated sugar
2 cups (12-ounce package) NESTLÉ® TOLL HOUSE® Semi-Sweet Chocolate Morsels
2 tablespoons seedless raspberry jam
Sweetened whipped cream (optional)
Fresh raspberries (optional)

**FOR CRUST: BEAT** flour, sugar, walnuts, butter and cocoa in large mixer bowl until a soft dough forms. Press dough onto bottom and side of ungreased 9- or 9½-inch fluted tart pan with removeable bottom.

**BAKE** in preheated 350°F oven for 12 to 14 minutes or until puffed. Cool completely on wire rack.

**FOR FILLING: HEAT** cream and sugar in medium saucepan just until boiling, stirring occasionally. Remove from heat. Stir in morsels and jam; let stand for 5 minutes. Whisk until smooth. Transfer to small mixer bowl. Cover; chill for 45 to 60 minutes or until mixture is cool and slightly thickened.

**BEAT** for 20 to 30 seconds, just until color lightens slightly. Spoon into crust.

Chill until firm. Remove rim of pan; garnish with whipped cream and raspberries. *Makes 1 (9-inch) tart*

# Apple Strudel

1 sheet (½ of a 17¼-ounce package) frozen puff pastry
1 cup (4 ounces) shredded ALPINE LACE® Reduced Fat Cheddar Cheese
2 large Granny Smith apples, peeled, cored and sliced ⅛ inch thick (12 ounces)
⅓ cup golden raisins
2 tablespoons apple brandy (optional)
¼ cup granulated sugar
¼ cup packed light brown sugar
½ teaspoon ground cinnamon
2 tablespoons unsalted butter substitute, melted

**1.** To shape the pastry: Thaw the pastry for 20 minutes. Preheat the oven to 350°F. On a floured board, roll out the pastry into a 15×12-inch rectangle.

**2.** To make the filling: Sprinkle the cheese over the pastry, leaving a 1-inch border. Arrange the apples on top. Sprinkle with the raisins, then the brandy, if you wish. In a small cup, mix both of the sugars with the cinnamon, then sprinkle over the apple filling.

**3.** Starting from one of the wide ends, roll up jelly-roll style. Place on a baking sheet, seam side down, tucking the ends under. Using a sharp knife, make 7 diagonal slits on the top, then brush with the butter. Bake for 35 minutes or until golden brown. *Makes 18 servings*

*Apple Strudel*

# Raspberry-Filled
## – Chocolate Ravioli –

- 2 squares (1 ounce each) bittersweet or semisweet chocolate
- 1 cup butter or margarine, softened
- ½ cup granulated sugar
- 1 egg
- 1 teaspoon vanilla
- ½ teaspoon chocolate extract
- ¼ teaspoon baking soda
  Dash salt
- 2½ cups all-purpose flour
- 1 to 1¼ cups seedless raspberry jam
  Powdered sugar

Melt chocolate in top of double boiler over hot, not boiling, water. Remove from heat; cool. Mix butter and granulated sugar in large bowl until blended. Add melted chocolate, egg, vanilla, chocolate extract, baking soda and salt; beat until blended. Blend in flour to make stiff dough. Divide dough in half. Cover; refrigerate until firm.

Preheat oven to 350°F. Lightly grease cookie sheets or line with parchment paper. Roll out dough, half at a time, ⅛ inch thick between two sheets of plastic wrap. Remove top sheet of plastic. (If dough gets too soft and sticks to plastic, refrigerate until firm.) Cut dough into 1½-inch squares. Place half of the squares, 2 inches apart, on prepared cookie sheets. Place about ½ teaspoon jam on center of each square; top with another square. Using fork, press edges of squares together to seal, then pierce center of each square. Bake 10 minutes or just until edges are browned. Remove to wire racks to cool. Dust lightly with powdered sugar.

*Makes about 6 dozen ravioli*

# – Cherry Envelopes –

- 2 packages (3 ounces each) cream cheese, softened
- ⅓ cup butter or margarine, softened
- ⅓ cup granulated sugar
- ⅓ cup milk
- 2¼ cups all-purpose flour
- 1 teaspoon baking powder
- 1 teaspoon grated lemon peel
- ½ teaspoon salt
- 1 can SOLO® *or* 1 jar BAKER'S® Cherry or Blueberry Filling
- 1 egg beaten with 1 tablespoon water for brushing
  Powdered sugar

**PREHEAT** oven to 350°F. Grease 2 baking sheets; set aside. Beat cream cheese, butter, granulated sugar and milk in large bowl with electric mixer until well blended. Stir in flour, baking powder, lemon peel and salt. Knead dough in bowl 8 to 10 times or until smooth. Divide dough into equal halves.

**ROLL** out one half on lightly floured surface to 15×10-inch rectangle. Cut into six (5-inch) squares. Spoon 1 heaping tablespoonful cherry filling onto center of each pastry square. Brush edges of pastry with beaten egg mixture and bring corners into center to enclose filling. Pinch edges to seal. Place filled pastries on prepared baking sheets and brush with beaten egg mixture. Repeat with remaining pastry and cherry filling.

**BAKE** 20 to 25 minutes or until golden brown. Remove from baking sheets and cool on wire racks. Dust with powdered sugar just before serving.

*Makes 12 pastries*

# Chocolate Tassies

**PASTRY**

> 2 cups all-purpose flour
> 2 packages (3 ounces each) cold cream cheese, cut into chunks
> 1 cup cold butter or margarine, cut into chunks

**FILLING**

> 2 tablespoons butter or margarine
> 2 squares (1 ounce each) unsweetened chocolate
> 1½ cups packed brown sugar
> 2 eggs, beaten
> 2 teaspoons vanilla
> Dash salt
> 1½ cups chopped pecans

Place flour in large bowl. Cut in cream cheese and butter. Continue to mix until dough can be shaped into a ball. Wrap dough in plastic wrap; refrigerate 1 hour. Shape dough into 1-inch balls. Press each ball into ungreased miniature (1¾-inch) muffin pan cup, covering bottom and side of cup with dough.

Preheat oven to 350°F. Melt butter and chocolate in heavy, medium saucepan over low heat. Remove from heat. Blend in brown sugar, eggs, vanilla and salt; beat until thick. Stir in pecans. Spoon about 1 teaspoon filling into each unbaked pastry shell. Bake 20 to 25 minutes or until pastry is lightly browned and filling is set. Cool in pans on wire racks. Remove from pans; store in airtight containers.

*Makes about 5 dozen tassies*

# Chocolate Pecan Tassies

**CRUST**

> ½ cup (1 stick) margarine or butter
> 1 package (3 ounces) PHILADELPHIA BRAND® Cream Cheese, softened
> 1 cup all-purpose flour

**FILLING**

> 1 square BAKER'S® Unsweetened Chocolate
> 1 tablespoon margarine or butter
> ¾ cup packed brown sugar
> 1 egg
> 1 teaspoon vanilla extract
> 1 cup chopped pecans
> Powdered sugar (optional)

**MICROWAVE DIRECTIONS: BEAT** ½ cup margarine and cream cheese until well blended. Beat in flour until just blended. Wrap dough in plastic wrap; refrigerate 1 hour.

**HEAT** oven to 350°F. Microwave chocolate and 1 tablespoon margarine in large microwavable bowl on HIGH 1 minute or until margarine is melted. *Stir until chocolate is completely melted.*

**BEAT** in brown sugar, egg and vanilla until thickened. Stir in pecans.

**SHAPE** chilled dough into 36 (1-inch) balls. Flatten each ball and press onto bottoms and up sides of ungreased miniature muffin cups. Spoon about 1 teaspoon filling into each cup.

**BAKE** 20 minutes. Cool in pans on wire racks 15 minutes. Remove from pans. Sprinkle with powdered sugar.

*Makes 36 tassies*

# CHEESECAKES & CAKES

*Kick off any celebration with one of these awesome cheesecakes, cakes, shortcakes or tortes—each one overflowing with memorable made-from-scratch flavor. There's even a great selection of kid-pleasing cakes that are sure to make any child's party outstanding.*

## Marble Cheesecake

HERSHEY®S Chocolate
   Crumb Crust (page 318)
3 packages (8 ounces each)
   cream cheese, softened
1 cup sugar, divided
½ cup dairy sour cream
2½ teaspoons vanilla extract,
   divided
3 tablespoons all-purpose
   flour
3 eggs
¼ cup HERSHEY®S Cocoa
1 tablespoon vegetable oil

Prepare HERSHEY®S Chocolate Crumb Crust. Heat oven to 450°F. In large mixer bowl on medium speed of electric mixer, beat cream cheese, ¾ cup sugar, sour cream and 2 teaspoons vanilla until smooth. Gradually add flour, beating well. Add eggs, one at a time, beating well after each addition. In medium bowl, stir together cocoa and remaining ¼ cup sugar. Add oil, remaining ½ teaspoon vanilla and 1½ cups cream cheese mixture; blend well. Spoon plain and chocolate batters alternately into prepared crust, ending with spoonfuls of chocolate batter; gently swirl with knife for marbled effect. Bake 10 minutes. *Without opening oven door, reduce temperature to 250°F;* continue baking 30 minutes. Turn off oven; without opening door, leave cheesecake in oven 30 minutes. Remove from oven to wire rack. With knife, immediately loosen cheesecake from side of pan; cool completely. Refrigerate several hours or overnight; remove side of pan. Cover; refrigerate leftover cheesecake.

*Makes 10 to 12 servings*

*continued on page 318*

*Marble Cheesecake*

*Marble Cheesecake (continued)*

## HERSHEY'S Chocolate Crumb Crust

**1¼ cups vanilla wafer crumbs (about 40 wafers)**
**⅓ cup powdered sugar**
**⅓ cup HERSHEY'S Cocoa**
**¼ cup (½ stick) butter or margarine, melted**

Heat oven to 350°F. In medium bowl, stir together crumbs, powdered sugar and cocoa; blend in butter. Press mixture onto bottom and ½ inch up side of 9-inch springform pan. Bake 8 minutes; cool completely.

# Sour Cherry Cheesecake with Macadamia Nut Crust

**Macadamia Nut Crust (recipe follows)**
**1 can (16 ounces) tart red pitted cherries**
**3 packages (8 ounces each) cream cheese, softened**
**1 cup sugar**
**3 eggs**
**1 teaspoon vanilla extract**
**1⅔ cups (10-ounce package) HERSHEY'S Vanilla Milk Chips**
**Sour Cherry Sauce (recipe follows)**

Heat oven to 350°F. Prepare Macadamia Nut Crust. Drain cherries, reserving juice for sauce. Chop cherries; drain. In large mixer bowl, beat cream cheese until smooth. Add sugar, eggs and vanilla; beat until blended. In medium microwave-safe bowl, place vanilla milk chips. Microwave at HIGH (100%) 1 minute; stir. If necessary, microwave at HIGH an additional 15 seconds at a time, just until chips are melted when stirred. Blend into cream cheese mixture. Stir in chopped cherries. Pour over prepared crust. Bake 50 to 55 minutes or until almost set in center. Remove from oven to wire rack. With knife, loosen cake from side of pan. Cool completely; remove side of pan. Refrigerate about 3 hours. Prepare Sour Cherry Sauce; spoon over cheesecake. Garnish as desired. Cover; refrigerate leftover cheesecake.

*Makes 10 to 12 servings*

## Macadamia Nut Crust

**1 jar (3½ ounces) macadamia nuts, very finely chopped**
**¾ cup graham cracker crumbs**
**2 tablespoons sugar**
**¼ cup (½ stick) butter or margarine, melted**

In medium bowl, combine all ingredients. Press mixture onto bottom of 9-inch springform pan. Bake at 350°F for 8 minutes. Cool.

## Sour Cherry Sauce

**1 tablespoon cornstarch**
**2 tablespoons cherry brandy *or* ½ teaspoon almond extract**

In medium saucepan, combine cornstarch and reserved cherry juice (from cheesecake). Cook and stir over medium heat until mixture comes to a boil. Remove from heat; stir in brandy. Cool.

# Teddy Drum Cheesecake

- 2 (11-ounce) packages ROYAL® No-Bake Cheesecake
- ⅓ cup sugar
- 2 tablespoons cocoa
- ½ cup FLEISCHMANN'S® Margarine, melted
- 3 cups cold milk
- 1¾ cups TEDDY GRAHAMS® Graham Snacks, any flavor, divided
- 1 tablespoon colored sprinkles
  Black shoe string licorice, for garnish
- 2 plastic drinking straws, for garnish
- 2 large gum drops, for garnish

Mix contents of graham cracker crumb packets, sugar and cocoa; stir in margarine. Reserve ½ cup crumb mixture; press remaining crumb mixture onto bottom of 8- or 9-inch springform pan.

In large bowl, with mixer at low speed, blend milk and contents of cheesecake filling packets. Beat at medium speed 3 minutes, scraping bowl occasionally. Fold in 1½ cups graham snacks; spread into prepared pan. Sprinkle reserved crumbs and colored sprinkles around cake edge. Chill 3 to 4 hours.

To serve, remove side of pan. Decorate side of cheesecake with licorice and remaining graham snacks to resemble drum. Insert a straw in each gum drop; place on top of cake to resemble drumsticks.

*Makes 12 servings*

# Oreo® Cheesecake

- 1 (20-ounce) package OREO® Chocolate Sandwich Cookies
- ⅓ cup FLEISCHMANN'S® Margarine, melted
- 3 (8-ounce) packages cream cheese, softened
- ¾ cup sugar
- 4 eggs, at room temperature
- 1 cup dairy sour cream
- 1 teaspoon vanilla extract
  Whipped cream, for garnish

Preheat oven to 350°F. Finely roll 30 cookies; coarsely chop 20 cookies. In bowl, combine finely rolled cookie crumbs and margarine. Press onto bottom and 2 inches up side of 9-inch springform pan; set aside.

In bowl, with electric mixer at medium speed, beat cream cheese and sugar until creamy. Blend in eggs, sour cream and vanilla; fold in chopped cookies. Spread mixture into prepared crust. Bake at 350°F for 60 minutes or until set.

Cool on wire rack at room temperature. Chill at least 4 hours. Halve remaining cookies; remove side of pan. To serve, garnish with whipped cream and cookie halves.

*Makes 12 servings*

# German Chocolate Cheesecake

Coconut-Pecan Graham Crust (recipe follows)
4 bars (1 ounce each) HERSHEY᾽S Semi-Sweet Baking Chocolate, broken into pieces
3 packages (8 ounces each) cream cheese, softened
¾ cup sugar
½ cup dairy sour cream
2 teaspoons vanilla extract
2 tablespoons all-purpose flour
3 eggs
Coconut-Pecan Topping (recipe follows)

Prepare Coconut-Pecan Graham Crust. Heat oven to 450°F. In small microwave-safe bowl, place chocolate. Microwave at HIGH (100%) 1 to 1½ minutes or until chocolate is melted and smooth when stirred. In large mixer bowl on medium speed of electric mixer, beat cream cheese, sugar, sour cream and vanilla until smooth. Add flour; blend well. Add eggs and melted chocolate; beat until blended. Pour into prepared crust. Bake 10 minutes. *Without opening oven door, reduce oven temperature to 250°F.* Continue baking 35 minutes. Remove from oven to wire rack. With knife, loosen cake from side of pan. Cool completely; remove side of pan. Prepare Coconut-Pecan Topping; spread over cheesecake. Refrigerate several hours. Garnish as desired. Cover; refrigerate leftover cheesecake. *Makes 10 to 12 servings*

# Coconut-Pecan Graham Crust

1 cup graham cracker crumbs
2 tablespoons sugar
⅓ cup butter or margarine, melted
¼ cup MOUNDS® Sweetened Coconut Flakes
¼ cup chopped pecans

Heat oven to 350°F. In small bowl, combine graham cracker crumbs and sugar. Stir in butter, coconut and pecans. Press mixture onto bottom and ½ inch up side of 9-inch springform pan. Bake 8 to 10 minutes or until lightly browned. Cool completely.

## Coconut-Pecan Topping

½ cup (1 stick) butter or margarine
¼ cup packed light brown sugar
2 tablespoons light cream
2 tablespoons light corn syrup
1 cup MOUNDS® Sweetened Coconut Flakes
½ cup chopped pecans
1 teaspoon vanilla extract

In small saucepan, melt butter; add brown sugar, light cream and corn syrup. Cook over medium heat, stirring constantly, until smooth and bubbly. Remove from heat. Stir in coconut, pecans and vanilla. Cool slightly.

*Top to bottom: German Chocolate Cheesecake, Sour Cherry Cheesecake with Macadamia Nut Crust (page 318)*

# Triple Layer Cheesecake

**Chocolate Crumb Crust (recipe follows)**
**3 packages (8 ounces each) cream cheese, softened**
**¾ cup sugar**
**3 eggs**
**⅓ cup dairy sour cream**
**3 tablespoons all-purpose flour**
**1 teaspoon vanilla extract**
**¼ teaspoon salt**
**1 cup HERSHEY'S Butterscotch Chips, melted***
**1 cup HERSHEY'S Semi-Sweet Chocolate Chips, melted***
**1 cup HERSHEY'S Vanilla Milk Chips, melted***
**Triple Drizzle (recipe follows)**

*\*To melt chips, place chips in separate medium microwave-safe bowls. Microwave at HIGH (100%) 1 minute; stir. If necessary, microwave at HIGH an additional 15 seconds at a time, stirring after each heating, just until chips are melted when stirred.*

Heat oven to 350°F. Prepare Chocolate Crumb Crust. In large mixer bowl, beat cream cheese and sugar until smooth. Add eggs, sour cream, flour, vanilla and salt; beat until blended. Stir 1⅓ cups batter into melted butterscotch chips until smooth; pour into prepared crust. Stir 1⅓ cups batter into melted chocolate chips until smooth; pour over butterscotch layer. Stir remaining batter into melted vanilla milk chips until smooth; pour over chocolate layer. Bake 55 to 60 minutes or until almost set in center. Remove from oven to wire rack. With knife, loosen cake from side of pan.

Cool completely; remove side of pan. Prepare Triple Drizzle, if desired; drizzle, one flavor at a time, over top of cheesecake. Refrigerate about 3 hours. Cover; refrigerate leftover cheesecake.

*Makes 12 to 14 servings*

## Chocolate Crumb Crust

**1½ cups vanilla wafer crumbs (about 45 wafers)**
**½ cup powdered sugar**
**¼ cup HERSHEY'S Cocoa**
**⅓ cup butter or margarine, melted**

Heat oven to 350°F. In medium bowl, stir together all ingredients. Press mixture onto bottom and 1½ inches up side of 9-inch springform pan. Bake 8 minutes. Cool completely.

## Triple Drizzle

**1 tablespoon *each* HERSHEY'S Butterscotch Chips, HERSHEY'S Semi-Sweet Chocolate Chips and HERSHEY'S Vanilla Milk Chips**
**1½ teaspoons shortening (do not use butter, margarine or oil), divided**

**MICROWAVE DIRECTIONS:** In small microwave-safe bowl, place butterscotch chips and ½ teaspoon shortening. Microwave at HIGH (100%) 30 seconds; stir. If necessary, microwave on HIGH an additional 15 seconds at a time, stirring after each heating, just until chips are melted when stirred. Repeat procedure with chocolate chips and vanilla milk chips, using ½ teaspoon shortening for each.

## Chocolate Nut Cheesecake

1½ cups finely crushed chocolate wafer
    cookies
1 cup chopped toasted almonds
½ cup chopped toasted hazelnuts
    (skins removed)
⅓ cup sugar
6 tablespoons butter, melted
1 cup sugar
3 (8-ounce) packages cream cheese,
    softened
4 eggs
⅓ cup whipping cream
¼ cup hazelnut-flavored liqueur
1 teaspoon vanilla
    Topping (recipe follows)

Preheat oven to 350°F. Grease bottom and
side of 9-inch springform pan. Combine
crumbs, almonds, hazelnuts, ⅓ cup sugar
and butter in medium bowl; blend well.
Press onto bottom and up side of
prepared pan.

Beat together 1 cup sugar and cream
cheese in large bowl until smooth and
creamy. Add eggs, 1 at a time, beating well
after each addition. Blend in whipping
cream, liqueur and vanilla. Pour into crust.
Bake 40 minutes or until firm to the
touch. Let stand on wire rack 5 minutes.
Meanwhile, prepare Topping; carefully
spread over cheesecake. Return
cheesecake to oven; continue baking 5
minutes. Loosen cake from rim of pan;
cool before removing rim of pan.
Refrigerate.          *Makes 1 (9-inch) cheesecake*

**Topping:** Combine 2 cups light sour cream,
1 tablespoon sugar and 1 teaspoon vanilla in
small bowl, mixing until well blended.

## Bavarian Forest Cheesecake

**WHOPPERS® CRUST**
1 package (8 ounces) WHOPPERS®
    Malted Milk Candy, crushed
½ cup graham cracker crumbs
¼ cup butter or margarine, melted

**FILLING**
3 packages (8 ounces each) cream
    cheese, softened
½ cup sugar
1 teaspoon vanilla
6 eggs
1 package (8 ounces) WHOPPERS®
    Malted Milk Candy, crushed
    Whipped cream, additional
    WHOPPERS® Malted Milk Candy
    and maraschino cherries for
    garnish

For Whoppers® Crust, in small bowl,
combine all crust ingredients; mix well.
Grease bottom of 9-inch springform pan.
Press crust mixture onto bottom of pan.
For Filling, preheat oven to 350°F. In large
bowl, beat cream cheese until fluffy.
Gradually add sugar, beating constantly;
beat in vanilla. Add eggs, 1 at a time,
beating thoroughly after each addition.
Pour batter onto prepared crust.

Bake 30 minutes. Remove from oven;
sprinkle 1 package crushed Whoppers®
over top. Continue baking 10 minutes or
until set. Loosen cake from rim of pan;
cool completely in pan on wire rack.
Cover; refrigerate at least 2 hours. Before
serving, remove side of springform pan.
Garnish cake with whipped cream,
additional Whoppers® and cherries. Store,
covered, in refrigerator.

*Makes 10 to 12 servings*

## Mediterranean — Chocolate Cake —

### CAKE
- ¾ cup all-purpose flour
- ½ cup unsweetened cocoa powder
- ¼ teaspoon baking soda
- ¼ teaspoon ground cinnamon
- 4 large eggs
- ¼ teaspoon salt
- 1 cup granulated sugar
- 2 teaspoons finely grated lemon peel
- ⅔ cup FILIPPO BERIO® Olive Oil

### GLAZE
- 2 tablespoons water
- 1 cup powdered sugar
- ¼ cup unsweetened cocoa powder
- 1 tablespoon FILIPPO BERIO® Olive Oil
- Pinch salt

For cake, preheat oven to 350°F. Grease 9-inch round cake pan or 9-inch springform pan with olive oil. Line bottom of pan with parchment paper or waxed paper.

In small bowl, combine flour, cocoa, baking soda and cinnamon. In large bowl, whisk together eggs and salt until blended. Slowly whisk in granulated sugar and lemon peel until combined. Sift flour mixture over egg mixture; fold in with rubber spatula until blended. Fold in olive oil, 2 tablespoons at a time. Pour batter into prepared pan. Bake 30 minutes or until cake springs back when pressed lightly in center. Cool on wire rack 10 minutes. Loosen cake from pan with knife or spatula. Invert onto wire rack; remove paper. Invert again; cool completely. Place cake on serving plate. Meanwhile, for Glaze, in small saucepan, blend water and powdered sugar. Sift cocoa over sugar mixture; blend well. Stir in olive oil and salt. Cook over low heat, stirring constantly, until warm. Drizzle Glaze over top of cake. Allow to set before serving.

*Makes 8 to 10 servings*

## Chocolate — Mayonnaise Cake —

- 2 cups all-purpose flour
- ⅔ cup unsweetened cocoa
- 1¼ teaspoons baking soda
- ¼ teaspoon baking powder
- 3 eggs
- 1⅔ cups sugar
- 1 teaspoon vanilla
- 1 cup HELLMANN'S® or BEST FOODS® Real or Light Mayonnaise or Low Fat Mayonnaise Dressing
- 1⅓ cups water

Preheat oven to 350°F. Grease and flour bottoms of two 9-inch round cake pans. In medium bowl, combine flour, cocoa, baking soda and baking powder; set aside. In large bowl, with mixer at high speed, beat eggs, sugar and vanilla, scraping bowl occasionally, 3 minutes or until smooth and creamy. Reduce speed to low; beat in mayonnaise until blended. Add flour mixture in 4 additions alternately with water, beginning and ending with flour mixture. Pour into prepared pans. Bake 30 to 35 minutes or until cakes spring back when touched lightly in centers. Cool in pans on wire racks 10 minutes. Remove from pans; cool completely on racks. Fill and frost as desired.

*Makes 1 (9-inch) layer cake*

*Chocolate Mayonnaise Cake*

# Bumpy Highway Cake

## CAKE

1 can (14 ounces) sweetened condensed milk (not evaporated), divided
1 BUTTER FLAVOR* CRISCO® Stick or 1 cup BUTTER FLAVOR CRISCO all-vegetable shortening
1 cup granulated sugar
1 cup firmly packed light brown sugar
4 eggs
2 teaspoons vanilla
1 cup buttermilk or sour milk**
½ cup unsweetened baking cocoa
2½ cups all-purpose flour
1 teaspoon baking soda
1 teaspoon ground cinnamon
½ teaspoon salt
1 cup hot water

## DRIZZLE

⅓ cup unsweetened baking cocoa***
3 tablespoons CRISCO Oil or CRISCO PURITAN Canola Oil

## FROSTING

¼ BUTTER FLAVOR CRISCO Stick or ¼ cup BUTTER FLAVOR CRISCO all-vegetable shortening
Reserved sweetened condensed milk
1 cup confectioners' sugar
½ cup miniature marshmallows, halved
1 cup chopped nuts

*Butter Flavor Crisco® is artificially flavored.

**To sour milk: Combine 1 tablespoon white vinegar plus enough milk to equal 1 cup. Stir. Wait 5 minutes before using.

***Substitute 4 bars (1 ounce each) HERSHEY®S Unsweetened Baking Chocolate, melted, for cocoa and oil, if desired.

**1. Heat** oven to 350°F. **Grease** 10-inch (12-cup) Bundt pan with shortening. **Flour** lightly.

**2. Measure** ⅓ cup condensed milk for cake. **Reserve** remaining milk for frosting.

**3. *For Cake,* combine** 1 cup shortening, granulated sugar, brown sugar, eggs, ⅓ cup condensed milk and vanilla in large bowl. **Beat** at medium speed of electric mixer until creamy. **Add** buttermilk and ½ cup cocoa. **Beat** until well blended.

**4. Combine** flour, baking soda, cinnamon and salt in medium bowl. **Add** to creamed mixture. **Beat** at low speed to blend. **Beat** at medium speed 5 minutes. **Stir** in hot water with spoon just until blended. *Do not overmix.* (Batter will be thin.) **Pour** into pan.

**5. Bake** at 350°F for 35 to 50 minutes or until top springs back when touched lightly in center or until toothpick inserted in center comes out clean. **Cool** 5 minutes before removing from pan. **Place** cake, fluted side up, on serving plate. **Cool** 15 minutes.

**6. *For Drizzle,* combine** ⅓ cup cocoa and oil in small bowl. **Stir** to blend.

**7. *For Frosting,* combine** ¼ cup shortening, reserved condensed milk and confectioners' sugar in medium bowl. **Beat** at high speed until glossy and of desired consistency. **Spread** on warm cake. **Sprinkle** with marshmallows and then nuts. **Decorate** with chocolate drizzle. **Serve** warm or cool completely.

*Makes 12 to 16 servings*

*Bumpy Highway Cake*

# Bittersweet Chocolate Pound Cake

## CAKE
2 cups all-purpose flour
1 teaspoon baking soda
1 teaspoon baking powder
1½ cups water
2 tablespoons instant coffee granules
4 bars (8 ounces) NESTLÉ®
    Unsweetened Baking Chocolate,
    broken up, divided
2 cups granulated sugar
1 cup butter, softened
1 teaspoon vanilla extract
3 eggs

## CHOCOLATE GLAZE
3 tablespoons butter or margarine
1½ cups sifted powdered sugar
2 to 3 tablespoons water
1 teaspoon vanilla extract
    Powdered sugar (optional)

**FOR CAKE:**
**COMBINE** flour, baking soda and baking powder in small bowl. Bring water and coffee to a boil in small saucepan; remove from heat. Add *3 bars (6 ounces)* baking chocolate; stir until smooth.

**BEAT** sugar, butter and vanilla in large mixer bowl until creamy. Add eggs; beat on high speed for 5 minutes. Beat in flour mixture alternately with chocolate mixture. Pour into well-greased 10-inch Bundt pan.

**BAKE** in preheated 325°F oven for 50 to 60 minutes until long wooden pick inserted near center of cake comes out clean. Cool in pan on wire rack for 30 minutes. Remove from pan; cool completely. Drizzle with chocolate glaze; sprinkle with powdered sugar.

**FOR CHOCOLATE GLAZE:**
**MELT** *remaining baking bar (2 ounces)* and butter in small, heavy saucepan over low heat, stirring until smooth. Remove from heat. Stir in powdered sugar alternately with water until desired consistency. Stir in vanilla.

*Makes 12 servings*

*Bittersweet Chocolate Pound Cake*

# — Cappuccino Cake —

½ cup (3 ounces) semisweet chocolate chips
½ cup chopped hazelnuts, walnuts or pecans
1 (18.25-ounce) package yellow cake mix
¼ cup instant espresso coffee powder
2 teaspoons ground cinnamon
1¼ cups water
3 large eggs
⅓ cup FILIPPO BERIO® Pure or Extra Light Olive Oil
 Powdered sugar
1 (15-ounce) container ricotta cheese
2 teaspoons granulated sugar
 Additional ground cinnamon

Preheat oven to 325°F. Grease 10-inch (12-cup) Bundt pan or 10-inch tube pan with olive oil. Sprinkle lightly with flour.

In small bowl, combine chocolate chips and hazelnuts. Spoon evenly onto bottom of prepared pan. In large bowl, combine cake mix, coffee powder and 2 teaspoons cinnamon. Add water, eggs and olive oil. Beat with electric mixer at low speed until dry ingredients are moistened. Beat at medium speed 2 minutes. Pour batter over topping in pan.

Bake 60 minutes or until toothpick inserted in center comes out clean. Cool on wire rack 15 minutes. Remove from pan. Place cake, fluted side up, on serving plate. Cool completely. Sprinkle with powdered sugar. In medium bowl, combine ricotta cheese and granulated sugar. Sprinkle with cinnamon. Serve alongside slices of cake. Serve cake with cappuccino, espresso or coffee, if desired.

*Makes 12 to 16 servings*

# Chocolate Glazed Citrus Poppy Seed Cake

1 package (about 18 ounces) lemon cake mix
⅓ cup poppy seed
⅓ cup milk
3 eggs
1 container (8 ounces) plain low-fat yogurt
1 teaspoon freshly grated lemon peel
 Chocolate Citrus Glaze (recipe follows)

Heat oven to 350°F. Grease and flour 12-cup fluted tube pan or 10-inch tube pan. In large mixer bowl, combine cake mix, poppy seed, milk, eggs, yogurt and lemon peel; beat until well blended. Pour batter into prepared pan. Bake 40 to 45 minutes or until wooden pick inserted in center comes out clean. Cool 20 minutes; remove from pan to wire rack. Cool completely. Prepare Chocolate Citrus Glaze; spoon over cake, allowing glaze to run down sides. *Makes 12 servings*

## Chocolate Citrus Glaze

2 tablespoons butter or margarine
2 tablespoons HERSHEY®'S Cocoa or HERSHEY®'S European Style Cocoa
2 tablespoons water
1 tablespoon orange-flavored liqueur (optional)
½ teaspoon orange extract
1¼ to 1½ cups powdered sugar

In small saucepan over medium heat, melt butter. With whisk, stir in cocoa and water until mixture thickens slightly.

Remove from heat; stir in liqueur, if desired, orange extract and 1¼ cups powdered sugar. Whisk until smooth. If glaze is too thin, whisk in remaining ¼ cup powdered sugar. Use immediately.

# Toll House®
## Carrot Cake

    2 cups all-purpose flour
    1 teaspoon baking powder
    1 teaspoon baking soda
    1 teaspoon salt
    1 teaspoon ground cinnamon
    ¼ teaspoon ground nutmeg
 1¼ cups sugar
    ¾ cup vegetable oil
    3 eggs
    1 teaspoon vanilla extract
 1¾ cups shredded carrots
    1 (8-ounce) can crushed juice-packed
       pineapple, undrained
    1 cup chopped nuts
    1 cup (6-ounce package) NESTLÉ®
       TOLL HOUSE® Semi-Sweet
       Chocolate Mini Morsels
    Citrus Cream Cheese Frosting
       (recipe follows)

**PREHEAT** oven to 350°F. Grease and flour 13×9-inch baking pan.

**COMBINE** flour, baking powder, baking soda, salt and spices in small bowl. In large mixer bowl, beat sugar, oil, eggs and vanilla until well blended. Gradually beat in flour mixture. Stir in carrots, pineapple with juice, 1 cup nuts and mini morsels. Pour into pan.

**BAKE** 45 to 50 minutes until wooden toothpick inserted into center comes out clean. Cool completely on wire rack. Spread with Citrus Cream Cheese Frosting. Garnish with additional chopped nuts, if desired.     *Makes 12 to 16 servings*

**Citrus Cream Cheese Frosting:** In small mixer bowl, combine 4 ounces softened cream cheese and 2 tablespoons softened butter or margarine. Add 3 cups sifted powdered sugar; mix thoroughly. Stir in 1 tablespoon orange juice and 1 tablespoon lemon juice. Add additional orange juice if necessary until frosting is of spreading consistency.

# Brownie Cake
## Delight

    1 package fudge brownie mix
    ⅓ cup strawberry all-fruit spread
    2 cups thawed reduced-fat nondairy
       whipped topping
    ¼ teaspoon almond extract
    2 cups strawberries, stems removed,
       halved
    ¼ cup chocolate sauce

Prepare brownies according to package directions, substituting 11×7-inch baking pan. Cool completely in pan. Whisk fruit spread in small bowl until smooth. Combine whipped topping and almond extract in medium bowl. Cut brownie crosswise in half. Place 1 half of brownie, flat-side down on serving dish. Spread fruit spread and 1 cup whipped topping onto bottom layer. Place second half of brownie, flat-side down, onto bottom layer. Spread remaining whipped topping over top layer of brownie. Arrange strawberries over whipped topping. Drizzle chocolate sauce over cake before serving.     *Makes 16 servings*

# Pineapple Upside-Down Cake

- 1 (8-ounce) can crushed pineapple in juice, undrained
- 2 tablespoons margarine, melted, divided
- ½ cup firmly packed light brown sugar
- 6 whole maraschino cherries
- 1½ cups all-purpose flour
- 2 tablespoons baking powder
- ¼ teaspoon salt
- 1 cup granulated sugar
- ½ cup MOTT'S® Natural Apple Sauce
- 1 whole egg
- 3 egg whites, beaten until stiff

**1.** Preheat oven to 375°F. Drain pineapple; reserve juice. Spray sides of 8-inch square baking pan with nonstick cooking spray.

**2.** Spread 1 tablespoon melted margarine evenly onto bottom of prepared pan. Sprinkle with brown sugar; top with pineapple. Slice cherries in half. Arrange cherries, cut side up, so that when cake is cut, each piece will have cherry half in center.

**3.** In small bowl, combine flour, baking powder and salt. In large bowl, combine granulated sugar, apple sauce, whole egg, remaining 1 tablespoon melted margarine and reserved pineapple juice.

**4.** Add flour mixture to apple sauce mixture; stir until well blended. Fold in egg whites. Gently pour batter over fruit, spreading evenly.

**5.** Bake 35 to 40 minutes or until lightly browned. Cool on wire rack 10 minutes.

Invert cake onto serving plate. Serve warm or cool completely. Cut into 12 pieces.
*Makes 12 servings*

# Cocoa Marble Gingerbread

- ½ cup shortening
- 1 cup sugar
- 1 cup light molasses
- 2 eggs
- 1 teaspoon baking soda
- 1 cup boiling water
- 2 cups all-purpose flour
- 1 teaspoon salt
- ¼ cup HERSHEY®S Cocoa
- ½ teaspoon ground cinnamon
- ½ teaspoon ground ginger
- ¼ teaspoon ground cloves
- ¼ teaspoon ground nutmeg
  Sweetened whipped cream (optional)

Heat oven to 350°F. Grease and flour 13×9×2-inch baking pan. In large mixer bowl, beat shortening, sugar and molasses until blended. Add eggs; beat well. Stir baking soda into water to dissolve; add to shortening mixture alternately with combined flour and salt, beating well after each addition. Remove 2 cups batter to medium bowl. Add cocoa; blend well. Add spices to remaining batter in large mixer bowl. Alternately spoon batters into prepared pan; gently swirl with knife for marbled effect. Bake 40 to 45 minutes or until wooden pick inserted in center comes out clean. Serve warm or at room temperature with sweetened whipped cream, if desired.

*Makes 10 to 12 servings*

*Pineapple Upside-Down Cake*

# — Rocky Road Cake —

1¾ cups all-purpose flour
⅓ cup unsweetened cocoa powder
2 teaspoons baking powder
1 teaspoon baking soda
½ teaspoon salt
1 cup granulated sugar
¾ cup MOTT'S® Natural Apple Sauce
½ cup skim milk
4 egg whites
1 teaspoon vanilla extract
¾ cup marshmallow topping
½ cup frozen light nondairy whipped
    topping, thawed
2 tablespoons chopped unsalted
    peanuts
    Powdered sugar (optional)
    Fresh red currants (optional)
    Mint leaves (optional)

**1.** Preheat oven to 350°F. Line 15½ ×10½-inch jelly-roll pan with waxed paper.

**2.** In medium bowl, sift together flour, cocoa, baking powder, baking soda and salt.

**3.** In large bowl, whisk together granulated sugar, apple sauce, milk, egg whites and vanilla.

**4.** Add flour mixture to apple sauce mixture; stir until well blended. Pour batter into prepared pan.

**5.** Bake 12 to 15 minutes or until top springs back when lightly touched. Immediately invert onto clean, lint-free dish towel sprinkled with powdered sugar; peel off waxed paper. Trim edges of cake. Starting at narrow end, roll up cake and towel together. Cool completely on wire rack.

**6.** In small bowl, whisk marshmallow topping until softened. Gently fold in whipped topping.

**7.** Unroll cake; spread with marshmallow mixture to within ½ inch of edges of cake. Sprinkle peanuts over marshmallow mixture. Reroll cake; place seam side down, on serving plate. Cover; refrigerate 1 hour before slicing. Sprinkle with powdered sugar and garnish with currants and mint leaves, if desired, just before serving. Cut into 14 slices. Refrigerate leftovers.     *Makes 14 servings*

*Rocky Road Cake*

# Chocolate Angel Fruit Torte

1 package chocolate angel food cake mix, prepared, cooled
2 bananas, thinly sliced
1½ teaspoons lemon juice
1 can (12 ounces) evaporated skim milk, divided
⅓ cup sugar
¼ cup cornstarch
⅓ cup cholesterol-free egg substitute
3 tablespoons nonfat sour cream
3 teaspoons vanilla
3 large kiwis, peeled, thinly sliced
1 can (11 ounces) mandarin oranges, rinsed, drained

Cut cake horizontally in half to form 2 layers; set aside. Place banana slices in medium bowl. Add lemon juice; toss to coat. Set aside. Whisk ¼ cup milk, sugar and cornstarch in small saucepan until smooth. Whisk in remaining milk. Bring to a boil over high heat, stirring constantly. Boil 1 minute or until mixture thickens, stirring constantly. Reduce heat to medium-low. Whisk ⅓ cup hot milk mixture and egg substitute in small bowl. Add to saucepan. Cook 2 minutes, stirring constantly. Remove saucepan from heat. Let stand 10 minutes, stirring frequently. Add sour cream and vanilla; blend well. Place bottom half of cake on serving plate. Spread with half of milk mixture. Arrange half of banana slices, kiwi slices and mandarin orange segments on milk mixture. Place remaining half of cake, cut-side down, over fruit. Spread remaining milk mixture onto cake; top with remaining fruit.  *Makes 12 servings*

# Chocolate Angel Food Rolls

**CAKE**
1 package DUNCAN HINES® Angel Food Cake Mix
3 tablespoons unsweetened cocoa
Confectioners sugar

**FILLING**
½ square (½ ounce) grated semi-sweet chocolate
1 container (8 ounces) frozen whipped topping, thawed

**DRIZZLE**
2 squares (2 ounces) semi-sweet chocolate, chopped
2 teaspoons CRISCO® Stick or CRISCO all-vegetable shortening

**1.** Preheat oven to 350°F. Line two 15½×10½×1-inch jelly-roll pans with aluminum foil.

**2.** For cake, place cake mix, cocoa and water (per package) in large bowl. Prepare cake following package directions. Divide batter into pans. Spread evenly. Cut through batter with knife or spatula to remove large air bubbles. Bake at 350°F for 15 minutes or until set. Invert cakes at once onto lint-free kitchen towels dusted with confectioners sugar. Remove foil carefully. Starting at short end, roll up each cake with towel jelly-roll fashion. Cool completely.

**3.** For filling, fold grated chocolate into whipped topping. Unroll cakes. Spread half of filling to edges on each cake. Reroll and place seam-sides down on serving plate.

**4.** For drizzle, combine chocolate and shortening in small resealable plastic bag. Place bag in bowl of hot water for several minutes. Dry with paper towel. Knead until blended and chocolate is smooth. Snip pinpoint corner in bag. Drizzle over rolls. Refrigerate until ready to serve.

*Makes 16 to 20 servings*

# Marble Chiffon Cake

**2 tablespoons plus 1½ cups sugar, divided**
**2 tablespoons plus ½ cup vegetable oil, divided**
**⅓ cup HERSHEY®S Cocoa**
**1 cup cold water, divided**
**2 cups all-purpose flour**
**1 tablespoon baking powder**
**1 teaspoon salt**
**7 eggs, separated**
**2 teaspoons vanilla extract**
**½ teaspoon cream of tartar**
  **Vanilla Glaze or Quick Cocoa Glaze (recipes follow)**

Preheat oven to 325°F. In small bowl, combine 2 tablespoons sugar, 2 tablespoons oil, cocoa and ¼ cup cold water; stir until smooth. Reserve. In small mixer bowl, stir together flour, remaining 1½ cups sugar, baking powder and salt. Add remaining ¾ cup cold water, ½ cup oil, egg yolks and vanilla. Beat on low speed until combined; continue beating on high speed 5 minutes. In large mixer bowl, with clean set of beaters, beat egg whites with cream of tartar until stiff peaks form. Pour batter in thin stream over beaten whites, gently folding with rubber spatula just until blended. Remove one third of batter to separate bowl; gently fold in reserved cocoa mixture. Pour half of light batter into ungreased 10-inch tube pan; top with half of chocolate batter. Repeat layers. With spatula or knife, swirl gently through batters to marbleize.

Bake 65 to 70 minutes or until top springs back when touched lightly. Invert pan on heatproof funnel or bottle; cool cake completely. Loosen cake from pan; invert onto serving plate. Spread Vanilla Glaze or Quick Cocoa Glaze over top of cake, allowing glaze to drizzle down sides.     *Makes 12 to 16 servings*

**Vanilla Glaze:** In small saucepan over low heat, melt ¼ cup butter or margarine; remove from heat. Gradually stir in 2 cups powdered sugar, 2 to 3 tablespoons hot water and 1 teaspoon vanilla extract; beat with wire whisk until smooth and slightly thickened.

## Quick Cocoa Glaze

**2 tablespoons butter or margarine**
**¼ cup HERSHEY®S Cocoa**
**3 tablespoons water**
**½ teaspoon vanilla extract**
**1¼ cups powdered sugar**

In small saucepan over low heat, melt butter. Stir in cocoa and water. Cook, stirring constantly, until mixture thickens. *Do not boil.* Remove from heat. Stir in vanilla. Gradually add powdered sugar, beating with wire whisk until smooth. Add additional water, ½ teaspoon at a time, until desired consistency.

# Raspberry Shortcake

1½ cups frozen raspberries, thawed, divided
6 tablespoons sugar, divided
1 cup all-purpose flour
1 teaspoon baking powder
¼ teaspoon baking soda
1 tablespoon cold margarine
⅓ cup evaporated skim milk
1 egg white
¼ teaspoon almond extract
¾ cup 1% low-fat cottage cheese
1 teaspoon lemon juice

Preheat oven to 450°F. Spray cookie sheet with nonstick cooking spray. Combine 1¼ cups raspberries and 2 tablespoons plus 1½ teaspoons sugar in small bowl; cover and refrigerate until ready to serve.

Combine flour, 2 tablespoons sugar, baking powder and baking soda in medium bowl. Cut in margarine using 2 knives or pastry blender until mixture forms coarse crumbs; set aside.

In separate small bowl, beat together milk, egg white and almond extract until well blended. Add to dry ingredients; mix lightly. Place dough on lightly floured board; knead about 5 minutes or until dough is no longer sticky to the touch. Roll out dough to ½-inch thickness. Cut 8 biscuits from dough using 2½-inch biscuit cutter; place on cookie sheet. Bake 10 minutes or until tops are lightly browned. Remove to wire rack; cool.

Place cottage cheese, remaining 1 tablespoon plus 1½ teaspoons sugar and lemon juice in food processor; process until smooth. Transfer mixture to medium bowl. Gently stir in remaining ¼ cup raspberries.

Split biscuits horizontally in half; place bottom halves on individual serving plates. Top each half with about 2 tablespoons reserved raspberry mixture and 1 tablespoon cottage cheese mixture; cover with biscuit top. Top with remaining reserved raspberry and cottage cheese mixtures.  *Makes 8 servings*

# Butterfly Cupcakes

1 (16-ounce) package OREO® Chocolate Sandwich Cookies, divided
1 (18.25-ounce) package yellow cake mix
Prepared frosting, any flavor
Red string licorice

Cut 24 cookies in half; coarsely chop remaining 17 cookies. Prepare cake mix batter according to package directions; fold in chopped cookies. Spoon batter into 24 (2½-inch) paper-lined muffin cups. Bake according to cake mix package directions for time and temperature. Cool. Frost and decorate to form butterflies using 2 cookie halves and licorice for each cupcake.

*Makes 24 cupcakes*

*Raspberry Shortcake*

## Jack-O'-Lantern Cupcakes

1 package DUNCAN HINES® Moist
   Deluxe Devil's Food Cake Mix
2 containers (16 ounces each)
   DUNCAN HINES® Creamy
   Homestyle Vanilla Frosting,
   divided
1 tablespoon unsweetened cocoa
   Green, yellow and red food
      colorings
   Candy corn
   Mini semi-sweet chocolate chips
   Peanut butter chips
   Vanilla milk chips
   Miniature marshmallows

**1.** Preheat oven to 350°F. Line 24 (2½-inch) muffin cups with paper baking cups.

**2.** Prepare cake mix following package directions for basic recipe. Pour batter evenly into 24 baking cups. Bake 19 to 22 minutes or until toothpick inserted in center comes out clean. Cool in pans 5 minutes. Remove to cooling racks. Cool completely.

**3.** Place ¼ cup Vanilla Frosting in small bowl. Stir in cocoa; fill small resealable plastic sandwich bag with cocoa frosting mix. Place ½ cup Vanilla Frosting in another small bowl. Stir in several drops of green food coloring; fill another small resealable plastic sandwich bag with green frosting mix. Remove excess air from each bag; seal. Squeeze frosting to one corner in each bag. Snip off tiny corner of each bag; set aside. Place remaining Vanilla Frosting in medium bowl. Stir in 12 drops yellow food coloring and 8 drops red food coloring to tint frosting orange.

**4.** Spread orange frosting on 1 cupcake. Run edge of table knife through frosting to make grooves like real pumpkins. Repeat with remaining cupcakes. Create jack-o'-lantern faces on each frosted cupcake with candy corn, chips and marshmallows, and piped cocoa frosting. Pipe green frosting to make stems.

*Makes 24 cupcakes*

*Jack-O'-Lantern Cupcakes*

# Hot Fudge Pudding Cake

1¼ cups granulated sugar, divided
1 cup all-purpose flour
3 tablespoons plus ¼ cup HERSHEY'S Cocoa, divided
2 teaspoons baking powder
¼ teaspoon salt
½ cup milk
⅓ cup butter or margarine, melted
1½ teaspoons vanilla extract
½ cup packed light brown sugar
1¼ cups hot water
Whipped topping (optional)

Heat oven to 350°F. In large bowl, stir together ¾ cup granulated sugar, flour, 3 tablespoons cocoa, baking powder and salt. Stir in milk, butter and vanilla; beat until smooth. Pour batter into 8- or 9-inch square baking pan. Stir together remaining ½ cup granulated sugar, brown sugar and remaining ¼ cup cocoa; sprinkle mixture evenly over batter. Pour water over top. *Do not stir.* Bake 35 to 40 minutes or until center is almost set. Cool 15 minutes; spoon into dessert dishes. Spoon sauce from bottom of pan over top of cake. Serve warm with whipped topping, if desired. Garnish as desired.

*Makes 8 servings*

# Gummy Purple Dinosaur Cake

1 tub (8 ounces) COOL WHIP® Whipped Topping, thawed
Few drops blue and red food colorings
1 baked 13×9-inch cake, any flavor except angel food, cooled
Gumdrops
Assorted small candies

**TINT** whipped topping purple with blue and red food colorings in small bowl with wire whisk.

**CUT** cake as shown in Diagram 1.

**USING** small amount of whipped topping to hold pieces together, arrange cake on serving tray as shown in Diagram 2. Frost cake with remaining whipped topping. Decorate with gumdrops and candies. Serve immediately. Store leftover cake in refrigerator.

*Makes 12 to 16 servings*

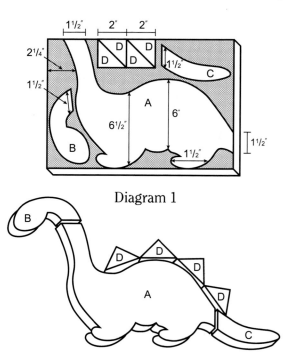

Diagram 1

Diagram 2

*Gummy Purple Dinosaur Cake*

# Macho Monster Cake

## INGREDIENTS

1 package (18.25 ounces) cake mix, any flavor, plus ingredients to prepare mix

1 container (16 ounces) cream cheese or vanilla frosting

Green and yellow food color

Black decorating gel

1 white chocolate baking bar (2 ounces)

## SUPPLIES

1 (13×9-inch) cake board, covered, or large tray

Preheat oven to 350°F. Grease and flour 13×9-inch baking pan. Prepare cake mix according to package directions. Pour into prepared pan. Bake 30 to 35 minutes until wooden toothpick inserted into center comes out clean. Cool in pan on wire rack 10 minutes. Remove from pan to rack; cool completely. Color cream cheese with green and yellow food color to make ugly monster green as shown in photo. Using Diagram 1 as guide, cut pieces out of cake. Position pieces on prepared cake board as shown in Diagram 2, connecting with some frosting. Frost cake. Using decorating gel, pipe eyes, mouth, hair and scars as shown. Break white chocolate baking bar into irregular pieces; position inside mouth as teeth.

*Makes 12 servings*

**Note:** *For cleaner cutting lines and fewer crumbs, place the cooled cake in the freezer for 30 to 45 minutes before cutting.*

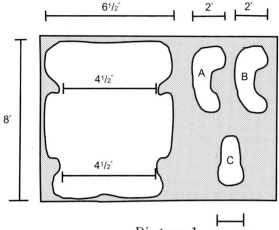

Diagram 1

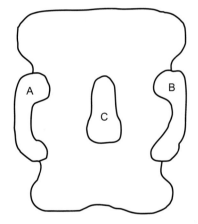

Diagram 2

*Macho Monster Cake*

# GRAND FINALES

*Say "yes" to dessert and indulge in one of these dazzling goodies for an encore that's sure to please. Your family and friends will savor every last bite of these velvety mousses, creamy trifles and feathery-light soufflés.*

## Poached Pears in Cranberry Syrup

1 quart (4 cups) cranberry
    juice cocktail
1 cup KARO® Light Corn
    Syrup
8 slices (¼ inch thick)
    unpeeled fresh ginger
2 cinnamon sticks (2 to 3
    inches)
8 slightly underripe pears

In heavy 4-quart saucepan combine cranberry juice, corn syrup, ginger and cinnamon sticks; bring to boil over medium-high heat. Peel pears, leaving stems attached. Add to cranberry liquid; cover. Reduce heat and simmer 15 to 20 minutes or until pears are tender. With slotted spoon transfer pears to shallow serving dish. Remove ginger slices and cinnamon sticks. Discard all but 2 cups syrup in saucepan. Bring to boil; boil 10 to 12 minutes or until syrup thickens slightly. Spoon sauce over pears. *Makes 8 servings*

*Poached Pear in Cranberry Syrup*

## — Bananas Flambé —

1 large banana
4 teaspoons honey
4 teaspoons chopped walnuts
4 teaspoons brandy (optional)

Halve unpeeled banana lengthwise; place in small flameproof dish. Drizzle cut surface of each half with 2 teaspoons honey and sprinkle with walnuts. On top rack of preheated oven broiler, broil banana about 5 minutes or until heated but not burnt. Remove from broiler. If desired, pour brandy over top and flame.

*Makes 2 servings*

**Tip:** Orange blossom honey is particularly good in this dessert.

Favorite recipe from **National Honey Board**

## Vanilla Cream — and Fruit Brûlée —

2 cups half-and-half or light cream
1 cup milk
1 (4-serving size) package ROYAL®
    Vanilla Pudding & Pie Filling
1 medium banana, sliced
½ cup fresh or frozen blueberries
¼ cup firmly packed light brown sugar

In saucepan, over medium-high heat, heat half-and-half or light cream and milk to a simmer. Briskly whisk in pudding mix. Cook and stir until pudding thickens and begins to boil. Cool slightly. Layer pudding, banana slices and blueberries in 1-quart heat-proof dish. Chill 2 hours.

Sprinkle surface of layered pudding mixture with brown sugar. Broil 3 inches from heat source 1½ to 2 minutes or until sugar is bubbly and melted. Serve immediately. *Makes 7 to 8 servings*

## — Crème Caramel —

½ cup sugar, divided
1 tablespoon hot water
2 cups skim milk
⅛ teaspoon salt
½ cup cholesterol-free egg substitute
½ teaspoon vanilla
⅛ teaspoon maple extract

Heat ¼ cup sugar in heavy saucepan over low heat, stirring constantly until melted and caramel colored. Remove from heat; stir in hot water. Return to heat; stir 5 minutes until mixture is a dark caramel color. Divide melted sugar evenly among 6 custard cups. Set aside.

Preheat oven to 350°F. Combine milk, remaining ¼ cup sugar and salt in medium bowl. Add egg substitute, vanilla and maple extract; mix well. Pour ½ cup mixture into each custard cup. Place cups in heavy pan; pour hot water into pan to 1- to 2-inch depth. Bake 40 to 45 minutes or until knife inserted near edge of cup comes out clean. Cool on wire rack. Refrigerate at least 4 hours or overnight.

When ready to serve, run knife around edge of custard cup. Invert custard onto serving plate; remove cup.

*Makes 6 servings*

*Crème Caramel*

# Cinnamon-Raisin — Bread Pudding —

1 can (12 ounces) evaporated skim milk
⅓ cup cholesterol-free egg substitute
2 tablespoons sugar
3 teaspoons maple syrup, divided
¼ teaspoon vanilla
⅛ teaspoon ground cinnamon
4 slices cinnamon-raisin bread, torn into 1-inch pieces

Preheat oven to 350°F. Spray 4 custard cups with nonstick cooking spray. Pour 2 cups water into 8×8-inch baking pan; set aside. Combine milk, egg substitute, sugar, 2 teaspoons maple syrup, vanilla and cinnamon in medium bowl. Stir in bread. Spoon evenly into prepared custard cups. Place cups in prepared pan. Bake 40 minutes or until bread pudding is set. Drizzle remaining 1 teaspoon syrup over servings. Serve immediately.

*Makes 4 servings*

# Hot Chocolate — Soufflé —

¾ cup HERSHEY₂S Cocoa
1 cup sugar, divided
½ cup all-purpose flour
¼ teaspoon salt
2 cups milk
6 egg yolks, well beaten
2 tablespoons butter or margarine
1 teaspoon vanilla extract
8 egg whites
¼ teaspoon cream of tartar
Sweetened whipped cream

Adjust oven rack to lowest position. Preheat oven to 350°F. Lightly butter 2½-quart soufflé dish; sprinkle with sugar. For collar, cut a length of heavy-duty aluminum foil to fit around soufflé dish; fold in thirds lengthwise. Lightly butter one side. Attach foil, buttered side in, around outside of dish allowing foil to extend at least 2 inches above dish. Secure foil with tape or string.

In large saucepan, stir together cocoa, ¾ cup sugar, flour and salt; gradually stir in milk. Cook over medium heat, stirring constantly with wire whisk, until mixture boils; remove from heat. Gradually stir small amount of chocolate mixture into beaten egg yolks; blend well. Add egg mixture to chocolate mixture in pan, blending well. Cook and stir 1 minute. Add butter and vanilla, stirring until blended. Set aside; cool 20 minutes. In large mixer bowl, beat egg whites with cream of tartar until soft peaks form; gradually add remaining ¼ cup sugar, beating until stiff peaks form. Gently fold about one third of beaten egg white mixture into chocolate mixture. Lightly fold chocolate mixture, half at a time, into remaining beaten egg white mixture just until blended; do not overfold.

Gently pour mixture into prepared dish; smooth top with spatula. Gently place dish in larger baking pan; pour hot water into larger pan to depth of 1 inch.

Bake 65 to 70 minutes or until puffed and set. Remove soufflé dish from water. Carefully remove foil. Serve immediately with sweetened whipped cream.

*Makes 8 to 10 servings*

*Hot Chocolate Soufflé*

# Fudge Sundae Pudding

- 1 cup all-purpose flour
- 2 teaspoons baking powder
- ⅔ cup granulated sugar
- 4 tablespoons unsweetened cocoa, divided
- ½ teaspoon salt
- ½ cup skim milk
- 1 teaspoon vanilla
- ½ cup firmly packed brown sugar
- ¼ cup granulated sugar
- 1 cup water
- 1 cup MOTT'S® Natural Apple Sauce

**1.** Preheat oven to 350°F. Spray an 8×8×2-inch baking pan with cooking spray.

**2.** In medium-size bowl combine flour, baking powder, ⅔ cup granulated sugar, 2 tablespoons cocoa and salt. Add milk and vanilla. Mix well. Spread into prepared pan.

**3.** In small bowl combine brown sugar, ¼ cup granulated sugar and remaining 2 tablespoons cocoa. Sprinkle evenly over batter.

**4.** Add Mott's® Natural Apple Sauce to water in saucepan. Bring to a rolling boil. Pour over batter. Do not stir in.

**5.** Bake for 35 to 40 minutes. Serve immediately with fat-free ice milk or sweetened whipped evaporated skim milk, if desired. *Makes 10 servings*

# Individual Fudge Soufflés

- ½ cup (1 stick) butter or margarine, softened
- 1¼ cups granulated sugar
- 1 teaspoon vanilla extract
- 4 eggs
- ⅔ cup milk
- ½ teaspoon powdered instant coffee
- ⅔ cup all-purpose flour
- ⅔ cup HERSHEY®S Cocoa
- 1½ teaspoons baking powder
- 1 cup (½ pint) whipping cream
- 2 tablespoons powdered sugar

Preheat oven to 325°F. Grease and sugar eight 6-ounce ramekins or custard cups; set aside. In large mixer bowl, beat butter, granulated sugar and vanilla until light and fluffy. Add eggs, one at a time, beating well after each addition. Scald milk; remove from heat and add powdered coffee, stirring until dissolved. Combine flour, cocoa and baking powder; add alternately with milk mixture to butter mixture. Beat 1 minute on medium speed.

Divide batter evenly among prepared ramekins. Place ramekins in two 8-inch square pans; place pans in oven. Pour hot water into pans to a depth of ⅛ inch.

Bake 45 to 50 minutes, adding more water if necessary, until wooden toothpick inserted in centers comes out clean. Remove pans from oven; allow ramekins to stand in water 5 minutes. Remove ramekins from water; cool slightly. Serve in ramekins or invert onto dessert dishes. Beat cream with powdered sugar until stiff; spoon onto warm soufflés.                    *Makes 8 servings*

# Kahlúa® White Chocolate Fondue

**2 cinnamon sticks**
**⅔ cup whipping cream**
**6 ounces white chocolate, chopped**
**¼ cup KAHLÚA®**
**Bite-size pieces of fruit, such as strawberries, raspberries, bananas, pineapple chunks, apple or orange wedges and cubes of pound cake or cookies**

Cut cinnamon sticks in half lengthwise; break each half into several pieces.

Combine cream and half of cinnamon pieces in small saucepan. Bring to a rolling boil; remove from heat. Cover and let stand 15 minutes. Add remaining cinnamon pieces; return to a boil. Remove from heat. Cover and let stand 15 minutes more.

Place white chocolate in medium bowl. Return cream to a boil once more; pour through strainer into bowl with white chocolate. Let stand 1 to 2 minutes; stir until smooth. Stir in Kahlúa®. Serve warm in fondue pot with bite-size pieces of fruit, cake or cookies.          *Makes 2 cups*

# Chocolate Plunge

**⅔ cup KARO® Light or Dark Corn Syrup**
**½ cup heavy cream**
**8 squares (1 ounce each) semisweet chocolate**
**Assorted fresh fruit**

In medium saucepan combine corn syrup and cream. Bring to boil over medium heat. Remove from heat. Add chocolate; stir until completely melted. Serve warm as a dip for fruit.          *Makes 1½ cups*

**Prep Time:** 10 minutes

**Note:** *Chocolate Plunge can be made a day ahead. Store covered in refrigerator. Reheat before serving.*

**Try some of these "dippers":** *Candied pineapple, dried apricots, waffle squares, ladyfingers, macaroons, pretzels, croissants, mint cookies or peanut butter cookies.*

**Microwave Directions:** In medium microwavable bowl combine corn syrup and cream. Microwave on HIGH (100%), 1½ minutes or until boiling. Add chocolate; stir until completely melted. Serve as above.

# Frozen Brandy Cream in Brandy Lace Cups

4 egg yolks
⅓ cup KARO® Light Corn Syrup
⅓ cup sugar
2 tablespoons brandy*
1 cup heavy or whipping cream
    Brandy Lace Cups, prepared (recipe follows)

*Or, use 2 tablespoons orange juice plus ½ teaspoon grated orange peel.*

In small bowl with mixer at high speed, beat egg yolks until light and fluffy, about 10 minutes. Meanwhile, in 1-quart saucepan combine corn syrup and sugar. Stirring frequently, bring to full boil over medium heat. Without stirring, boil 2 minutes or until temperature on candy thermometer reaches 240°F. Beating constantly, gradually pour hot syrup in a thin, steady stream into egg yolk mixture. Continue beating until thick and completely cool, about 20 minutes. Gently fold in brandy.

In chilled mixer bowl beat cream until stiff. Lightly fold about half of brandy mixture into whipped cream. Gently fold in remaining brandy mixture. Cover; freeze 4 to 5 hours or overnight. Just before serving, spoon into Brandy Lace Cups. If desired, garnish each cup with fruit.                 *Makes about 2½ cups*

**Prep Time:** 45 minutes, plus freezing

## Brandy Lace Cups

¼ cup KARO® Light or Dark Corn Syrup
¼ cup (½ stick) MAZOLA® margarine or butter
¼ cup sugar
½ cup flour
¼ cup very finely chopped pecans or walnuts
2 tablespoons brandy
1 ounce semisweet chocolate, melted (optional)

Preheat oven to 350°F. Grease 2 (15½ × 12-inch) cookie sheets. In small saucepan combine corn syrup, margarine and sugar. Stirring constantly, bring to full boil over medium heat. Remove from heat. Stir in flour, nuts and brandy.

Drop 4 rounded tablespoonfuls of batter about 7 inches apart onto each prepared cookie sheet. Bake 6 to 8 minutes or until golden. Cool on cookie sheet 1 minute or until cookies can be lifted from sheet but are still pliable. Remove cookies with spatula; drape shiny-side down over bottoms of drinking glasses or 6-ounce custard cups, pressing gently to form cups. If cookies harden before shaping, reheat briefly on cookie sheets. Cool cups completely. Store in airtight container. If desired, drizzle cups with melted chocolate just before filling.

*Makes 8 to 10 dessert cups*

*Frozen Brandy Cream in Brandy Lace Cup*

## Tiramisù

2 packages (8 ounces each) cream
    cheese, softened
⅔ cup sugar
¼ cup Marsala wine
2 teaspoons vanilla extract
2 cups whipping cream, whipped
1 cup strong coffee or espresso,
    chilled
2 tablespoons almond liqueur *or*
    1 teaspoon almond extract
2 packages (3 ounces each)
    ladyfingers (24 ladyfingers)
1 cup HEATH® Bits

In a mixing bowl, beat cream cheese and
sugar until light. Blend in wine and
vanilla. Fold in whipped cream. In a small
bowl or measuring cup, combine coffee
and liqueur. To assemble, split each
ladyfinger in half horizontally and
vertically. Place four pieces in each of
eight footed dessert or wine glasses.
Drizzle ladyfingers with the coffee
mixture. Top with about ¼ cup cream
mixture and several teaspoons Heath®
Bits. Repeat with two more layers ending
with Heath® Bits. Cover and refrigerate at
least 2 hours before serving.

*Makes 8 servings*

## Tiramisù

1½ cups cold 2% low fat milk, divided
1 container (8 ounces) pasteurized
    process cream cheese product
2 tablespoons MAXWELL HOUSE® or
    YUBAN® Instant Coffee or SANKA®
    Brand 99.7% Caffeine Free Instant
    Coffee
1 tablespoon hot water
2 tablespoons brandy (optional)
1 package (4-serving size) JELL-O®
    Vanilla Flavor Fat Free Sugar Free
    Instant Reduced Calorie Pudding
    & Pie Filling
2 cups thawed COOL WHIP LITE®
    Whipped Topping
1 package (3 ounces) ladyfingers, split
1 square (1 ounce) BAKER'S® Semi-
    Sweet Chocolate, grated

**POUR** ½ cup of the milk into blender
container. Add cream cheese product;
cover. Blend until smooth. Blend in the
remaining 1 cup milk.

**DISSOLVE** coffee in water; add to
blender with brandy. Add pudding mix;
cover. Blend until smooth, scraping down
side occasionally; pour into large bowl.
Gently stir in whipped topping.

**CUT** ladyfingers in half crosswise. Cover
bottom of 8-inch springform pan with
ladyfinger halves. Place remaining halves,
cut-ends down, around side of pan. Spoon
pudding mixture into pan. Chill until firm,
about 3 hours. Remove side of pan.
Sprinkle with grated chocolate.

*Makes 12 servings*

*JELL-O® Tiramisù*

# Chocolate
## — Raspberry Trifle —

### CHOCOLATE CUSTARD

    3 tablespoons cornstarch
    1 tablespoon granulated sugar
    ⅛ teaspoon salt
    2 cups milk
    3 egg yolks
    2 cups (11½-ounce package) NESTLÉ®
        TOLL HOUSE® Milk Chocolate
        Morsels, divided

### TRIFLE

    1 cup heavy whipping cream
    1 tablespoon granulated sugar
    1 (10¾-ounce) frozen pound cake,
        thawed
    2 tablespoons crème de cacao, divided
    ¼ cup seedless raspberry jam

**FOR CHOCOLATE CUSTARD: COMBINE**
cornstarch, sugar and salt in medium,
heavy saucepan. Gradually add milk.
Whisk in egg yolks until smooth. Cook
over medium heat, stirring constantly,
until mixture comes to a boil; boil for 1
minute. Remove from heat. Add *1½ cups*
morsels; stir until melted and smooth.
Press plastic wrap on surface; chill.

**FOR TRIFLE: BEAT** cream and sugar
until stiff peaks form. Cut cake into
½-inch-thick slices. Cut one slice into thin
strips; reserve for top. In 2-quart straight-
sided bowl, layer half of cake slices, half
of crème de cacao, half of jam, half of
chocolate custard and half of whipped
cream. Repeat cake, crème de cacao, jam
and custard layers. Top with reserved
cake strips, *¼ cup* morsels, remaining
whipped cream and *remaining* morsels.
Chill.              *Makes 8 to 10 servings*

# Crunchy Nutty
## Ice Cream
### — Sundaes —

    **Peanut Butter Sauce (recipe follows)**
    **Coconut Crunch (recipe follows)**
    1 pint vanilla ice cream

Prepare Peanut Butter Sauce and Coconut
Crunch. Scoop ice cream into sundae
dishes. Spoon prepared sauce over ice
cream; sprinkle prepared crunch over
top. Serve immediately.

*Makes 4 to 6 servings*

## Peanut Butter Sauce

    1 cup REESE'S® Peanut Butter Chips
    ⅓ cup milk
    ¼ cup whipping cream
    ¼ teaspoon vanilla extract

In medium saucepan over low heat, heat
peanut butter chips, milk and whipping
cream, stirring constantly until chips are
melted. Remove from heat; stir in vanilla.
Cool to room temperature.

## Coconut Crunch

    ½ cup MOUNDS® Sweetened Coconut
        Flakes
    ½ cup chopped nuts
    1 tablespoon butter or margarine

Heat oven to 325°F. In shallow baking
pan, combine coconut, nuts and butter.
Toast in oven 6 to 8 minutes or until
mixture is very lightly browned, stirring
occasionally. (Watch carefully.) Cool to
room temperature.

*Chocolate Raspberry Trifle*

## – Honey Ice Cream –

2 cups milk
¾ cup honey
Dash salt
2 eggs, beaten
2 cups heavy cream
1 tablespoon vanilla

Heat milk in medium saucepan over medium heat but do not boil; stir in honey and salt. Pour small amount of hot liquid into eggs; add to milk mixture. Cook and stir over medium-low heat 5 minutes. Cool thoroughly at room temperature. Stir in cream and vanilla. Refrigerate until cold. Freeze in ice cream maker according to manufacturer's directions.          *Makes about 5 cups*

Favorite recipe from **National Honey Board**

## Honey Praline
## ——— Sauce ———

¾ cup pecan halves
2 tablespoons butter or margarine
½ cup honey
1 teaspoon all-purpose flour
Dash salt
⅓ cup heavy cream

Spread pecans in shallow pan. Bake in preheated 300°F oven 15 minutes. Melt butter in small saucepan over medium heat. Blend in honey, flour and salt.

Reduce heat to low and simmer 5 minutes, stirring constantly. Remove from heat and let cool. Blend in cream, mixing until smooth. Stir in pecans.

*Makes 1½ cups*

Favorite recipe from **National Honey Board**

## — Charlotte Russe —

2 packages (4-serving size each) *or*
  1 package (8-serving size) JELL-O®
  Brand Gelatin, any red flavor
2 cups boiling water
1 quart vanilla ice cream, softened
12 ladyfingers, split
  COOL WHIP® Whipped Topping, thawed (optional)
  Fresh raspberries (optional)
  Mint leaves (optional)

**COMPLETELY** dissolve gelatin in boiling water. Spoon in ice cream, stirring until melted and smooth. Chill until thickened but not set.

**TRIM** about 1 inch off one end of each ladyfinger; reserve trimmed ends for snacking or other use. Vertically place ladyfingers, cut-ends down, around side of 8-inch springform pan. Spoon gelatin mixture into pan. Chill until firm, about 3 hours. Remove side of pan. Garnish with whipped topping, raspberries and mint leaves, if desired.

*Makes 10 servings*

## Frozen Pudding Bars

1 package (4-serving size) JELL-O®
     Instant Pudding and Pie Filling,
     any flavor
2 cups cold milk

**PREPARE** pudding mix with milk as directed on package. Pour into pop molds or paper or plastic cups. Insert wooden stick or spoon into each cup. Freeze until firm, about 5 hours.          *Makes 6 pops*

**Prep Time:** 10 minutes
**Freezing Time:** 5 hours

## Frozen Fruity Bars

1 package (4-serving size) JELL-O®
     Brand Gelatin, any flavor
½ cup sugar
2 cups boiling water
2 cups cold water

**DISSOLVE** gelatin and sugar in boiling water. Add cold water. Pour into pop molds or paper or plastic cups. Freeze until almost firm, about 2 hours. Insert wooden stick or spoon into each cup. Freeze until firm, about 8 hours or overnight.          *Makes 8 pops*

**Prep Time:** 15 minutes
**Freezing Time:** 8 hours

## Peach Melba Freeze

1 container (8 ounces) peach low fat
     yogurt
¼ cup peach fruit spread
1 tub (8 ounces) COOL WHIP LITE®
     Whipped Topping, thawed
½ cup fresh raspberries
1 package (10 ounces) frozen
     raspberries in lite syrup, thawed
2 teaspoons cornstarch

**STIR** yogurt and fruit spread in large bowl. Gently stir in whipped topping and fresh raspberries with wire whisk until blended.

**RINSE** and dry COOL WHIP LITE® tub. Spray with no stick cooking spray. Spoon yogurt mixture into tub. Cover with plastic wrap. Freeze 4 hours or until firm.

**MIX** raspberries in lite syrup and cornstarch in small saucepan. Stirring constantly, bring to boil on medium heat; boil 1 minute. Strain to remove seeds, if desired. Refrigerate sauce until ready to serve.

**RUN** small warm wet knife or spatula around edge of tub to unmold dessert. Place serving dish on top of tub. Invert, holding tub and dish together; shake gently to loosen. Carefully remove tub; cut dessert into wedges. Serve with raspberry sauce.          *Makes 8 servings*

## Dish of Dirt

14 OREO® Chocolate Sandwich Cookies, finely crushed (about 1 cup crumbs), divided
1 pint chocolate ice cream
¼ cup chocolate-flavored syrup
 Gummy worms, for garnish
 Prepared whipped topping, for garnish

In each of 4 dessert dishes, place 2 tablespoons cookie crumbs. Top each with ½ cup ice cream, 2 tablespoons cookie crumbs and 1 tablespoon syrup. Garnish with gummy worms and whipped topping. *Makes 4 servings*

## Mud Slides

2 cups cold milk
1 package (4-serving size) JELL-O® Chocolate Flavor Instant Pudding & Pie Filling
14 chocolate sandwich cookies, finely crushed (about 1½ cups)
2 cups thawed COOL WHIP® Whipped Topping

LINE bottoms and sides of 2 loaf pans with wet paper towels. Tilt 2 (12-ounce) glasses in each pan.

POUR milk into 1-quart container with tight-fitting lid. Add pudding mix; cover tightly. Shake vigorously at least 45 seconds; pour evenly into glasses.

GENTLY stir 1¼ cups of the cookies into whipped topping with wire whisk in medium bowl until blended. Spoon evenly over pudding in glasses; sprinkle with remaining ¼ cup cookies.

REFRIGERATE until ready to serve.
*Makes 4 servings*

## Citrus Sorbet

1 can (12 ounces) frozen DOLE® Mandarin Tangerine or Orchard Peach Juice Concentrate
1 can (8 ounces) DOLE® Crushed Pineapple or Pineapple Tidbits, drained
½ cup nonfat or low-fat plain yogurt
2½ cups cold water

•**Combine** frozen concentrate, pineapple and yogurt in blender or food processor container; blend until smooth. Stir in water.

•**Pour** mixture into container of ice cream maker.* Freeze according to manufacturer's directions.

•**Serve** sorbet in dessert dishes.
*Makes 10 servings*

*Or, pour sorbet mixture into 8-inch square, metal pan; cover. Freeze 1½ to 2 hours or until slightly firm. Place in large bowl; beat with electric mixer on medium speed 1 minute or until slushy. Return mixture to metal pan; repeat freezing and beating steps. Freeze until firm, about 6 hours or overnight.*

**Prep Time:** 20 minutes
**Freeze Time:** 20 minutes

*Dish of Dirt*

## Easy Éclair Dessert

27 whole graham crackers, halved
3 cups cold milk
2 packages (4-serving size) JELL-O® Vanilla Flavor Instant Pudding & Pie Filling
1 tub (12 ounces) COOL WHIP® Whipped Topping, thawed
1 container (16 ounces) ready-to-spread chocolate fudge frosting
Strawberries

ARRANGE ⅓ of the crackers on bottom of 13×9-inch baking pan, breaking crackers to fit, if necessary.

POUR milk into large bowl. Add pudding mixes. Beat with wire whisk 2 minutes. Gently stir in whipped topping. Spread ½ of the pudding mixture over crackers. Place ½ of the remaining crackers over pudding; top with remaining pudding mixture and crackers.

REMOVE top and foil from frosting container. Microwave frosting in container on HIGH 1 minute or until pourable. Spread evenly over crackers.

REFRIGERATE 4 hours or overnight. Cut into squares to serve. Garnish with strawberries.          *Makes 18 servings*

## Frozen Cherry Terrine

1 can (8 ounces) pitted dark sweet cherries in light syrup, undrained
1 package (4-serving size) JELL-O® Brand Cherry Flavor Sugar Free Gelatin
1 cup boiling water
1 container (8 ounces) plain low fat yogurt
2 cups thawed COOL WHIP LITE® Whipped Topping

•LINE bottom and sides of 9×5-inch loaf pan with plastic wrap; set aside.

•DRAIN cherries, reserving syrup. If necessary, add enough cold water to reserved syrup to measure ½ cup. Cut cherries into quarters.

•COMPLETELY dissolve gelatin in boiling water. Add measured syrup. Stir in yogurt until well blended. Chill until mixture is thickened but not set, about 45 minutes to 1 hour, stirring occasionally. Gently stir in cherries and whipped topping. Pour into prepared pan; cover. Freeze until firm, about 6 hours or overnight.

•REMOVE pan from freezer about 15 minutes before serving. Let stand at room temperature to soften slightly. Unmold terrine onto serving plate. Remove plastic wrap. Cut into slices.          *Makes 12 servings*

*Easy Éclair Dessert*

# Acknowledgments

The publisher would like to thank the companies and organizations listed below for the use of their recipes and photographs in this publication.

Alpine Lace Brands, Inc.

American Lamb Council

Beef Industry Council

Best Foods, a Division of CPC International Inc.

Blue Diamond Growers

Bob Evans Farms®

Canned Food Information Council

Chef Paul Prudhomme's Magic Seasonings Blends®

Christopher Ranch Garlic

Dean Foods Vegetable Company

Del Monte Foods

Dole Food Company, Inc.

Domino Sugar Corporation

Filippo Berio Olive Oil

Florida Department of Agriculture and Consumer Services, Bureau of Seafood and Aquaculture

Golden Grain/Mission Pasta

Heinz U.S.A.

Hershey Foods Corporation

The HVR Company

Kahlúa Liqueur

Kellogg Company

Kikkoman International Inc.

The Kingsford Products Company

Kraft Foods, Inc.

Lawry's® Foods, Inc.

Leaf®, Inc.

Thomas J. Lipton Co.

McIlhenny Company

MOTT'S® Inc., a division of Cadbury Beverages Inc.

Nabisco, Inc.

National Beef Cook-Off®

National Cattlemen's Beef Association

National Honey Board

National Pasta Association

National Pork Producers Council

National Turkey Federation

Nestlé Food Company

Newman's Own, Inc.

Norseland, Inc.

North Dakota Wheat Commission

Perdue® Farms

The Procter & Gamble Company

The Quaker Oats Company

Ralston Foods, Inc.

Reckitt & Colman Inc.

Riviana Foods Inc.

Sargento Foods Inc.®

Sokol and Company

Southeast United Dairy Industry Association, Inc.

StarKist Seafood Company

The Sugar Association, Inc.

USA Rice Council

Walnut Marketing Board

Wisconsin Milk Marketing Board

# Index

# Metric Chart

## VOLUME MEASUREMENTS (dry)

⅛ teaspoon = 0.5 mL

¼ teaspoon = 1 mL

½ teaspoon = 2 mL

¾ teaspoon = 4 mL

1 teaspoon = 5 mL

1 tablespoon = 15 mL

2 tablespoons = 30 mL

¼ cup = 60 mL

⅓ cup = 75 mL

½ cup = 125 mL

⅔ cup = 150 mL

¼ cup = 175 mL

1 cup = 250 mL

2 cups = 1 pint = 500 mL

3 cups = 750 mL

4 cups = 1 quart = 1 L

## VOLUME MEASUREMENTS (fluid)

1 fluid ounce (2 tablespoons) = 30 mL

4 fluid ounces (½ cup) = 125 mL

8 fluid ounces (1 cup) = 250 mL

12 fluid ounces (1½ cups) = 375 mL

16 fluid ounces (2 cups) = 500 mL

## WEIGHTS (mass)

½ ounce = 15 g

1 ounce = 30 g

3 ounces = 90 g

4 ounces = 120 g

8 ounces = 225 g

10 ounces = 285 g

12 ounces = 360 g

16 ounces = 1 pound = 450 g

## DIMENSIONS

1/16 inch = 2 mm

⅛ inch = 3 mm

¼ inch = 6 mm

½ inch = 1.5 cm

¾ inch = 2 cm

1 inch = 2.5 cm

## OVEN TEMPERATURES

250°F = 120°C

275°F = 140°C

300°F = 150°C

325°F = 160°C

350°F = 180°C

375°F = 190°C

400°F = 200°C

425°F = 220°C

450°F = 230°C

## BAKING PAN SIZES

| Utensil | Size in Inches/ Quarts | Metric Volume | Size in Centimeters |
|---|---|---|---|
| Baking or Cake Pan (square or rectangular) | 8×8×2 | 2 L | 20×20×5 |
| | 9×9×2 | 2.5 L | 22×22×5 |
| | 12×8×2 | 3 L | 30×20×5 |
| | 13×9×2 | 3.5 L | 33×23×5 |
| Loaf Pan | 8×4×3 | 1.5 L | 20×10×7 |
| | 9×5×3 | 2 L | 23×13×7 |
| Round Layer Cake Pan | 8×1½ | 1.2 L | 20×4 |
| | 9×1½ | 1.5 L | 23×4 |
| Pie Plate | 8×1¼ | 750 mL | 20×3 |
| | 9×1¼ | 1 L | 23×3 |
| Baking Dish or Casserole | 1 quart | 1 L | — |
| | 1½ quart | 1.5 L | — |
| | 2 quart | 2 L | — |